D1572806

He Was Some Kind of a Man

Film and Media Studies Series

Film studies is the critical exploration of cinematic texts as art and entertainment, as well as the industries that produce them and the audiences that consume them. Although a medium barely one hundred years old, film is already transformed through the emergence of new media forms. Media studies is an interdisciplinary field that considers the nature and effects of mass media upon individuals and society and analyzes media content and representations. Despite changing modes of consumption—especially the proliferation of individuated viewing technologies—film has retained its cultural dominance into the 21st century, and it is this transformative moment that the WLU Press Film and Media Studies series addresses.

Our Film and Media Studies series includes topics such as identity, gender, sexuality, class, race, visuality, space, music, new media, aesthetics, genre, youth culture, popular culture, consumer culture, regional/national cinemas, film policy, film theory, and film history.

Wilfrid Laurier University Press invites submissions. For further information, please contact the Series editors, all of whom are in the Department of English and Film Studies at Wilfrid Laurier University:

Dr. Philippa Gates
Email: pgates@wlu.ca

Dr. Russell Kilbourn
Email: rkilbourn@wlu.ca

Dr. Ute Lischke
Email: ulischke@wlu.ca

Department of English and Film Studies
Wilfrid Laurier University
75 University Avenue West
Waterloo, ON N2L 3C5
Canada
Phone: 519-884-0710
Fax: 519-884-8307

He Was Some Kind of a Man

Masculinities in the B Western

RODERICK MCGILLIS

Wilfrid Laurier University Press

This book has been published with the help of a grant from the Canadian Federation for the Humanities and Social Sciences, through the Aid to Scholarly Publications Programme, using funds provided by the Social Sciences and Humanities Research Council of Canada. We acknowledge the support of the Canada Council for the Arts for our publishing program. We acknowledge the financial support of the Government of Canada through the Book Publishing Industry Development Program for our publishing activities.

    Canada Council for the Arts / Conseil des Arts du Canada

   ONTARIO ARTS COUNCIL / CONSEIL DES ARTS DE L'ONTARIO

Library and Archives Canada Cataloguing in Publication

McGillis, Roderick
He was some kind of a man : masculinities in the B western / Roderick McGillis.

(Film and media studies series)
Includes bibliographical references and index.
ISBN 978-1-55458-059-0

1. Masculinity in motion pictures. 2. Western films—History and criticism. I. Title.
II. Title: Masculinities in the B western. III. Series: Film and media studies series

PN1995.9.M46M345 2009   791.43'6278   C2008-907742-3

For Frances, as always

The western does not age.
— André Bazin

Men with guns. Guns as physical objects, and the postures associated with their use, form the visual and emotional center [of the western].
— Robert Warshow

Contents

Preface

In the Warner Brothers film *Casablanca* (1941), when the innocent young woman from Bulgaria asks cynical American saloon owner Rick Blaine (Humphrey Bogart) what the prefect of police, Captain Renault (Claude Raines), is like and whether he will keep his word, Rick replies: "He's just like any other man, only more so." And at the end of Orson Welles's *Touch of Evil* (1958), as the prostitute Tanya (Marlene Dietrich) gazes on the bloated body of just-deceased Hank Quinlan (played by Welles), she remarks, "He was some kind of a man. What does it matter what you say about people?"

Both Hank Quinlan and Louis Renault are men of exorbitant appetite; such men either learn to control that appetite and become self-denying and state-serving men (as Renault does at the end of *Casablanca*) or they die (as Quinlan does). As we see them in the movies, they are aberrations, foiled by the greater heroism, moral commitment, and self-denial of another man—Rick in *Casablanca* and Vargas (Charlton Heston) in *Touch of Evil*. What interests us about these "other" men is that both are models of masculinity devoutly to be imitated by the male viewer, and yet both are clearly outside conventional social structures: when Colonel Strasse (Conrad Veidt) asks Rick what nationality he is, Rick replies that he is a drunkard; Vargas is a Mexican. In other words, both men hail from places the films encourage viewers to associate with darkness and dissolution, places mysterious and strange, places beyond the familiar American towns and cities, liminal places that seem to offer no room for conventional family backgrounds but plenty of room for behaviour rich in libidinous, or at least transgressive, possibility.

What I am touching on here is, of course, the popular mythic notion of the charismatic male invested with the power to take charge, to set things in order, to shoulder responsibility in a world helpless without his skill, determination, and moral authority. This guy can cross the line, even join the bad people for a while, because he is, in the end, strong, reliable, straight, and morally stiff as a two-by-four. I grew up knowing this man as the cowboy. He is the subject of this book—more precisely, the cowboy of the Saturday-afternoon B western, who fashioned my sense of masculinity, is the subject of this book.

Acknowledgements

Obviously, this book has been in the making for a long time—since I regularly went to the movies on Saturday afternoons to see Roy Rogers and Gene Autry and the others. In those days, my sister, Sandra Meyer, rode with me some of the time, and my mother endured hours of simulated shooting and riding inside and outside our house. All that play was early preparation for this study. Thanks to my mother and my sister. More recently, I found impetus in Quentin Tarantino's homage to Roy Rogers in his 2004 film, *Kill Bill, Volume 2*. The writing of this book, however, is the work of some half-dozen years, and during that time I have had the good fortune to share ideas and drafts of chapters with several people who are, as it were, pardners in this effort.

Thanks to continuing support from Uli Knoepflmacher, David Kent, Laurent Chabin, Wayne Gearey, Clara Joseph, Barbara Belyea, Jeanne Perreault, Maria Nikolajeva, Kimberly Reynolds, Clare Bradford, Perry Nodelman, Peter Hunt, Thomas Van Der Walt, Dieter Petzold, Keath Fraser, John Kerr, David Rudd, Jan Susina, Sandra Beckett, and Jean Perrot. I owe a debt to my teacher Northrop Frye. Shaobo Xie and Liya Yuen gave me a useful book on the cowboy life. Chris Olbey helped me to reach a better understanding of the black westerns of the 1930s than I could have had without his interest and suggestions. Craig Werner and Karen Sands-O'Connor gave me the opportunity to test ideas about nostalgia at the 2001 ChLA Conference in Buffalo, and Rolf Romoren gave me a similar opportunity at the 2003 IRSCL Congress in Kristiansand, Norway. Karen also read individual chapters and made valuable comments, and she also shared a book or two. Nancy Stewart allowed me to read her work on cowboy fiction, and she made valuable suggestions concerning my own work. I exchanged ideas with Ira Wells and Jordan Petty. Jean Webb returned to those yesteryears to share her memories of cowboys in London's East End. John Stephens generously allowed me to ride my hobby horse as a contributor to *Ways of Being Male* (Routledge, 2002), and some of what appears in that book creeps into chapter 1 of this book. Thanks to Kerry Mallan and Queensland University of Technology in Brisbane for the opportunity to read sections of one chapter to a small but kind audience (including Geraldine and Raylee), and thanks also to Kerry for co-presenting a paper in Norway that has resulted in a co-authored article that contains a reference or two to cowboys. Bob and Tamara Seiler have ridden along with me on this project since before it began; I have benefited from their work on western themes (especially the Calgary Stampede). Mark Palmer generously donated three Roy Rogers novels to spur me along when I began to flag. Vic Ramraj and I won our spurs riding the same territory for many years. John and Carole Moroz (and Jolyene and Frank and Buddy) offered sanctuary from the trail. Jack Zipes gave me early and continuing encouragement; he is an inspiration. Jacqueline Larson showed the patience of an experienced tracker. More recently, Lisa Quinn and Leslie Macredie of Wilfrid Laurier University Press have shown a commitment to this project long in the making, and the copy-editing and the suggestions of Rob Kohlmeier have made this a better book than it was when I submitted it to the Press. A sidekick whose voice sounds in several chapters of this book is Nancy Ellen Batty, and she kept me from at least one egregious moment. She also taught me something about the sound of two hands slapping. No one can write about B westerns without acknowledging the work of Chuck Anderson; his website, The Old Corral (www.b-westerns.com), is not only a labour of love but a definitive source for information on these westerns and the people who worked in them. For the photographs of Roy Rogers, Dale Evans, and Trigger in chapters 5 and 6, I have to thank Roy Rogers, Jr., and the administrator of the Roy Rogers–Dale Evans Museum, in Branson, Missouri (www.royrogers.com/museum-index.html). Mr. Rogers asked for nothing in return for permission to use these photos—a generosity I associate with Roy Rogers, Dale Evans, and the whole Rogers family. I owe gratitude to Mr. Monte Hale for permission to use the photograph that graces the cover of this book. Mr. Hale has also graciously provided me with a few more photographs, three of which you will find in the pages that follow. Now that I have communicated with Mr. Hale, I regret not having done so years ago. And I would not have reached Mr. Hale had I not had the assistance of Maxine Hansen of the Gene Autry Western Heritage Museum in Los Angeles. Ms. Hansen has been unflaggingly helpful and kind. As always, Kate and Kyla endured their father's hobby horse with equanimity. And for watching quite literally hundreds of films with me, for being the best partner anyone could ever wish for, my deepest thanks go to Frances Batycki.

Introduction
Ride the High Country, or "They Went Thataway"

for Sam Peckinpah and Sunset Carson

> *The myth [of the American frontier] has been remarkably resilient. Not only did it inform American expansion globally during the presidencies of FDR and Truman, but the uncertainties posed by the Cold War (which used cowboy-and-Indians iconography time and again), the nuclear arms race, and subsequent crises of confidence (particularly urban crime, oil price explosions, the 1979 hostage taking in Tehran, and the 9/11 attacks) led to the embrace in popular culture and politics of the comforting narrative of civilization versus savages. The myth remains vibrant, but the frontier itself is disappearing again.* ₁
> —Tirman, 32

Many men of my generation can remember, often with the help of an old family photo album, their childhood fascination for what sometimes we see referred to as the Silver Screen Cowboys. I am one of these men. What interests me now is the role the cowboys and the films they starred in played in forming a general notion of masculinity that we now call hegemonic. The continuing notion of the man as steadfast, independent, resourceful, self-reliant, aggressive, rational, and controlling remains hegemonic, and by hegemonic I simply mean that this notion of masculinity remains the ideal, although it is by no means the only notion we have of what it means to be masculine. Competing notions of the sensitive male, the vulnerable male, and the compromising and non-competitive male have arisen in the wake of the cinematic era that is my subject. Could those cowboys have contributed to a sense of masculinity that challenges the very hegemonic masculinity that they most obviously

1

promote? To take just one example, I note that perhaps the most famous celluloid cowboy, John Wayne, began his career appearing in forty-two series or B western films, and then went on to enduring fame in big-budget A productions. The character he played in the B westerns differs markedly from those he played in the films we remember most vividly. In the B western, the Wayne character manifests all those solid characteristics of the hegemonic male, but he also takes care of children and the elderly, he sings and plays a guitar (or at least he pretends to sing and play), he wears rather fancy clothes, and he lives intimately with other men. Of course, Wayne does these things, after a fashion, in his more famous films, but with an edge missing in the one-dimensional roles he had in the B westerns. He had yet to develop the fully competent, unbending man we associate with characters such as Ethan Edwards, Rooster Cogburn, or Wil Andersen.

The B western hero appealed to young boys (and girls, too) in a manner similar to the way cinematic superheroes appeal today. Like the heroic male figure in both comics and film, the silver screen cowboy is ostensibly one-dimensional; he represents goodness. From a cultural perspective, however, he is a complex figure, passing from film to the culture generally, through a whole range of products from books to pyjamas. Although adults and children both enjoyed the exploits of these heroes, they appealed strongly to a youth audience, and for this reason I think of them as functioning in a manner familiar to us from the study of children's literature. In what follows, I focus on the B western film from the 1930s to the early 1950s but expect an excursion or two into books for the young and in one chapter to the wider area of economic production we call the marketplace. In every chapter, I remain concerned with the notion of masculinity. And I confess an autobiographical agenda: I am interested in one aspect of our culture that fashioned me into the sixty-year old heterosexual male who is writing this book. I begin with some general reflections.

Those Six-Gun Heroes

My subject is masculinity as conceived in the Hollywood Poverty Row B Western movie. The B western developed from the silent western movies of such cowboys as Tom Mix, Buck Jones, Fred Thompson, and Ken Maynard. As the British Film Institute's *Companion to the Western* notes, these films differed from those of William S. Hart by placing "action and excitement over complexities of character and theme" (Buscombe, 35).

Whereas the characters Hart portrayed were not above drinking and smoking, Mix and Maynard represented clean living and appealed to a juvenile audience. Further, as the BFI *Companion* observes, "Tom Mix leads in a straight line to Gene Autry" (35). When sound became the norm for Hollywood films, after 1929, many small studios churned out genre films for a Depression-era audience eager for escape from the worries brought on by failed crops and lost jobs. Cowboys such as Ken Maynard and Buck Jones made the transition to sound in a series of short, inexpensively made films that stayed close to the western formula worked out since at least the publication of Owen Wister's novel *The Virginian* in 1902. (For studies of formula in narrative and the western formula, see Cawelti 1976 and Wright 1975.) The B western, also known as the series western and the Poverty Row westerns, developed in the later 1930s into the Singing Cowboy westerns, and by the mid-1940s any number of cowboy stars rode across small-town screens, from the well known such as Gene Autry and Roy Rogers to the less well known such as Eddie Dean and Jimmy Wakely. By 1954 the B western had come to an end, replaced by big-budget westerns, with stars such as John Wayne, Randolph Scott, and Joél McCrea, and by the TV western, then in the ascendant. Indeed, several of the B western stars made the move to TV, most prominently Roy Rogers, Hopalong Cassidy, and Gene Autry.

In the pages that follow I discuss or mention in passing a great number of B westerns. Because many hundreds of such films appeared between 1930 and 1954, I cannot claim to have seen all of them. I have, however, seen several hundred. I mention in passing certain films because they illustrate a point I am making, and I provide extended treatment of others because they are either unusual (e.g., *The Crooked Trail* as an example of male affection or *The Frontiersman* because it sums up the various features of my subject) or because the film provides a strong element of what I am discussing (e.g., *Starlight over Texas* and its treatment of guns). Now and again, I mention an A western (e.g., *Shane* or *The Searchers*) because it extends the discussion and provides a contrast with the B pictures. B westerns differ from the bigger-budget A productions in a variety of ways. The production values of the A westerns are higher, for one thing. The A westerns use a range of locations, whereas the B films show the same locations in film after film. The running times of A films are generally twenty to sixty minutes longer than those of B films. The longer durations accommodate the complications in plot and theme that are absent from the comparatively one-dimensional B films. Characters remain stock in the B films, while the A westerns attempt to develop characters in more rounded ways. Moreover, audiences for the two kinds of film differ. The B western appealed to rural audiences and youthful audiences. The singing cowboy versions of the B western attempted to draw an audience of women, as well as a youthful male audience. Interesting here is the connection between children and females, a connection deeply imbedded in the history of children's literature and cultural assumptions regarding women and children. The A westerns were made to appeal to adults, even an audience of urban sophisticates. Sex, social concerns, moral ambiguity, psychological complexity—all are features of the A western. These films thrive on emotional intensity. The B film is more serene, predictable, and formulaic.

I may have begun to watch B westerns when I was a boy, but in the 1980s Public Television aired a weekly program called *Those Six-Gun Heroes*, hosted by Sunset Carson. This program began and ended with a song, and with this I begin. The song is a tribute to B western films:

> There was justice in his six-gun
> There was magic in his name
> And I always tried to be him
> When we played our cowboy games
> I stood in line to see him
> Ride across our small-town screen
> I rode with him in every scene
> And he would ride off to the sunset
> With that friendly western smile
> He would ride into the sunset
> No goodbyes, just so long for a while.

The song that graced *Those Six-Gun Heroes* gives as full an account of the B western cowboy as we could wish for. Overall, the tone of the song is elegiac, and elegy is built into the vision of manhood almost as a warning, as well as a substitution. The warning is that no boy aspiring to become the hero he desires to emulate can accomplish such becoming because the hero is always a man of the past, always already out of touch with changing times, always a figure of regression, and paradoxically always already old even though he never ages. He is both brother and father. He takes a beating and he is also the stern lawgiver who metes out beatings. He is a protector, and a defender of the law. He is the law—the law of the father. And yet he often acts outside the law. He is, in short, a fantasy. He represents the Ideal-I and all the accoutrements we associate with him function as *objets petits a*, those metonymic substitutions for a reality we can never have. What I attempt to do in this book is simply to look at the cowboy, only to do so awry (see Žižek, *Looking Awry*). In order to put nostalgia into perspective, I have to consider the cowboy as an elegiac substitution for that which we cannot have. As substitution, elegy serves to offer the vision of the male a touch of sentiment, a touch of feeling, that which the male supposedly does not show because feeling is a feminine weakness. The glow of sentiment, even sadness, that emanates from so much heroic palaver serves to soften the masochistic self-denial of the hero. Moral masochism is his preserve. The hero lives a life of denial: he is often alone, beyond the comforts of domesticity and home, without a sense of place. Sometimes he carries a mysterious burden, a guilt sometimes objectified in a former failure of nerve or a mistaken shooting or the sight of death. His seemingly attractive freedom to roam, to spend his life unconstrained by the ties of home and work, has its price, and that price is the very thing that seems to attract: the apparent freedom is available only because the cowboy accepts the life of exile from community and he represses his desire for the comforts of home. The elegiac tone of so much western lore, then, disguises so much paradox. Riding into the sunset appears quite romantic, and Thanatos remains barely discernable.

If the cowboys taught my generation anything, they taught discipline, denial, self-control, in short the virtues of repression, or what Herbert Marcuse calls "surplus-repression," that extra bit of restraint worked into us by social, economic, and political means in order to ensure we are compliant citizens and eager consumers. Elegy is a disguised lament for the masochistic acceptance of conformity. Heroes may exist in silhouette, but their power remains available to a society constructed on what we might call "masculine" conventions: they are the patriarchs. Masculine power is a function of masculine pain. Happy on the outside, crying on the inside—we all know the refrain. As David Savran notes in his articulation of how masochism works in the male psyche, "the cultural texts constructing masochistic masculinities characteristically conclude with an almost magical restitution of phallic power" (37). Western films often put this crudely, but powerfully nonetheless: some way through the film the hero receives a beating, he suffers and finds himself restrained and under threat of death, but by the end he reasserts his power and defeats the forces of anarchy, pride, and excess. Once again powerful beyond measure, he rides into limbo until his next appearance.

But let's explore the song.

There was justice in his six-gun. Justice from the barrel of a gun. Richard Slotkin, in *Gunfighter Nation*, points out that from its inception the United States constructed its sense of destiny as a dynamic and progressive civilization on a myth that depends largely on aggression (10–21). The country was created by men who tamed the wilderness, intent on subduing by violent means a violent land and its savage inhabitants. Or, as Savran says more bluntly in his discussion of the emergence of the masculine self since the seventeenth century, "male subjectivity is founded on *violence*" (25; italics in original). Both social and psychological versions of manhood involve the necessity for active control of an Other that requires stewardship and taming. That Other is either a barbarous bunch (native or foreign) in need of a civilizing force, or it consists of the libidinous drives in the psyche in need of chastening by Mr. Strong Superego. To accomplish the work of order, the good force of manly civilization carries a big stick, a "weepin" (see Fritz Lang's *The Return of Frank James*, 1940) of some type, more often than not manifesting itself as a gun. The gun, as we all know, sublimates; the male is gun crazy precisely because the gun is a tool that does the work of subduing that which the gun paradoxically stands for. The title of the 1950 film *Annie Get Your Gun* is, from one perspective, just another way of saying "Annie Get Your Man." A more progressive reading might render the title "Annie Get Your Phallus."

The gun, as we hear again and again, is a necessary adjunct to justice. It is the gun that ensures peace and order and fair play and freedom. A person has the right to bear arms, and the Second Amendment to the American Constitution certifies this right. The western film has always placed emphasis on the gun as a magic weapon; the hero's pistols often sport ivory or even pearl handles, or they have some other distinctive design such as an engraved paladin or maybe, more sinisterly, notches. Some weapons have modifications; for example, the Winchester rifle with its rounded lever that John Wayne carried and twirled in many films beginning with his entrance in *Stagecoach* (1939) or the long-barrelled six-gun, the Buntline Special associated with Wyatt Earp. Some cowboy heroes used both a gun and a bullwhip to disarm or disable an enemy (Whip Wilson, "Lash" LaRue), and some carried their pistols reversed in their holsters (Rex Allen, Wild Bill Elliott). In the hands of a hero, the gun can even be benign, capable of shooting a weapon from the hand of an enemy even from a horse at full gallop. In one film, *Powdersmoke Range* (1935), the hero goes into a gunfight carrying two Colt single-action .32-20s on a forty-four frame precisely so he will not kill his opponent. (This brings to mind Nancy Reagan's "tiny little gun.")

In *West of Everything*, Jane Tompkins recounts her visit to the Buffalo Bill Museum in Denver, Colorado, in June 1988, where she saw "case after case of rifles and pistols," "rows and rows of guns." Expressing her failure to respond to this display of firepower in the manner intended by the curator, she writes:

> Awe and admiration are the attitudes the museum invites. You hear the ghostly march of military music in the background; you imagine flags waving and sense the implicit reference to feats of courage in battle and glorious death. The place had the air of an expensive and well-kept reliquary, or of the room off the transept of a cathedral where the vestments are stored. These guns were not there merely to be seen or even studied; they were there to be venerated. (194)

As children, we (myself and the boys I played with) did precisely this: we venerated guns. Guns occupied much of our waking lives, our games and fantasies, and perhaps even our dreams. I can recall the passion I expended vainly trying to convince my mother to buy me a Red Ryder BB gun. The gun was not a weapon; it was a tool every real man should have in order to accomplish his work as provider and protector. The gun revealed its owner's mastery. Many will recall Alan Ladd as Shane instructing young Joey Starrett in the use of firearms. A gun, he says, is the measure of a man's moral strength, not his physical strength (*Shane*, 1953). I confess that at the age of ten, I too believed, at least in one lazy corner of my mind, that "there was justice in his six-gun."

There was magic in his name. Yes, the names sing like an incantation: Allan "Rocky" Lane, "Wild Bill" Elliott, Hoot Gibson, Larry "Buster" Crabbe, Battling Bob Steele, Sunset Carson, Al "Lash" LaRue, Buck Jones, Colonel Tim McCoy, Johnny Mack Brown, Tex Ritter, Tom Mix, Ray "Crash" Corrigan, Hopalong Cassidy, Rex Allen, Don "Red"' Barry, Roy Rogers, King of the Cowboys, or Gene Autry and his Wonder Horse Champion. You can add your own magic names. The names conjure the sense of wild abandon, recklessness, and natural toughness and savvy; they also conjure strength and order, discipline and natural majesty. They are simple names, yet distinctly memorable. They are names fit for characters in fiction: Cisco Kid, the Virginian, Buffalo Bill Cody, Wild Bill Hickok, Davy Crockett, Kit Carson, Daniel Boone, Jim Bridger, Hawkeye. Already we see the confusion of history and fiction, fantasy and reality; as Seiler and Seiler point out, the historical, fictional, and mythic levels on which the cowboy exists "are so interrelated that determining where the historical figure ends and the fictional character begins is difficult, if not impossible" (51).

The westerns I focus on deal fast and loose with history, as their depictions of Billy the Kid, Jesse James, or Pat Garrett testify (e.g., *Billy the Kid Returns*, 1938; *Days of Jesse James*, 1939; or *Outcasts of the Trail*, 1949). In the movies this blurring of the relationship between history and fiction was deliberate; depictions of historical figures such as Jesse James or Billy the Kid often had nothing to do with historical accuracy. The folding of reality into fantasy also occurs in the many western stars themselves. The western star merged with the characters we see on the screen. William Boyd *was* Hopalong Cassidy, Rex Allen *was* the Oklahoma Cowboy, and Roy Rogers *was* the King of the Cowboys. As Richard Slotkin points out (referring to John Wayne), the "idea was to suggest that what the audience saw on the screen was not just 'an actor in a role' but somehow a 'real' cowboy-adventurer" (273). Characters such as Roy Rogers and Hopalong Cassidy (William Boyd) made personal appearances wearing their cowboy duds and sporting their cowboy pistols. To the kids who were witness to these personal appearances, Roy and Hoppy were cowboys; they were the characters who appeared on screen. If these good guys on the screen and in the comics were somehow real, then what they stood for was worth all our attempts to achieve. And what they stood for, besides the value of a good gun, was independence, responsibility, self-denial, and the repression of anything that might smack of bodily indulgence. These guys drink nothing but milk, sleep in their clothes and rarely change them, carry no toiletries on their long journeys, sometimes sleep two abed, and avoid—at times reluctantly—marriage. Yes, *I always tried to be him ...*

When we played our cowboy games. What should leap out at anyone who has grown up with the films I write about is not simply the nostalgia redolent in memories of childhood play with toy guns and holsters and tin marshal's badges, but the deeply insistent regressive tendency of what we experienced on the screen. The image of masculinity we received appeared innocent, offering the young male viewer nothing but solid moral value for the fifteen- or twenty-five-cent admission fee. And it was true that we left the theatre on a Saturday afternoon to return to our neighbourhood and, invariably, acted out what we had seen on the screen. For us, the life of a cowboy was a game. Games, we know, are preparation for life. In games, as Johan Huizinga pointed out long ago in *Homo Ludens*, we learn order and civilized behaviour. The catch here is that playing cowboys involves dragging into adulthood the fantasies of childhood; something of Peter Pan adheres to this play. The actors we see on the screen are playing; they act in front of a camera, and in turn we act out the roles we see on screen. One result of such play is its perpetuation in such absurd "adult" activities as paintball and in the proliferation of gun clubs. The desire to remain "boys" (our heroes, after all, were cow*boys*) results in a fetishization of the gun and in games of pretend violence. But a short step takes us from paintball to warrior magazines such as *Soldier of Fortune: The Journal of Professional Adventurers* and *Combat Handguns* and *Gung-Ho*, and to "combat pistol shooting at Gunsight Ranch" (see Gibson, *Warrior Dreams*). Male culture can be, and often is, a culture of violence. These games, as Rosalind Miles suggests in *Rites of Man*, are passage rituals, tests of manhood. Paradoxically, these ritual games are passages that lead nowhere; they are designed to maintain the fiction of male boyishness even in the midst of adult activity.

Our sense of masculinity derives to a great extent from notions of boyhood and "boy culture." In the last century, as Anthony Rotundo points out, boyhood was a "distinct cultural world with its own rituals and its own symbols and values." The boys' world was separate from that of girls and women and from the world of business; in their closed world, "boys were able to play outside the rules of the home and the marketplace" (31). Sanctioned activities in this boy world included hunting, fighting, competitive games involving physical exertion, and games that mimicked certain of the activities of men, especially those associated with war and aggression. The boys' world emphasized "energy, self-assertion, noise, and a frequent resort to violence" (Rotundo, 37). Loyalty to groups was also important. Courage in the face of threat, both physical and emotional, was a virtue (Rotundo, 41–46), and courage implied stoicism. No self-respecting boy wanted to be known as a crybaby. The boy, or at least the Good Bad Boy as Leslie Fiedler named him some years ago, could transgress with impunity. Boys will, after all, be boys. So it was and so it is.

I stood in line to see him / Ride across our small-town screen. Obviously, the films I am discussing played all across North America and elsewhere in the world. But it is true to say that the main market for these films was small-town America (and Canada), the so-called Heartland. The films speak to those in relatively rural areas who still believe spaces are wide open and fresh, whose fantasies may legitimately include horses, and whose houses most likely contain 12-gauge shotguns and 30.30 rifles for hunting, and who eat duck and venison in season. Postwar urbanization saw those guns move into the cities, and the forests and rocks of the western landscape become the canyons and alleys of the naked city. The transformation is nicely captured in the title of a film from 1981,

Fort Apache, the Bronx. The seepage of western lore, language, and ethos into modern urban life is exhaustively set out in Slotkin's *Gunfighter Nation.* Small-town idol worship has become big-town fear, violence, and intolerance.

I mention intolerance because an insistent message in these films is that the hero is white, a descendant of good European stock. Insistent but silent. Race never becomes an issue in these films, because the fantasy is that race does not count. People in small towns have little to do with matters of race, and when they do the racial categories are clear: white/Other. *White* is a word we can hear in these films spoken as a synonym for *generous, caring*—in short, *good.* Being white is tantamount to being morally upright, clean, and in control. By implication, anyone who is other than white is immoral, unclean, and uncontrolled. White equals safely repressed; non-white equals the wildly savage, the libidinous, or the downright silly.

The heroes in these films often conform to cliché; they wear white hats and ride white horses—not always, but often. They are invariably clean-shaven; indeed, their skin appears smoothly prepubescent. Their clothes rarely show wear and tear. The villains, on the other hand, are often grizzled, even hirsute. Moustaches are common—bushy ones for bad-guy cowboys and thin ones for the oily banker, the large landowner, and the eastern businessman. Sometimes the villains are ethnically or racially coded: a Mexican or Native American, a French Canadian or Chinese person. Villains have a tendency to travel in gangs, sometimes organizing into paramilitary groups with uniforms or into mysterious bands such as the Hooded Horsemen (*The Mystery of the Hooded Horsemen*, 1937) or the Purple Vigilantes (*The Purple Vigilantes*, 1938). The good guy usually travels alone or at most with two sidekicks, and, although outnumbered, he and his friends defeat the baddies, sometimes with the assistance of a motley crew of local citizens that the hero has convinced to stand up and fight. The fiction is that the small independent business person can successfully defend his or her land and business against the ruthless tyranny of big business or foreign incursion. All that is needed is pluck, the willingness to shoot a gun, and the leadership of the itinerant cowboy whose only permanent relationship is with his horse.

Speaking of permanent relationships, I note that women feature consistently in these films as playful love interests. I say *playful* because rarely do they have more than a token role in the plot. Whenever the hero travels with a sidekick or two, he chooses his male friends over the girl, who watches him longingly from her ranch-house porch as he rides away. As we might expect, the female represents an end to the hero's freedom, and unless she can be brought to accept his life of manly action and the guns that go with it, he will ride away, if not into the sunset, then to follow a wandering star. The woman finds herself situated with a parent (almost always a father) and/or children. She is never independent, except in the rare cases when she is a villain. Even when the woman does appear as villain capable of competing, after a fashion, with men, she is located in a saloon or gambling emporium. She does not have the freedom of the wandering hero. Her place is in town; his is under the stars, among the buttes, mesas, and forests of a landscape as craggy and pure as the man himself.

And he would ride off to the sunset / With that friendly western smile. I have mentioned the necessarily elegiac quality of the western. The irony is that this character who obviously does not exist in the normal world of everyday responsibility, work, and family life, nevertheless comes to represent that which is of value in this world of everyday responsibility, work, and family life. No wonder the real man finds his life constricted, narrow, petty, and dull. The cowboy, always a bundle of contradictions, beckons the man to a more exciting life, while at the same time teaching him the virtues of restraint and austerity. The smile must be wry. "That friendly western smile" is both comforting and frightening. "When you call me that, smile," we remember the Virginian saying in his laconic manner. And we know he is smiling as he says this. The smile communicates self-assurance, friendship, and a willingness to explode at any time. This smile reflects the duplicity of a masculinity based on aggression and arms. In the B western, perhaps the most baroque expression of what the smile communicates is Hopalong Cassidy's distinctive and hearty laugh. When Hoppy laughed, we knew the situation was well in hand.

No goodbyes, just so long for a while. And a short while it is. The cowboy keeps coming back like the tumbling tumbleweed. Roy, Gene, Rocky, "Lash," and the rest may be in hillbilly heaven along with Tex, but they are still with us in so many ways, telling us what it means to be a man. As I write this introduction, a piece appears in my local paper, the *Calgary Herald*, with the title "There's Something about a Well-Seasoned Cowboy That Makes Women Wild about the West." The writer of this report, Dina O'Meara, quotes an Edmonton woman named Kim Shanks: "I think cowboys are sexy because they're men, not wimps.... They're not going to whine or whimper if they get a scratch" (D1). Cowboys such as Clint Eastwood and John Wayne, O'Meara asserts, "squinted, sauntered and shot their way into our hearts." Strong and silent, the cowboy does his job and gets on with things. Squinting and sauntering may result from a life under the sun in boots made more for riding than walking, but shooting into our hearts is a deft reminder of how dangerous this image of manhood is. O'Meara and many others accept the shooting, along with the sauntering, as a sign of attractive manhood. Such attractiveness is what our culture has taught us for much of the past century. For me, and for many men of my generation, the attractions of the cowboy were as natural as going to the cinema on Saturday afternoon. The cowboy may have ridden into the sunset, but just so long for a while. He keeps coming back, and each time he does he carries a heavier load of hardware or gear we now generally hear referred to as ordnance.

Three Men and a Dummy: A Case History

for John Wayne and the gang

My heroes have always been cowboys. When I reflect on this, I can only conclude that something queer looks back at me. I cannot ride horses. I cannot abide guns. I know nothing of cows or of riding fence. I am not an advocate of violence in any form. But I do love cowboys. As a boy, I ran home from school to catch *Cowboy Corner* on TV, a program we received from Watertown, New York, in which a fellow called Danny B introduced daily a B western film from the previous two decades. These films featured such stars as "Lash" LaRue, Johnny Mack Brown, Eddie Dean, and Bob Steele. I went to the movies on Saturday afternoons, where we could see the likes of the Durango Kid and Roy Rogers. I read western comics. I ached to own the latest western paraphernalia: six-guns, stetsons, ropes, boots, badges, silver spurs—all the stuff I saw the western heroes wear in those wonderful western films that filled my days and nights with fantasies of power and self-confidence. In short, when I was a boy much of what formed my image of manhood derived from those B western films that thrived from the 1930s until the mid-1950s, when television sent them into the sunset.

What intrigues me now is the apparent paradox: raised on the violence of cowboy movies, I have emerged nonetheless as a pacifist, yet a pacifist who continues to feel attraction to those violent cowboy movies. Why? I shall argue that these films, like much popular culture, are ambiguous in their message in that they contain deeply conservative values edged with transgressive desire. In short, I argue that these films are "queer"—that is, they construct a masculinity that is distinctly other than the one-dimensional image we might have of the cowboy as the type of male we think of as aggressive, unemotional, laconic, action-oriented, and violent. Just as the films blend genres, they also blend gender. They produce a male figure who is communal, parental, sensitive, and Other. The rub here is *communal* and Other. These cowboys function as preservers, even nurturers, of community, and at the same time they remain outside community, uninterested in economic gain and political power. Often they interact with children (at least one, Red Ryder, travels with a child; his young companion is a Native American, Little Beaver), and when they do they are clearly role models for these children. Yet they do not marry, they do not hold jobs, they appear not to work. They exist on horseback, forever riding from one endangered community to another to set things right. I argue that these films construct a male figure who is "queer," and by *queer* I mean a person who does not fit comfortably into our binary categories heterosexual/homosexual, insider/outsider, masculine/feminine.

My sense of queer owes something to Judith Halberstam's study *In a Queer Time and Place* (2005). Halberstam notes that

> much of the contemporary theory seeking to disconnect queerness from an essential definition of homosexual embodiment has focused on queer space and queer practices. By articulating and elaborating a concept of queer time, I suggest new ways of understanding the nonnormative behaviours that have clear but not essential relations to gay and lesbian subjects. (6)

She goes on to relate queer to "nonnormative logics and organizations of community, sexual identity, embodiment, and activity in space and time" (6). More specifically, queer refers to the possibility of a life lived "outside of those paradigmatic markers of life experience—namely, birth, marriage, reproduction and death" (2). We will see more of this later, but for now we can note the cowboy hero's existence outside the paradigmatic markers Halberstam lists. Both the time and space the hero occupies are queer in the sense that they appear to collapse categories such as east and west (e.g., *Wall Street Cowboy*, 1939), past and present (horses and wagons and trucks and cars and airplanes often compete for our attention and compete for arrival at some significant destination), and even dimensions of space (a character in one shot is on a set but in the next he or she is in an outdoor location, or a character looks from one location to another that is clearly geographically different from the one he stands in, as in the opening of *Springtime in the Sierras*, 1947). Cowboy heroes exist in something of a liminal zone; they interact socially but for the most part do not lead conventional lives associated with marriage, home, and reproduction.

In this section I focus on a batch of western films made mostly by Republic Studios in the 1930s and '40s, films that starred the sagebrush trio known as the Three Mesquiteers (Stony Brook, Tucson Smith, and Lullaby Joslin), characters created by William Colt MacDonald in a series of books in the 1930s. Films starring these cowboy heroes constitute only a small fraction of the hundreds of westerns made by so-called Poverty Row Studios such as Monogram, Mascot, Tiffany, Grand National, and PRC (Producers Releasing Corporation). These films were made quickly and cheaply; they were formulaic; they were immensely popular. Many of them delight in breaking down distinctions in genre: blended with the western are such film genres as the detective mystery, science fiction, war stories, gangster films, comedy, the musical, the circus story, and even the jungle adventure tale. Sometimes this play with genre has strange results, as in many of the Mesquiteer films which feature as their d'Artagnan figure Elmer, the ventriloquist's dummy. Elmer often appears to speak and act independently of his ventriloquist, Lullaby (Max Terhune), giving the films something of the surreal quality of the mid-1970s television situation comedy *Soap*. In one film, *Riders of the Whistling Skull* (1937), Elmer briefly comes under suspicion of murder. Elmer fulfills several roles in the films: companion, comic relief, diversion, child, and even ironic adult commentator on the Mesquiteers' adolescent behaviour. Lullaby carries Elmer in a large womblike sack across the saddle of his horse, and he "births" him whenever an occasion arises in which Elmer can be useful. This D'Artagnon doubles as a baby for the three men who are his bearers. Genre blending in these films is also gender blending; something queer wanders the west in these films, although, as Vito Russo notes in *The Celluloid Closet* (1981), "it is easy to see [because of the homophobia in American culture at the time] how directors could be blind to their own subtexts" (79).

In his discussion of the sissy in films of the 1930s and '40s, Russo points out that the inclusion of the sissy served to deflect any uncertainty concerning manhood away from the hero (31). Later, he contends, the sissy was "employed to protect heroism from defamation" (89). In the films of the early sound era, "homosexuality did not officially exist" and "homophobic sentiment was directed elsewhere. *Symbols* of masculinity were defended by the use of *symbols* for homosexuality" (32; italics in original). The sissy works to defend symbols of masculinity. In the B western, the sissy makes an appearance as sidekick to several of the heroes. The sidekick generally provides a counter to the strength and composure of the hero. Character actors such as "Gabby" Hayes, Andy Clyde, and Al St. John play older men who fondly recall the time when they were rough and tough. Now, however, they are creaky and bent with age. Gabby Hayes often rails against "persnickety women." Andy Clyde appears at least once in drag. Al St. John is interesting among these actors; he served as Fatty Arbuckle's foil in many of Fatty's silent comedies, and in many of these we find Fatty in drag being courted by St. John.

The ineffectual sidekick becomes more pointedly a "sissy"—that is, a character who is not overtly gay but who is swishy and quite possibly gay—in the late 1930s and the '40s with the appearance of actors such as Syd Saylor, Gordon Jones, Snub Pollard, and especially Pinky Lee in sidekick roles. The mannerisms (so to speak) of these characters, especially the latter two, are clearly of the sissy variety: soft-spoken, coy, fearful, hesitant, and limp-wristed. Syd Saylor employed a stutter, a sure sign of ambiguous masculinity in these films, and Pinky Lee spoke with a slight lisp, another sign of ambiguous masculinity. Snub Pollard had mannerisms reminiscent to those of Stan Laurel, an actor who often used the mannerisms of drag in his dealings with Oliver Hardy (Russo, 10; see also 25). The sidekick provides comic relief and also assurance that the hero is all man. The hero takes a paternal and patient attitude toward his sidekick, willing to accept his weaknesses because these weaknesses cannot threaten the hero's masculinity. Sidekicks serve as reminders of a weak masculinity that puts the hero's strong masculinity into sharp focus.

I do not, however, mean to imply that these films are homosexual in theme, either covertly or overtly, although for all I know they may be. But they do take an interest in such things as male bonding, single-sex families, and what we might call revisionary notions of masculinity. My interest here is in the manner in which these films present masculinity. Put another way, I intend to understand the west in these films as "queer space," a space for mixing things up and shaking our conventional notions of things. We might, I think, also understand the cultural moment of these films as queer space, since they construct their male heroes against the backdrop of the Depression and the emergence of America as a world power just prior to World War II. What we see in the films of the Three Mesquiteers and those of Gene Autry (and I use these only as representative of a whole range of other films with group heroes such as the Range Busters, the Trail Blazers, the Rough Riders, the Hopalong Cassidy films, and those with single heroic figures such as Monte Hale and Bob Steele and Buster Crabbe) is a strangely mixed configuration of the male. Something queer is going on in these films, and it is the queerness that I wish to interrogate. The title of this section already hints at something of this queerness: "three men and a dummy" invites us to think of the ménage as family.

The sheer number of these films indicates both their popularity and their pervasive influence on the filmgoing public. Between 1935 and 1943, fifty-three films appeared starring the Three Mesquiteers, fifty-one of these from Republic Studios. The three characters, as the title of the series indicates, derive from Alexander Dumas' *The Three Musketeers*, and just as the Three Musketeers are in fact four, so too are their cowboy counterparts (at least in the films with Max Terhune as Lullaby). The characters in the films are saddled with unlikely names: Stony Brook, Tucson Smith, Lullaby Joslin, and, in those films which starred Max Terhune, the wooden dummy Elmer. During the eight-year life of the series, several actors played the parts of the Mesquiteers, the most prominent of these being Al St. John, Hoot Gibson, John Wayne, Robert Livingston, and Tom Tyler as Stony, Guinn "Big Boy" Williams, Harry Carey, Ray "Crash" Corrigan, and Bob Steele as Tucson, Guinn Williams, Syd Saylor, Max Terhune, Rufe Davis, and Jimmy Dodd as Lullaby. Others who made appearances in major roles include Raymond Hatton, Duncan Renaldo, and Ralph Byrd. My focus here is the films that include Elmer, the dummy.

Why a dummy? Well, it is true that western films marketed to a mixed audience of adults and children in the 1930s and '40s had no truck with reality. Perhaps this is nowhere more evident than in the twelve-chapter western–science fiction film *Phantom Empire* (1935), starring Gene Autry and Smiley Burnett. Here is a mishmash that no one, young or old, could mistake for reality in the west—old west or new west. Westerns during this period clearly looked to provide satisfying fantasy for Depression-ridden audiences whose desire was for some sense of beauty and song amid the dreary wastes of failed markets and lost topsoil. Many of these films deal with dispossessed landowners, water shortages, failed crops, bank foreclosures, uprooted peoples seeking places to settle and work. But they also deal with what it means to be a male.

Let's look at the Mesquiteers. Again I have to ask the question: Why a dummy? To answer this, we need first to examine the construction of masculinity in each of the Mesquiteers themselves. Loosely, what these three represent are the hotheaded young man, the level-headed mature man, and the comical slightly older man. Here is a bizarre version of the Tin

Man, the Scarecrow, and the Cowardly Lion. Together they represent every-thing the male ought to be: adept at taking control, purposeful in action, thoughtful, loyal, adaptable, and capable of humour. These fellows don't take life completely seriously, although they do take such things as jus-tice, honour, and protection of the innocent seriously. Often the objects of their protective actions are children, sometimes children in orphanages (e.g., *Roarin' Lead*, 1936, and *Heroes of the Saddle*, 1940); at other times they protect women, once even pretending that their ranch belongs to a woman who mistakenly thinks it is hers (*Three Texas Steers*, 1939). Yes, the three men own a ranch, but they appear never to work it. Nor do they appear to have help keeping the place going. Most often we find them itin-erant cowboys who just happen to find trouble wherever they go. I men-tioned orphanages, and, when the plot requires, as it does in *Roarin' Lead*, the three are on the board of directors of an orphanage. They are ranch-ers, horse dealers, businessmen, undercover agents, archaeologists, engi-neers—just about anything you can imagine. They are footloose and fancy free, and they can turn their hands or their horses to just about anything.

Two of the Mesquiteers have eyes for women: Stony and Tucson. Stony is the one most taken with a woman, although at times Stony and Tucson are rivals for her attention. Dining out, dancing, serenading, and of course riding (often with the man saving the woman from disaster on a runaway horse or in a runaway buggy) are some of the courting ritu-als the films show. Perhaps the most persistent sign of a man's worth, besides his saving the woman from runaway animals, is his willingness to fist-fight. But it hardly matters. The viewer learns the importance of gallantry even as he learns the even more important lesson about free-dom; a man is free only when he is away from the domesticating ways of a woman. In one film, *Hit the Saddle* (1937), Stony is about to be mar-ried. Lullaby laments: "There must be some good way to bust up a mar-riage." A crestfallen Tucson can only rationalize: "He brought this on himself." Always resourceful, Lullaby convinces the would-be bride that if she marries Stony, she faces a life of sewing, washing, cooking, and other domestic chores. She quickly cuts out for New York, where she plans to become an actress—a sign that Stony is better off without this potential hoyden in his life. Stony's only response to her departure is "I'm cured," indicating that only while suffering from some disease could he have entertained the thought of marriage. A return to health means a return to the boys. At the end of many of these films, most of which do not bring the hero to the brink of marriage, the young man taken with a woman always chooses to leave the woman and ride off with his pals. This is the boys' loyalty that I mentioned earlier. For boys, allegiance to the group comes before all else.

Male companionship is what these films are about. But not simply male companionship; rather, the companionship of boys. As I indicated earlier, something of Peter Pan sweeps through these films; this sagebrush trio (dubbed the Trigger Trio in the 1937 film of that name) exemplifies what Leslie Fiedler calls the "good bad boy" (1972, 259–67; 1966, 254–87)—that young fellow with the sly grin and the cocky tilt to the head whom we forgive for his excesses of exuberance because we know that when the chips are down, m'am, he'll come through in spades, riding over the crest of a hill to rescue whatever needs rescuing and setting to right whatever has nearly toppled under the pressure of some bad man's greed. When you get right down to it, boys will be boys, and that is just the way we want it. These mature men can play at being boys because the "boy" is our ideal of masculinity. The opening sequence of *Range Defenders* (1937) makes the point. Here Tucson and Lullaby find Stony in a barber's chair, and like two schoolboys they play a trick on him and run away giggling. Practical jokes are part of the fun of being boys. So too are kibitzing and even quarrelling. Stony and Tucson often quarrel and even pout, but their quarrels reflect their intimacy. No matter what the reason for their tiffs, they always rally when one or the other is in trouble or when they can fight together against a gang of baddies.

Inseparable from the notion of manhood in these films is what I can only call the friendly gun. Guns these days are not so friendly, despite the strident call on the part of some for permission to own them. Charlton Heston has passed on, but his virility continues to impress those who insist on their right to carry arms. Still and all, in fiction and films sex may be preferable to violence nowadays (as Fiedler pointed out forty years ago), but we continue to defend the gun. In the films I am discussing, sex is attractive, but what Fiedler calls "good clean violence" (1972, 273) is preferable to just about anything. In the first of Republic Studio's Mesquiteer films, *The Three Mesquiteers* (1936), Stony turns quickly to Tucson as the two of them fire their pistols at a gang of bad guys and asks, "Isn't this better than ranching?" He and everyone watching the film know the answer. Not much has changed, only nowadays the bullets fly toward the innocent as well as the guilty. And they fly out here—in the land before the screen.

The opening sequence of the Mesquiteers films changed little over the years, but it did change. The first films in the series, mostly with Livingston, Corrigan, and Terhune, begin with an introduction of each of the Mesquiteers. First Stony, then Tucson, and finally Lullaby. Each smiles in turn at the camera in gestures of welcome to the audience. It's the Happy Gang, so come on in. Then we have the rest of the credits. The films with John Wayne as Stony alter this beginning in a manner that intensifies the myth of the friendly gun. We see each Mesquiteer in turn: Stony first, then Tucson, and finally Lullaby. All three shots are medium close-up, the actors facing the camera. Each smiles and draws his six-shooters, Stony with a twirl, Tucson with both guns aimed at the audience, and Lullaby with a gesture pointing his gun toward us. Clearly, these fellows are friendly, and they use their guns here as toys; part of their appeal comes in the direct way they draw, twirl, and point their weapons at us. The actions mimic the quick draw and remind us that these cowboys are proficient with their guns, fast on the draw, and accurate in their aim. It was precisely actions such as these that gave rise to my desire as a child for a set of toy guns. They would have to look as much like the real thing as possible. Plastic guns or any other obviously fake replicas would not do. We wanted Colt .45s, and we wanted them in real leather holsters cut low just the way the gunfighters on the screen had them, slung low on the hip and tied to the thigh with a rawhide cord.

Slung low on the hip so that we could be hipsters. I doubt that the connection is direct, but it is nevertheless nice. The rebel male of the 1950s is, as articulated by Norman Mailer in *The White Negro*, the new "frontiersman in the Wild West of American night life" (qtd. in Savran, 49). The hipster who developed out of the infantile heroics of the B western cowboys differed from that cowboy in that he no longer had a cause against which to rebel. When asked what he is rebelling against, the hipster (Johnny in László Benedek's *The Wild One*, 1953) can only reply: "Whaddya got?" As David Savran points out, Mailer's "white negro" has something akin to the psychopathic in his makeup; he is masochistic, undirected, and concerned with self-gratification. Savran notes that such a subject is "infantilized and potentially violent" (49). The childish behaviour and the capacity for violence are evident in the many films of the 1950s that present young men in gangs: *The Wild One* (1953), for example, and *Blackboard Jungle* (1955), *Rebel without a Cause* (1955), *High School Confidential* (1958), and even *Bucket of Blood* (1959). This was the time of the birth of the cool. We haven't come as far from that time as we sometimes like to think we have.

Let me return to the sly grin. This usually goes along with the swagger that accentuates the cowboy body. The Mesquiteers were nothing if not cocky in their masculinity (especially Stony as played by Robert Livingston). Boys learned the importance of self-assurance by watching these films.

Not only is the manner of projecting the body in movement important, but so too are clothes that set off the body. Trousers tend to be close fitting. Various paraphernalia accentuate hips and crotch: belts, holsters, buckles, and sometimes chaps. Some trousers have fancy stitched patterns to emphasize the length of the leg and/or the shape of the buttocks. Boots are often worn outside the trousers to show off the fine tooling. Shirts are clean, and some have embroidered designs or stitched pockets or fancy stitching on cuffs or shoulders. All this fashionable dress serves both to draw attention to the male body and to feature attractive items of merchandise for the young viewer who hopes to emulate his screen hero. The cowboy is, from one perspective, a fashion model. Guns and holsters are part of the fashion, exhibiting eye-catching shine and fancy patterns. No matter how long these fellows have been on the trail, no matter how frenetic the fist fights, they manage to remain clean, well groomed, and sartorially splendid.

So Stony, Tucson, and Lullaby are inseparable. But why a dummy? The addition of Elmer to the group only reinforces its paternal function. These guys not only fight and ride and shoot and stop runaway horses, but they also care for children. Children, either in ones, twos, or gaggles, frequently appear in these films, and when they do not Elmer serves as a good substitute. Bizarre as it may seem, when children are absent Elmer reminds us that these three cowboys are caregivers. Many of these films involve the trio defending family values, and they often serve as surrogate fathers to children whose parents have died or are for some reason ineffective. Realizing the distance between the vision of a John Ford and the directors (men such as Joe Kane, Mack Wright, and George Sherman) of the Mesquiteers series, we might nevertheless think of Stony, Tucson, and Lullaby as the "Three Godfathers."

As I noted earlier, Elmer rides in a large rounded bag that hangs from Lullaby's saddle horn. He goes wherever the other three go, and Lullaby takes him from his sack—births him—whenever the film requires a bit of comic relief or some nifty plot turn. For example, in one film, *Three Texas Steers* (1939), Elmer hangs on a barn wall and comments on a fight that takes place between Lullaby and a friendly circus gorilla (yes, a gorilla!). But mostly Elmer is a reminder that these three range riders are at heart defenders of domestic harmony, champions of the small and defenceless, and father figures who remain deeply attached to boyhood. When Elmer talks, he takes charge; he is a wiseacre—brash, quick, and ironic. The dummy speaks with authority and flips the three men around him into adolescence. Why a dummy?

The evocation of fantasy is undeniable in the presence of Elmer in the Mesquiteers films. And the fantasy perpetrated by the films has to do with a masculinity that is decidedly powerful. These boys whose home is on the range seldom voice a discouraging word. Together they represent a male who is complete and autonomous. The male here does not need a woman—for anything. Male companionship and a good horse provide all that is necessary for fulfillment. Furthermore, these men do not only ride, fight, shoot, break broncs, herd cows, fix fences; they can also run orphanages, make decisions on the building of dams and telegraph lines and the resettling of communities. Most importantly, they can care for children; they can cook, keep house, change diapers, and prepare milk for feeding an infant. And as the presence of Elmer suggests, they can even give birth to a living, talking, though not breathing, person. No fantasy of male independence could be more complete. We might recall Freud's conversation with Little Hans. The child asserts that he is going to have a little girl next year, but Freud tells him, "Only women, only mommies have children." Hans replies: "But why shouldn't I?" (247). Why not indeed? The Mesquiteers can have Elmer. The myth of parthenogenesis structures these films

I've made much of Elmer here, but note the comment of a school principal interviewed by Raphaela Best: "If I encourage boys to play in the dollhouse, the community will run me out" (qtd. in Miedzian, 110). The space occupied by the Mesquiteers may not be a dollhouse, but Elmer is surely a doll. Three men and a male doll, then, represent the family unit in these films. This is a world in which women have no permanent place. They can provide a bit of fun—some dancing or a flirtatious walk through town—but they are not a necessary aspect even of family life. This I find queer. What kind of man do we have in these films? And why did the community not run him out? The answer to the first question, we've heard before. Remember Tanya in Welles's *Touch of Evil*: "He was some kind of a man." An answer to the second question must come later.

"All I want is to enter my house justified": Becoming a Man

for Randolph Scott and Joel McCrea

The kind of man we have here is some kind of a man. But what kind? And how did he get to be this kind of a man? I've tried to indicate that the male hero as these films construct him includes both that which we would expect and that which is surprising. We expect the man to sport his guns, to flex his muscles, to assert his authority and power, to take command, to run things, to set the agenda for social and domestic order. This is the patriarchal role many of us have come to feel is discomfiting. When the male who plays this role also exhibits adolescent swagger and moodiness, we see this as part of his appeal: he's the good bad boy, remember. This is, after all, the male our culture continues to think will lead us to Armageddon. But the Mesquiteers, and many of their B western compadres, exhibit what I can only call "queer" traits. What do I mean by queer?

Quite simply, I mean that which is unconventional, against the grain, nonconformist, and most importantly mixed rather than fixed. (Perhaps it is no coincidence that the most famous western hero of the 1920s had the name Tom Mix.) From this perspective, using *queer* to describe the cowboy heroes of B westerns is somewhat perverse, because these paragons of manly virtue serve to champion convention. The films in which they appear could not be more convention-ridden; the values the films express could not be more traditional in terms of community and family; and the men by and large reflect what the patriarchy sees as most important for men: power and authority. But from the perspective of identity these men have no essence; rather, they are a bundle of disparate traits, a mixture of masculine and feminine. They may desire to be masculine in a conventional sense (shooting bad guys is more fun than ranching), but they also desire that which they cannot be—that is, other than they are.

What I'm referring to here is an interrogation of the male identity that common sense tells us is sure and meaningful. We all know what a man is, right? Wrong. We may think we know what a man is, and aspects of our market-driven culture harp on the same old version of masculinity, masculinity defined by certain clothes, by cigarettes, by hair style, by body shape, and of course by certain apparently gender-specific activities such as stock car racing, contact sports, running powerful companies, drinking beer, riding motorcycles, leering at women, wrestling, and so on. "Yippee kai-oh-kai-yay, motherfucker," just about says it all. I choose this apparently wry line from the Bruce Willis film *Die Hard* (1988) as typical of the kind of masculinity we seem unable to put behind us because the film evokes the cowboys I write about here. At one point in the action, the villain refers to Willis as a would-be John Wayne, but Willis replies that he's always preferred Roy Rogers, and he asks that the villain call him Roy. He adds that he is partial to sequins. Of course, he's being ironic. No self-respecting male who takes his sexual identity seriously can be partial to sequins.

Again, implied here is an unconflicted masculine identity. Willis can have fun with the image of the cowboy because he is so sure of himself as a male. The true male is a cowboy, but this means he can ride and shoot and rope and rescue women and defeat bad guys and leap off tall buildings and take any amount of pain and then after successfully dispatching wrongdoers either light out into the territories or have the woman he wishes. But the B westerns I've been examining don't give us this unconflicted male hero, even though they may think they do. Return to the clothes they wear. The sartorial splendour of many of the B western stars marks their interest in appearance, fashion, and material things. These guys not only dress prettily, they also often sing. This aspect of their identity conflicts with the hard riding and hard shooting they display in their pursuit of the scruffy villains who threaten community cohesion and peace. So too does their interest in cooking and child rearing and domestic life. These fellows have a feminine side, perhaps quietly apparent in their reluctance actually to shoot anyone. They shoot guns from bad guys' hands or wing them in the shoulders or only threaten to shoot. The world of the B western is a world in which violence very often has little effect, and when it does—for example, when a child or a brother dies (*Santa Fe Stampede*, 1938; *Trailing Double Trouble*, 1940)—the shock reminds us how terrible violence is. On the other hand, people, mostly men, do die, shot from their horses or from high ledges in grand shootouts, and the violence here is routine, without impact, just part of the action.

This might work in either of two ways. First, the routine shooting of members of the Hollywood Posse, extras who provide expert riding and exciting stunts, suggests a normalizing of violence. It is quite simply part of the scene here. In a world of masculine activity, acts of violence, including those that result in death, are expected. Second, such acts may be a necessary part of justice. We recall that justice comes from the barrel of a gun as often as not in these films. The celebration of violence here is genuinely troubling.

However, when we remember the reluctance of the hero to shoot to kill, and when we register shock at the violent deaths of children or siblings or fathers, we cannot but acknowledge that these films critique violence while they are apparently celebrating it. (This ambivalence with respect to violence continues to be apparent in recent films such as *Shoot 'Em Up* [2007] and *Ironman* [2008]. The former makes direct reference to the Second Amendment.) In other words, these films are unsure of just how to go about presenting violent acts. Obviously, they go to some lengths to remind viewers that what we see is a fantasy—anyone who has seen these films will know that the six-shooters appear to have an unlimited supply of bullets in those six chambers, and hats appear glued to the heroes' heads. In this fantasy world, violent acts allow the hero to display feats of courage, agility, strength, restraint, judgment, and proficiency. Violence serves to make a man. The best man knows how to fight both with and without weapons. But he fights well because he fights according to a code of honour.

Cowboy Codes
Straight and Pure and All Boy

I remember having an ambivalent relationship with codes when I was young. The codes of honour and conduct that I was supposed to accept as a Wolf Cub and a Boy Scout made me uneasy; I did not like the association of military discipline with codes of behaviour. On the other hand, I felt an attraction to the personal code (most often unstated in the films) of justice and fair play exemplified in the celluloid cowboys. I can remember pretending to carry out the blood brother ritual that my friends and I saw in films; we would pretend to cut our hands and then clasp each other in the mixing of blood that indicated a bond that could not be broken no matter what the suffering. Only later did I read of such boyish pretending in the works of Mark Twain. This play tried to make a distinction between the military codes of behaviour that stemmed from duty and the manly codes of honour and friendship that stemmed from something beyond the call of duty. Our cowboy heroes were honourable because they were men of integrity, fair play, and loyalty. Sometimes their honour was materialized in a badge, but just as often it had nothing to do with position and everything to do with character. Cowboys were honourable because they accepted the responsibilities of manhood—protecting the weak and setting an example for others. Cowboys were of a type with the Boy Scout ideal, as we shall see.

Talk of codes seems nearly synonymous with the west and with the cowboy. We can read about the code of the west (Rosenberg; Yoggy, 170), the Western hero's "simple code of justice" (White 1987, 28), codes of masculinity (Coyne, 84–104), the Virginian's Code (Manchel, 28), creeds (Durgnat and Simmons), and codes as "child-sized ten commandments" (Calder, 187). Many of the western's clichés attest to the notion of a manly code: "A man's gotta do what a man's gotta do." "Some things a man can't walk away from." "Will nothing make a man of you." "Take it like a man." "A man's man." There are others. The codifying of male behaviour has a long tradition in American culture, going back to the conduct books in the nineteenth-century Jacksonian period and even earlier. Lee Clark Mitchell connects the masculine guides of the Jacksonian era to James Fenimore Cooper's Natty Bumppo, and he contrasts the behaviour set out in these conduct books with "conduct books from the earlier Federalist period" that set out a "fixed set of behaviors: obedience to elders, honesty, frugality, sincerity," among other things (51). These manly virtues become the basis for the Scout Law, and this law in turn informs the same behaviours touted in the cowboy codes and creeds of the 1940s and '50s.

A scan of B western film titles illustrates how important the code was to these films: *Code of the Rangers* (1938), *Code of the Saddle* (1947), *Code of the West* (1947), *Code of the Cactus* (1939), *Gun Code* (1940), *Code of the Fearless* (1939), *Code of the Silver Sage* (1950), and so on. The rather absurd titles (can a cactus have a code?) function to intensify the importance of code. The code out west is ubiquitous: even the cactus and the sage function by a code. Rarely do the stories dwell on the code; rather, the sense of principle and honour activates a code of behaviour that rests on duty, loyalty, honesty, patriotism, and industry. The cowboy code is implicit. In the films, the hero does not have to speak his code because he lives it. By the late 1940s, cowboys begin to articulate their codes, as we will see.

The cowboy codes are an interesting social and cultural phenomenon because they set out rules of behaviour for boys that derive from a context of individual freedom. The ideal of freedom goes back to the frontiersman who was "his own man." He distrusted authority and military discipline and yet his characteristics become attached to the disciplinary notions of codes (see MacDonald 1993, 145). The characteristics of the frontiersman are ideologically linked to American constitutional values. As Mitchell sees in the work of Cooper, something contradictory is at work in the western mythos. The cowboy represents all those virtues of America and the American male that we continue to hear lauded today: freedom, independence, individualism, openness, exploration, newness, freshness, and ruggedness. The cowboy is unfettered by the restraints of civilization; he is a maverick. And yet the young cowpoke finds himself confronted with a set of rules for behaviour that must constrain his freedom and individuality. The cowboy is both above the law and an upholder of the law. The cowboy roams the range, but only so that he can come across injustices that require fixing or weaknesses in the social fabric that need mending. The cowboy, as a cultural icon, illustrates how our cultural practices work to give us the illusion of freedom while at the same time they interpellate us into a safely collective ideology, even a market ideology. In other words, the cowboy both expresses freedom and contains it. In many ways, the cowboy is the pure capitalist: interested in material things, supporting private enterprise and private property, selling his skills when and where needed, and resistant to change when change means a reduction in these freedoms. The cowboy upholds that which must defeat him.

Put another way, the cowboy is himself a text in which we find inscribed the pattern of capitalist manhood. Let's consider cultural practice, gender construction, and textuality as these relate both to the cowboy and to his young fan. Once we see how the cowboy functions as cultural practice, we can return to the codes of behaviour.

Cultural Practice

The word *culture* is famously slippery. Raymond Williams asserts that it is "one of the two or three most complicated words in the English language" (87). He traces it etymologically to the Latin words *cultura* (cultivation) and *colere* ("inhabit, cultivate, protect, honour with worship"). The connection with the notion of inhabiting leads to our word *colony*, and we know that one aspect of colonization is the spreading of culture in the sense of a set of approved practices. Williams points out that as early as Milton, in the seventeenth century, we find a connection between culture and government; in *The Readie and Easie Way to Establish a Free Commonwealth* (1660), Milton speaks of the "natural heat of Government and Culture" (qtd. in Williams, 88). Culture places people, and it keeps them in place; in a sense culture governs people. Mostly we experience culture engagingly; cultural practices appear benign. Cultural practices may refer to activities a group of people who are connected politically and economically engage in. These activities may be highly ritualized or spontaneous. For example, oral storytelling is often a ritual activity, whereas reading may be less ritualized and more of a random activity. A culture will, however, ritualize as much as possible its cultural practices.

In schools, for example, reading time may take place in a special area, at special times, and with special preparations. Book festivals, music festivals, and even academic conferences have ritualistic aspects. We can see ritual at work at soccer matches and theatre performances, at wrestling matches and wedding ceremonies. Even going to the movies has a ritual aspect, as theatres in the 1940s and '50s knew when they set their Saturday matinee program with a chapter serial, Movietone news, a cartoon, and a main feature that more often than not was a B western. Boys would go to the cinema, pay their fifteen cents to enter and ten cents for popcorn, and after the film return home to recreate actions they saw on the screen. Ritual, like the practices it organizes, serves to gather people together both physically and cognitively. Ritual shapes knowing.

As my example of wrestling matches or theatre performance should indicate, cultural practice sorts groups of people according to matters of civility and to a certain extent class; some activities manifest order and education, whereas other activities do not. Social groups form hierarchies of activities from the apparently disorganized to the highly regulated, and so we might think today that reading books or attending yoga classes is preferable to watching TV or playing video games or attending wrestling matches. We might think of cultural practices as either "high" or "low," the former indicating activities that the privileged engage in, whereas the latter are those activities thought by the privileged to be rather vulgar. Obviously, cultural practices in this sense of high and low relate to matters of class. Where I come from, we might expect people of privilege to eat in certain ways and those less privileged to eat in ways that differ from the ways of the privileged. The cultural practices of some might include attending the philharmonic or the opera, whereas those of others might include going to roller derbies or monster truck competitions.

In cinema, the distinction between film and movie is something most of us are familiar with. The early sound era in Hollywood saw prestige films made by big studios such as Paramount, Metro Goldwyn Mayer, and Warner Brothers. Intermediate studios such as Columbia, Republic, and RKO made a range of films, from the A feature to the B movie. And then there were the Poverty Row studios such as Monogram, Tiffany, Mascot, and Grand National. These studios churned out series films and chapter serials, making films in not much more than a week and catering to the rural and younger audiences. The division between popular and mainstream (between the A film and the B movie) mirrored to some extent the condition of literature. To some extent the division applies to genre. The costume drama, the melodrama, the psychological drama, the recreation of history, or the adaptation of great books usually form the narrative basis for big-budget films, whereas the horror story, the western, and the detective thriller take on a formulaic and ritual aspect in the small-budget B feature. The westerns that are my subject clearly belong to the "low" category. In this they share something with children's literature. The comparison is inexact, however, because film was (and is) valued less highly than literature. Some films straddle the boundary between high and low, however (and I think here of films by directors such as Alfred Hitchcock and John Ford), and in this they share a quality with the novels of Charles Dickens. But the B western remains the chapbook of film, a form impossible to revive and impervious to highbrow dismissal.

In literature, a distinction has always existed between those forms (such as the ode, the epic, the sonnet, and so on) that the prim and urbane read and those forms (such as the ballad, doggerel, the comic book, and so on) enjoyed by those from the rough edges of society. Children's literature used to find its place in the latter, or low, category (and perhaps for some it retains low status). In children's literature we can see a division between the books that gain institutional approval—we might even say gain canonical status—and those that do not. Often, people who champion books of high status decry those books they consider of low status. We saw this evaluation of literary products two centuries ago, when the cheap chapbooks gave rise to the Cheap Repository Tracts precisely because those responsible for the Cheap Repository Tracts (Hannah More, Sarah Trimmer, and others) thought the chapbooks hawked by travelling chapmen were "bawdy and subversive" (Jackson 1989, 177). Zohar Shavit has noted that the spread of literacy in the eighteenth century opened the way for the marketplace to sell "unsuitable material, at least from the point of view of the religious establishment" (169), and that people like More and Trimmer set out to provide "appropriate alternative reading matter" (170). The result was what Shavit calls the "stratification of a system" (158ff.). The next two centuries saw a continuous rift between the defenders of high culture and the purveyors of low culture.

From the point of view of ideology, this rift is interesting. Clearly, what passes as high culture (books or films that are acceptable to the defenders of good taste and urbane values) seldom contains messages detrimental to the social fabric. High culture is, by and large, safe culture. On the other hand, low culture is called low precisely because those redoubtable defenders of high culture fear the subversive potential of formulaic and sensational art. And yet, both high and low art may be deeply conservative or deeply radical. In the case of comics and series films, the content is often safely conservative while the form is transgressive. This transgression is a function not of the form as formulaic but rather of the form as perceived by the aesthetic-minded as vulgar and crude. The difference between the westerns I consider here and the popular literary material aimed at a young audience is that the popular literature was and continues to be the object of criticism by the defenders of moral value and polite culture, but the films with cowboy heroes such as Hopalong Cassidy or Roy Rogers were accepted as a safe pastime for children. These films presented no apparent threat to the moral fibre of the nation; they did not have their Fredric Wertham to decry their lack of proper values. On the contrary, they stood for precisely the values of nationhood, self-reliance, and self-control that seemed appropriate to pass on to the younger generation. The irony is that these films now appear quaint, old-fashioned, out-of-date, naive, even downright silly, but the values they promulgated remain in tact. These films are no longer a part of living culture, and yet what they said about masculinity remains with us. The contemporary audience for these films is an aging audience that seems unable to charge the films with meaning for today's youth. These films retain historical interest but not much aesthetic interest. While cultural studies has successfully democratized the study of the arts, it does not seem capable of resuscitating a popular form that never did take purchase among a cross-section of consumers. But the codes that are a part of the world of the B western cowboy maintain their relevance.

When we speak of the codes in any book or film as a system, or when we speak of the production of literary works or films as a system, we acknowledge how deeply embedded literature and film are within social, economic, and political systems. In short, systems generate cultural production, and cultural production, like production generally, is not disinterested. The producers of culture in these days of late capitalism are interested, at the very least, in the making of money. But even more important than that is the perpetuation of conditions in which to make money. Books must, as John Stephens has pointed out, "intervene in the lives of children" (8), and he means intervene in ways that socialize children. The same is true of the films I am exploring. Socialization takes place when children learn to behave according to certain expectations, expectations that are reflections of specific ideologies. And every book, as Stephens says, "has an implicit ideology" (9)—and, he might have added, every film, too. Ideology tends to be a pejorative word, but

Stephens reminds us that ideologies "are not necessarily undesirable" (8). We all need to make sense of the world, and ideologies provide values and beliefs that help us do just that—make sense of the world.

Gender Construction

I do not propose to delve into the subject of performance and perfomativity, but I need to mention the subject in order to point out that gender is a matter of construction, not biology. In other words, no essential masculinity or essential femininity exists. As Bob Connell and others have argued, we do not have a single notion of masculinity; rather, we have, and some of us practise, masculinities. The same is true of femininity and femininities. All girls do not just want to have fun, and all boys will not be boys. Individuals, as well as groups, define themselves through difference. At the same time, social and political systems have a stake in organizing gender, just as they organize other aspects of their systems— social hierarchies, living spaces, wages and benefits, and so on. The cultural practices any society engages in will affect certain ways of being male and being female. In children's literature, we have seen evidence of concern for traditional ways of being male and being female in the critical writing that focused on female characters in fairy tales or that worried about a lack of strong female protagonists or that encouraged the presentation of female characters in non-traditional roles. We now have a number of series for young readers that centre on females: the American Girls Series, the Royal Diary Series, the Polish American Girls Series, Our Canadian Girls Series, Cool Careers for Girls Series, and so on. The difference between such series and older series, such as the Nancy Drew or Trixie Belden books, is that these recent series establish girls in history; they participate in a revisioning of history so that readers may appreciate the contribution of females in the past as well as in the present. But what of masculinity? How far have we come from the hegemonic masculinity of the scout, the frontiersman, the cowboy, the Hardy boy?

Hegemonic masculinity focuses on our sense of capability. The hegemonic male rides tall in the saddle, as a recent picture book puts it. I refer to Anne Carter and David McPhail's *Tall in the Saddle* (1999; the title echoes that of a 1944 John Wayne movie), which presents a first-person narrative in which a little boy tells how each morning he and his Dad "play cowboys." When Dad leaves for work, "still wearing his boots," the boy follows him and discovers that his Dad spends the day riding the range, herding cattle, and rousting rustlers. The cover of the book (the picture is repeated within the story) shows the boy and his father, dressed as cow-boys, sitting astride their rearing horses in a pose reminiscent of Roy Rogers and Trigger and other western heroes of the 1940s and '50s. For boys of that generation the cowboy was the central icon of masculinity, and to a great extent he still is. I'll return to the cowboy in the next section.

The point is that gender is something we learn and we learn gender largely, although not exclusively, through the texts we experience. The texts we experience as youngsters prepare us for being boys and girls, men and women.

Textuality

Many of us think that the word *text* refers to a book. My *Webster's New Collegiate Dictionary* delivers this definition: "the original written or printed words and form of a literary work" (1974, 1206). Indeed, all seven of the definitions provided in this dictionary make reference to the writ-ten word. And of course we have the portmanteau word *textbook*. A text, then, is something material made out of words; it depends upon the larger system of language that it uses for its own purposes to formulate infor-mation or narrative or instruction or whatever the words in text form might intend. Textuality is the fashioning or weaving (from the Latin *tex-tus*, weaving) of material from a system of language into an object of communication. What we commonly mean by *a system of language* is words, the lexical repertory available to anyone who learns a particular language. But by *language* we might mean something more than just spo-ken or written words fashioned into grammatical units. Obviously, humans communicate with other sign systems—for example, that used by the deaf, or Morse code, or semaphore. Dance, silent film, painting and draw-ing, the way we dress—all these form systems of signs that constitute a language. Obviously, I am speaking of textuality and language as mani-festations of semiotics. Sign systems.

Roland Barthes designates the text as a "methodological field," and he says that it "*is experienced only in an activity*" (57, 58; italics in orig-inal). Such an activity is interpretation, at whatever level this takes place. By interpretation, I take my cue again from Barthes and intend a mean-ing close to one used in music when we say that an instrumentalist *inter-prets* a piece of music. To interpret, however, we need to be able to under-stand the codes that constitute the text we wish to interpret. The word *code* here has at least two meanings. First, we associate the code with a message; second, we think of code in a plural sense, as the various "codes, or subcodes, at work in any given communicational act" (Jameson, 27). Although both codes require interpretation, the former requires less interpretative activity than the latter. In literary textuality, we might think of the difference between openly didactic works and richly symbolic works. This difference, however, does not constitute a strict binary. Nor do the two senses of code necessarily appear sequentially, as may appear in children's literature in the move from the moral tale in the late eighteenth century to the more symbolic fantasies of the mid-nineteenth century. Didactic and symbolic codes overlap.

The same is true of film. Film too is text, and like literary text it communicates through a system of signs or codes. The white hat and clean clothes of the cowboy hero communicate goodness; it is this form's sign of moral strength, the way beauty is a sign of moral purity in the fairy tale. The convention of filming the hero in full frame as he rides his horse, the camera positioned just below mid level of the horse's body, constitutes another sign of goodness and heroism. Bad guys riding are usually shot from a distance, or when the close-up occurs the camera looks slightly down rather than up at the horse and rider. The films have their codes. The cowboys such as Gene Autry, Roy Rogers, and Hopalong Cassidy also had their codes; they took the idea of a code literally. They took the unwritten code the cowboy adhered to, and they turned it into text.

Cowboy Codes

The text, then, is not necessarily a written text. Nor need it be single, as in one book or one film or one comic, and so on. Like the fairy tale or the series western film, texts may be part of a system and the system consists of a network of codes. Since children of my generation and later more often than not experience textuality visually, I focus on film, specifically the cowboy film familiar to me when I was a boy in the 1950s. These films, variously referred to as the B western or the Poverty Row westerns or series westerns, were more often than not made as packages of four to six films to be sold as a single group to various film theatres, usually in rural towns. The term *series* reflects the self-conscious connectedness of these films in which some characters used the same name from one series to another or, in the case of certain of the heroes and sidekicks, used their own names as opposed to a strictly filmic name. For example, Smiley Burnette appeared in a number of films using his own name, but he also appeared in many films using the name Frog Milhouse. He was Frog in films in which he appeared with more than one hero.

Roy Rogers, after the early 1940s, used his own name in his films, whereas Tex Ritter used a variety of names, but these more often than not incorporated his first name, Tex. In short, we might take as a single text the Hopalong Cassidy films from Paramount Studios made between 1935 and 1948, or Republic's Three Mesquiteers films from 1936 to 1943, or Columbia's Durango Kid films from 1946 to 1952, and so on. Gene Autry seems aware of the collective textuality of his own films. In his autobiography he tells us: "Trying to single out one of my pictures is like trying to recall a particular noodle you enjoyed during a spaghetti dinner" (51). I will go further and say that, at least from the point of view of gender construction, the entire genre of the B western from the 1930s to the 1950s constitutes a single text, a single text made up of many ostensibly discrete texts. Collectively, these films constitute a code of masculinity; they informed young viewers just what characteristics made up the complete man, just as they informed the young viewer what made up the incomplete man.

The notion of a code as a strict set of behavioural values is common to our thinking about cowboys. Notice how easily Diana Serra Cary, in reminiscing about her childhood in Hollywood, slips into the description of "a man's true character," according to the "code" (she uses this word) of men who were extras and stuntmen in the early cowboy films:

> Was he trustworthy, or would he dry-gulch you in some arroyo for your horse, your saddle or your poke? How did he treat his horse? On a long trail was he a hazard or an asset, a gunsil [sic] or a good hand? Would he stand by you, or quit when the chips were down? (88)

Cary here uses the cowboy lingo—"dry-gulch," "good hand," and "when the chips were down." She writes as if the stuff of western fiction and film were the stuff of real life. A true man must measure up to a certain code that ultimately derives from fiction and film. This code designates a set of characteristics for an aspiring man to emulate: trustworthiness, kindness to animals, industriousness ("a good hand"), and loyalty.

In the B western of the early sound era, with stars such as Buck Jones, Tim McCoy, Ken Maynard, Bob Steele, and so on, the hero embodied this set of characteristics admirably. An early example is Wally Wales (a.k.a. Hal Taliaferro) in *Breed of the West* (1930). Wally plays a loyal and hardworking cowhand who romances the ranch owner's daughter, much to the consternation of the ranch foreman, an unpleasant fellow named Long-Rope Wheeler (Robert Walker). Long-Rope is a villain, in cahoots with the head bad guy, and his name most likely plays on the adage "Give him enough rope and he'll hang himself." Wally is not only trustworthy and loyal but also helpful to strangers and kind to animals. Swift on the draw, Wally avoids killing or even wounding, preferring to shoot the gun from the hands of those who threaten him. At one point, the sheriff (Hank Bell) sums up Wally's character when he remarks: "That's the breed of the west. He'll make good at anything."

The code of manliness set out in *Breed of the West,* and countless films like it, fits into what Gaylyn Studlar calls "the cultural framework of a boy-centred reform movement that sought to build character in American boys and ensure the proper development of a 'strenuous' masculinity" (64–65). Studlar refers to Robert Baden-Powell, Ernest Thompson Seton, and Daniel Carter Beard, all founders of the Boy Scout movement, as being at "the forefront of this movement to build character in boys" (65). One of the sources for the ideals of masculinity is Baden-Powell's *Scouting for Boys* (1908), in which Baden-Powell provides a code of behaviour for young boys. He explicitly connects the Scout with the knights of the Middle Ages: "In the old days the knights were the scouts of Britain" (22). Knights followed a set of seven guidelines that included honour, loyalty to God, politeness "to all women and children and infirm people," helpfulness to all, generosity, adeptness in the use of weapons, and fitness (23). Duty, obedience, and preparedness are the most important virtues of the Scout. Baden-Powell informs readers that laws for proper manly behaviour are ancient. "The Japanese have their Bushido," he says. The knights had their "chivalry or rules." The "Red Indians" have "their laws of honour," and so do Zulus, "the natives of India" and so on (44). And the Boy Scouts too have their Laws.

According to Boy Scout Law, a Scout is trustworthy, loyal, patriotic, helpful, friendly, courteous, kind, obedient, cheerful, thrifty, brave, clean, and reverent. With the possible exception of the last in this list, all the other characteristics apply nicely to the cowboy. And even the last of the list—reverence—fits by implication (and reverence is central in Roy Rogers's list of virtues). Bad guys often refer to clergymen as Sky Pilots, and in one film, *Wild Horse Canyon* (1938), a bad guy called Red (Charles King) calls the kindly ranch owner a "spavined old hymn chanter." Western star Tim McCoy often dressed in such a way that people mistook him for a preacher; the same mistake has Hoot Gibson taken for a parson in *The Fighting Parson* (1933). Sometimes the hero protects a man of the cloth (e.g., *Stone of Silver Creek,* 1935) or even is a man of God (e.g., *Hellfire,* 1949). And Roy Rogers made no secret of his Christian beliefs, having not only ten steps of conduct for members of his fan club but also a prayer. Clearly, the heroes are on the side of all the values that apply to a just civilization, including those that relate to a pious community. The pious community is God-fearing, Caucasian, family-loving, and law-abiding. Men run businesses and women tend to hearth and home. And the wandering cowboy hero keeps this society safe and ordered.

The connection with the Boy Scouts is self-conscious. Phil Hardy, in his exhaustive reference work *The Western* (1983), remarks: "Odd though it may seem, the Boy Scouts are frequently featured in Westerns" (40). At least one film focuses entirely on the Scouts, the twelve-chapter serial *Scouts to the Rescue* (1939). Given the films' interest in the same character traits that the Scout movement promoted, I do not think the appearance of Scouts in westerns is odd. At least two films from the 1930s present the Scouts working with the cowboy hero to thwart villains. In *Drum Taps* (1933), Ken Maynard receives the help of a Scout troop and, even more obviously, *Tex Rides with the Boy Scouts* (1937) lauds the virtues of the Scout movement. This film, starring Tex Ritter, contains a prologue about the Boy Scouts, with footage from a large jamboree in Washington, D.C. We hear a voice-over that celebrates "the glory of making upright, stalwart, responsible manhood, attained only through the medium of that far greater glory, a clean-living, clean-thinking boyhood." "No nobler" movement than the Boy Scouts—a "living symbol of the spirit of youth"—exists. The voice-over goes on to assert that character is essential in life, and the Boy Scouts mould the character of the growing boy and turn him into a citizen. We hear an appreciation of the twelve "noble rules" of the Scouts and the Boy Scout Oath.

The narrative then begins with a train at night heading for a tunnel. A robbery follows. Newspaper headlines indicate a million-dollar robbery has taken place. Cut to Tex riding with his two companions, Pee Wee and Stubby. Tex sings as the other two admire him. They come to the Black Hawk Mining and Development Company, where they have a run-in with Stark (Charlie King) and his henchmen. Then Tex and his partners proceed to the Boy Scout camp. Tex shows the boys his Silver Beaver badge. In his youth, he was a Boy Scout. Cut to the head bad guy, Dormand (Forrest Taylor), and his minions at the Black Hawk Mine. We hear Dormand advise his gang: "Don't let those boys [the Scouts] fool you. They are smarter than you think." Cut to Pee Wee and Stubby with the Scouts. Pee Wee wants to learn to be a Scout, and this gives opportunity for some tomfoolery. Buzzy (Tommy Bupp), one of the young scouts, has an older sister, Norma (Marjorie Reynolds), who works for Dormand. She does not know he is a baddie. Late in the film, Dormand shoots Buzzy, but of course he does not die. His Scout comrades help Tex round up the gang of bad guys by setting a rope trap for Stark and his henchmen, while Tex and a posse of adults catch Dormand and another group of henchmen. This film offers the clearest indication of just how self-conscious these films are about appealing to boys and about constructing a masculinity that conforms to scouting values.

The Scouts in both *Drum Taps* and *Tex Rides with the Boy Scouts* are shown camping, and we remember that Baden-Powell asserts that "Scouts must, of course, be accustomed to living in the open; they have to know how to put up tents or huts for themselves; how to lay and light a fire; how to kill, cut up, and cook their food," and so on (21). He notes that, "few fellows learn or practise these things when they are living in civilized places because they get comfortable houses and beds to sleep in" (22). Scouts must be prepared, and we see in these films that they are. They are resourceful and skilled in tying knots and camping. They are cowboys in the making—essentially just smaller versions of the cowboys. What differentiates the Boy Scout from the cowboy is individuality; the Scout is part of a troop and the cowboy is a loner who rides by himself or with one or two pals.

The films with Buzz Henry provide a nice transition from the Boy Scout pictures to the boy as heroic individual. In *Buzzy Rides the Range* (1940), for example, the boy cowpoke rides into the ranch on his white horse, Blue Rex, and proceeds to have a shooting match with Dude (George Morrell), the old retainer of the ranch. We see at the beginning that Buzzy, although a boy, is proficient with firearms. The plot has the woman rancher along with other local ranchers suffering from rustling. The girl's fiancé is, of course, the villain. The local cattlemen ask the government for help and feel abandoned when no help arrives. In the desert, Buzzy and his friend Dude come across a man sunburned and in bad shape. This is Ken Blair (Dave O'Brien). He is really the government agent working under cover. He befriends Buzzy, who overhears the bad guys chortling about how their boss is putting one over on the other ranchers, including the woman rancher. Buzzy rides to the rescue at the end, knocking the pistol from the bad guy's hand as he prepares to shoot Ken. At another point in the film, Buzzy writes a note and places it on his saddle and then sends Blue Rex home. Buzzy is a boy with the resourcefulness and skills of the cowboy. He is the viewer's fantasy.

What we have in these western movies is a filmic textuality, a series of formula films that in the early sound era began to present the cowboy as the type of heroic masculinity. Most of these films do not foreground their codes as directly as *Tex Rides with the Boy Scouts*, though many contain children, especially boys, who learn from the heroes what it means to be a "true man." But the inclusion of children in the stories is not necessary for these films to pass on their code of manliness. The hero always has someone to protect, be this a child or a woman or a group of settlers or farmers or animals or even the country. We might remember that the Boy Scout Oath, mentioned in the prologue to *Tex Rides with the Boy Scouts*, states that the Scout will do his "duty to God and my country" and "help other people at all times" and "keep myself physically strong, mentally awake, and morally straight." (I quote this from the film.) The cowboy admirably performs the ideal set out by the Scout Oath, even to the point of sedulously avoiding strong drink. Scouts are explicitly warned of the deleterious effects of alcohol and smoking (Baden-Powell, 26). The character traits a Scout ought to exhibit and the duties he ought to discharge allow for a great variety of plots in which the hero might save a ranch from rustlers or a bank from a corrupt businessman or his country from the Nazi menace.

As time goes on, the code of behaviour set out by the Boy Scouts finds its way directly into the world of individual cowboy heroes. What was implicit in most of the films of the 1930s and early '40s becomes reified in the most famous of the cowboy codes, the one set out by Gene Autry. In his autobiography, *Back in the Saddle Again* (1978), Autry confesses that the "set of rules I evolved to govern the role of the B Western hero . . . must sound naïve to today's do-your-own-thing disciples." But he acknowledges that "we took such matters seriously then and the code tapped a spirit that was alive in the land" (184). He then presents his code:

1. The cowboy must never shoot first, hit a smaller man, or take unfair advantage.
2. He must never go back on his word, or a trust confided in him.
3. He must always tell the truth.
4. He must be gentle with children, the elderly, and animals.
5. He must not advocate or possess racially or religiously intolerant ideas.
6. He must help people in distress.
7. He must be a good worker.
8. He must keep himself clean in thought, speech, and personal habits.
9. He must respect women, parents, and his nation's laws.
10. The cowboy is a patriot.

In short, the cowboy is as good as a Boy Scout. Masculinity finds its definition in this code.

Gene Autry's code brings together personal and public duty. The cowboy is a model of the good father, protector of the innocent, and defender of the state. He is everything the Wizard of Oz was supposed to be. When Autry says the code "tapped a spirit that was alive in the land," he is surely right. Many of the cowboy stars of the 1940s and '50s followed Autry with their own set of rules. Hopalong Cassidy offered his Creed for American Boys and Girls, the Lone Ranger had a creed, Roy Rogers had his steps of conduct and a prayer, and TV's Wild Bill Hickok had a Deputy Marshal's Code of Conduct. Creed, code, prayer—the language suggests words of power, scripture. The codes find their original in the Ten Commandments, as Baden-Powell well knew (see Rosenthal, 108–9). All the cowboy codes and creeds repeat the rules set out in Autry's code, rules pertaining to hard work and clean living and patriotic behaviour. These codes surface just after World War II, and they reflect a desire for clarity and coherence and certitude. They codify what it means to be all boy and all man. Implicit in these rules is a sense of stewardship that has national and racial and gender implications. Despite Hopalong Cassidy's inclusion of girls in his creed, the sense is that American boys are the inheritors of power. TV's *Rawhide* had its definition of the trail boss and "What It Means to Work Hard and Be in Charge":

> The Trail Boss is the man in charge. The man who rides herd on the hands as well as the cattle. The leader. The man whom experience has taught. The man who has learned from another trail boss. The man who sets the pace. The man who gives the orders—and must be obeyed. The man who has full responsibility for the safe conduct of the herd all the way. The man who knows everyone's job. The man who leads from start to finish. (http://www.tvacres.com/westerns_coverpage.htm)

In short, we have here hegemonic manhood.

All of these (and more) cowboy codes are collected on Rudy A. D'Angelo's website, The Spaghetti Western. D'Angelo is the author of a history of the cap gun and a fan of the old western films and television programs. In the section of his website devoted to the cowboy codes, he tells us that the westerns he grew up watching provided "good role models" and taught youngsters "right from wrong and the proper way to behave." He closes this section by telling his readers that "these wonderful cowboy stars and western heroes" were "partners with Mom and Dad in helping shape the characters and young minds to grow up to be good citizens." And he laments the "huge loss and void" felt now that "our role models have ridden off into the Sunset."

D'Angelo adds one code I have yet to mention. I began by noting that the cowboy is a good capitalist, an upholder of the market economy. Nothing could indicate this more than the Daisy Manufacturing Company's appeal to youngsters with their Red Ryder BB rifle and American Boys Bill of Rights. D'Angelo includes this bill of rights with the other cowboy codes, and it is also available on the Daisy Company's website. This bill of rights sounds all the familiar themes from the other codes: it speaks of rights to training and to happiness and to liberty, echoing the Declaration of Independence. But it adds a significant "right," one related to the second Amendment of the American Constitution and to the values championed by the National Rifle Association and other gun groups in the U.S.—"The Right to learn to shoot safely." D'Angelo adds a parenthetic comment after this bill of rights in which he gives "special thanks" to the Daisy Company, "one of America's leaders in wonderful rifles, BB guns, toy guns and safe toys for boys.... ASK DAD, HE HAD A 'DAISY.'" Effectively, D'Angelo accepts the connection between his cowboy heroes and the market economy. We see this connection also in the plethora of market items—clothing, toys, games, flashlights, pocket knives, lunch boxes, puzzles, pins, and so on—endorsed by Roy Rogers, Hopalong Cassidy, and others.

One set of rules missing from D'Angelo's collection of cowboy codes is the Smiley Burnette Fan Club Pledge. Smiley Burnette was one of the many comical sidekicks that populated the B western. In films, he was sometimes known as Frog Milhouse, and he appeared most often with Gene Autry, although he also rode alongside the likes of Sunset Carson, Roy Rogers, and Charles Starrett (the Durango Kid). Members of Smiley's fan club received the following pledge:

I promise to make every effort to see Smiley "Frog" Burnette in every picture he is in.

I promise always to let my friends know where and when they can see "Frog" in pictures.

I promise to show my loyalty to "Frog" by writing him once each month faithfully and will offer constructive and helpful suggestions regarding his pictures.

I promise to show my interest in our club by doing everything I can to get new members.

I promise to carry my membership card with me at all times and to obey the pledges guiding our fan club. (The Old Corral, http://www.b-westerns.com/pals-sb3.htm)

These fans do not have a creed or code or prayer to recite or commit to memory; instead, they have a pledge. What they pledge makes reference to such attributes as loyalty, helpfulness, industriousness, and trust. But the pledge is consumer oriented: see Smiley Burnette movies whenever it is possible to do so. This is a parody of the cowboy codes, an ironic exposé of the star-centred nature of fandom. Smiley makes fun of the narcissistic side of celebrity status. The humour in this pledge shares a sensibility, if not a form, with that of Mark Twain in *The Adventures of Huckleberry Finn* (1884), in which Tom Sawyer makes his gang take an oath and write their names in blood.

Of course Smiley Burnette is himself not the main man; he is not the cowboy hero. He is the comical sidekick who by his very presence in a western film helps define the hero and set off the hero's superior masculinity. Mostly, the comical sidekick serves to highlight the capabilities and leadership of the hero. However, in the case of Smiley and his pledge, we have a sidekick who punctures the overly serious hero. The hero takes himself too seriously; Smiley is willing to laugh at himself. In the opening sequence of the Gene Autry film, *Public Cowboy #1* (1937), Smiley sits backward on his horse and wears a false face on the back of his head so he can check for villains behind while he appears to be looking forward. The two-way looking of Smiley is a nifty metaphor for looking back to the past; it represents the nostalgic longing that pretends to be current, forward looking, while all the time gazing at the past, yearning for what is behind. The Smiley Burnette brand of masculinity comments on the impossible masculinity of the hero. The masculinity represented in the figure of the cowboy remains always in the past. No one can live up to the measure of Gene or Roy or Hoppy, but anyone can relate to Smiley.

Continuing Codes

The western heroes who once offered young boys models of masculinity are long gone, and even when they did ride the range they did so only in the imaginations of their young viewers and fans. The cowboy heroes were the stuff of pretend, and consequently they may have ridden into the sunset, but this does not mean that they are gone. If these cowboy heroes are the stuff of pretend, then they are fantasies. In other words, they are aspects of our unconscious. The unconscious continually works on the conscious, as we think we know. Boys and men continue to pretend, and their pretend continues to take a form reminiscent of the cowboy masculinity. In popular culture for kids, we have a number of computer games with cowboy themes: *Dead Man's Hand, Hangman: The Wild West, Showdown, the Gunfighting Game, High Noon Drifter.* The *Toy Story* films (1995, 1999) indicate the continuing appeal of the cowboy, and the Buzz Lightyear character illustrates the connection between the heroic cowboy and his reincarnation as a science fiction hero. The group of youngsters known as the Power Rangers might remind us of the Texas Rangers or the Range Riders or the Lone Ranger. The cowboy has not so much left as he has morphed. And for adults whose desire is to prolong their boyhood, the fast-draw clubs that began "in Southern California in 1982" "play strongly to the fantasies of the child within grown men and women" (Diaz, 175). According to James William Gibson, paintball, a game in which grown men pretend to be soldiers, complete with assault rifles and other ordnance, "offers men the opportunity to act against the adult world in two ways: first, by approximating real violence, and second, by essentially playing a child's game" (138–39). Gibson says war movies and novels (and, I would add, fast-draw competitions), along with paintball, provide "a ritual transition to warrior adulthood through regression to childhood" (139).

The ritualistic aspect of games such as fast-draw and paintball carry us back to cowboy mentality and its code. William Pollack has considered the damaging effect of the Boy Code. According to Pollack, this code has "four injunctions":

Men should be stoic, stable, and independent.

Men should "*Give 'em hell*," or assume the John Wayne stance based on "daring, bravado, and attraction to violence."

Men should strive for "status, dominance, and power."

Men should exhibit "*No sissy stuff.*" (24; Pollack's italics)

Pollack ends his book with the hopeful suggestion that society is "starting to revise the old Boy Code" (396), and he offers as an example the story of a popular high-school teenager, Chris Jackson, and his friend Dan. Chris and Dan had been friends for many years, but when they got to high school Dan started "becoming a jerk" (393). What this means is that Dan assumed the role of the bully. The crisis came when Chris made friends with a new girl in school, Allison. Dan "seemed really to hate her" (394), and he began to tease her because she had a stutter. Chris stepped up and defended Allison, and his defence threatened to escalate into a fight between the two boys. Just before the fists begin to fly, several level-headed kids interrupted the two young men and stopped the fight.

Pollack concludes from this story that the present generation of boys is "beginning to question the double standard of masculinity that has pushed boys and men to feel they must choose between being the kind of tough, competitive, unfeeling, uncommunicative man traditionally celebrated as 'masculine' and being the kind of open, expressive, egalitarian man now heralded as ideal by much of contemporary society" (396). This sounds positive, but for me the story of young Chris is redolent of the stuff of the cowboy. Here are two young male friends who find tension growing between them as one gravitates towards anti-social behaviour and the other remains committed to the common good. When Allison appears on the scene, the tension between the male friends increases. We have seen this situation in countless westerns, beginning possibly with Owen Wister's novel *The Virginian* (1902) and reprised in many western films. And the outcome closely resembles the western scenario. Chris plays the hero and defends the helpless Allison. That the two boys do not come to blows seems important to Pollack. But Dan and Chris do not fight because others stop them from fighting. The message here is not that Chris necessarily represents a new type of masculinity, but that we need collective action to stop the kind of male posturing that leads to violence. We need, perhaps, not "to codify a new set of rules for boys and men, a code for the Real Boy" (Pollack 397), but rather to uncode boyhood and masculinity altogether. We need, perhaps, to reconsider our own nostalgic relationship to what it means to be a boy.

I return to the Boy Scouts. The patriotic duty of the Scout was clearly connected to maintaining the British Empire. Baden-Powell exhorts his reader, the Scout, to "prepare himself, by learning to shoot and to drill, to take his share in defence of the Empire, if it should ever be attacked" (277). In the westerns so intimately connected to my own boyhood, I saw not only men but boys too prepared to shoot and defend. The charm for me was not the codes, the set of rules I had to memorize for Scouts or the creeds and pledges of the cowboy clubs, but rather the independence and apparent freedom from rules that the cowboy hero seemed to represent, despite the rules and codes he urged on young boys. What matters now is the fondness with which some look back on those days of yesteryear with their paradoxically roaming cowboy tied to a set of virtues that now have largely vanished. How do we deal with the nostalgia that clings to these codes and their champions?

When We Were Young
Nostalgia and the Cowboy Hero

To take an interest in the past, especially one's personal past, does not necessarily mean that one is nostalgic, at least in any sentimental sense. I have no desire to return to a childhood past that I remember as troubled and difficult. If nostalgia is a feeling of loss and a desire to restore or renovate what is lost, then I have no nostalgia for my own past. And I certainly have no intention to lament the passing of the cowboys that are my subject.

However, to study things of the past is to indulge to some extent in nostalgia; we indulge ourselves by dwelling on what has been and can never be again. Those who study children and their culture study, to some extent, their own past—what has been and can never be again. Children are what we were, and some people look back wistfully at that which they were. Jacqueline Rose has noted how children's fiction sets the child up as a "pure point of origin" (8). We cling (or at least some people do) to the notion of childhood innocence in order to preserve a sense of the rightness of an older form of culture—a culture that we associate with the past and with childhood and with messing about with things in an easy, carefree manner. Perhaps inevitably the association with the past and with childhood leads to a longing not only for what we were but also for where we were; and where we were, many of us, was a place called *home*. Maybe you can't go home again, but maybe you can't stop trying to go home again either, even if you were never there in the first place. Home is where the imagination rests. And home is what the imagination cannot quite capture. Home is ever so far away in the palm of your hand, as George MacDonald once said (225). Or to put this in a nicely ambivalent way, we might echo the famous sentiment "There's no place like home." That's right: there is *no place* like home, not even a grey farm on the Kansas prairie. Not yet, anyway. Despite the elusiveness of home, many people continue to think of home, the place whence they came, as mistily comfortable and desirable. Home is that imperial, palace whence we came and to where we wish to return; home is where the heart is, and where children feel safe. At least this is how home is supposed to be: home, sweet home (see Reimer).

The study of children's literature and culture with its return to childhood and its emphasis on home smacks of nostalgia. To read as a child, to reconnect with the inner child—"to reenter and reevaluate [our] own childhood experience as part of a personal emancipatory human project" (Galbraith, 188)—is to wish for the chance to return and redo and reconstitute the past in order to transform the present. I quote in the previous sentence words from an article by Mary Galbraith on childhood studies. Galbraith calls for a continuation of "the project of the Enlightenment" (192), and she does so in an impassioned voice. If we were to attach the notion of nostalgia to Galbraith's "urgent call to develop this academic field [i.e., childhood studies]" (200), then we would need to qualify our notions of nostalgia in some way in order both to account for the "emancipatory" call in Galbraith's "manifesto" and to avoid the kind of nostalgia James Kincaid speaks of as either an "ingredient" of eroticism or a "trifle" (25). The return to childhood is a return intended not as a holiday to some pastoral retreat where children are perceived as innocently sweet and perhaps even androgynously nubile, but as an emancipatory journey intended to free us from the haunting of the past and from oppressive forces in the present. Rather than nostalgia, we have in the trauma of childhood an anti-nostalgia. Yet the allure of even such anti-nostalgia is strong; humans have a capacity to transform anti-nostalgia into nostalgia. The desire to connect with a past that was good despite the fear and trembling it may have contained takes the form of nostalgia for that which we imagine may have been or should have been. Nostalgia may just grow stronger as the ghost of a traumatic past flickers through our time. Would that the past we know existed never had existed; perhaps nostalgia can eradicate that hated and haunting past.

But we may also yearn for certain aspects of a former life that actually did exist. All things past are not trauma laden. Some things past might well be humanly positive and to yearn for them might well be productive of positive action in the present. We might term this a "practical nostalgia." I take the term "practical nostalgia" from Debbora Battaglia, who argues that nostalgia "may in fact be a vehicle of knowledge, rather than only a yearning for something lost"; she detaches "the notion of nostalgia from the merely sentimental attitude with which we may too easily associate it" (77).

Her example is the urban Trobrianders in Papua New Guinea, whose yam-growing competitions are not simply a mourning "for what is missing from the present" (Battaglia, 78, quoting Strathern, 111) but a "transformative action with a connective purpose" (77). Battaglia concludes: "the rupture from present conduct permitted by this social action of *extension toward sources* [i.e., the Trobrianders' growing of yams and the creation of gardens in their place of displacement] opens subjects to creative reconfiguration: nostalgic practice invites self-problematization" (93).

What Battaglia calls practical nostalgia seems to me to have some connection with what Sveltana Boym calls "reflective nostalgia," which she distinguishes from "restorative nostalgia" (41–55). The latter sets out to rebuild the lost home, to have again the past that seems so attractive, whereas the former (reflective nostalgia) is set upon thinking through the past. One attempts "to conquer and spatialize time" and the other "cherishes shattered fragments of memory and temporalizes space" (49). Reflective nostalgia "reveals that longing and critical thinking are not opposed to one another, as affective memories do not absolve one from compassion, judgment or critical reflection" (48–49). The person who indulges in reflective nostalgia is aware of the distance between past and present and that this distance cannot be materially bridged. The past is of use when we use it to reflect upon the present and future. We cannot go home again, but we can use our attachment to a past home as an incentive to build a better one.

To study children's literature and culture may be to indulge in a form of nostalgia—a glance at the series of books by Lemony Snicket will indicate how self-conscious this harkening back to older times (or should I say younger times?) may be for publishers of books for children. Peritextual matter in the Lemony Snicket books strongly resembles books that now appear in antiquarian catalogues: the covers with their framed pictures, smaller lozenges, and ribbon-like banners bring to mind late-nineteenth-century and early-twentieth-century books for children; the endpapers (the front ones containing on the recto an *ex libris* plate) and the uneven or uncut page edges are evocative of older books and more likely to make their parodic (or is it really nostalgic?) point with adult readers than with children. Daphne Merkin, in the *New York Times Magazine*, puts it this way: "The series has been cunningly packaged to suggest a Victorian dime-store novel—the unimposing, bijou trim size is both elegant and kid-friendly; the margins are temptingly wide; the thick paper has deckle edges. And there are enough innovative design touches—including witty pencil drawings by Brett Helquist, a personalized ex libris bookplate, patterned endpapers and bindings that pick up on the subtle colorations of the laminated illustrative inlay on the nonjacketed cover—to make the most obsessive art director swoon with joy."

The books have an ironically detached adult narrator who clearly keeps children informed as to what they should know; this narrator reminds us of narrative voice as it sounds in many nineteenth-century children's books. Another recent series that evokes older books is the Royal Diaries series. The decorations (covers, uncut pages, endpapers, and so on) in the books in this series, like those of the Lemony Snicket books, are meant to recall the past. The Royal Diaries series even has the gilt-edged pages of what we might suppose were the finer books from the past. The very appearance of the books in these two series is a conscious call to nostalgia. We might have here what Svetlana Boym calls "inculcation of nostalgia," the creation of ersatz objects from the past "as a marketing strategy that tricks consumers into missing what they haven't lost" (38). Boym goes on to cite Arjun Appadurai, who calls market-driven nostalgia "'ersatz nostalgia' or armchair nostalgia, 'nostalgia without lived experience or collective historical memory'" (Boym, 38).

Perhaps the staying power of a book such as Grahame's *The Wind in the Willows* (1908) owes as much to its nostalgic evocation of safe and comfortable homes and to a pastoral good life adults can yearn for as it does to its continuing appeal to children. Indeed, the strong pastoral element in children's literature seems meant to appeal to adults as much or more than it appeals to the young (see Nodelman, 219–22). The young like the gothic and the ghoulish; adults like to remember things past, whether those things actually belonged to the past or not. And so we might conclude that the nostalgia evident in both the look and the content of children's books appeals to the adults who are, more often than not, the purchasers of the books, whereas the emphasis on child protagonists and plots that may approach and even at times cross over the borders of transgression appeals to children who are the ostensible target audience for these books.

I'm not, however, convinced that this is the whole story. A book such as Philippa Pearce's *Tom's Midnight Garden* (1958) might remind us that children too can feel nostalgic. Staying with his aunt and uncle in a strange house, Tom longs for his own home. His longing takes him to a long-ago past when gardens graced ground that was later paved and fenced for garbage cans. Time-slip fantasies often give us young characters who move to the past in order to escape a present that is less than satisfying. I think of Janet Lunn's *The Root Cellar* (1981) or some of William Mayne's works. Children as well as adults can find the present intolerable and wistfully imagine a time and place—perhaps in the past—that seems preferable. C.S. Lewis's Narnia books offer children such a place, a place where the protagonists can be kings and queens and accomplish great deeds; these books are nostalgic for a heroic past. We might well think of examples of books for young readers that work on the reader in ways we might relate to nostalgia.

This notion of child nostalgia in books is relevant to films. For me and my friends, at least, watching the cowboys round up the bad guys was deeply satisfying, so much so that we went home and re-enacted what we saw on the screen. Playing cowboys was just about all we did for a few years way back when, and while playing we indulged in a fantasy of control and authority. This fantasy, performed with the aid of a number of *objets petits a* (pretend pistols, rifles, spurs, horses, and so on) filled a lack we felt in our own lives. It played out the inescapable nostalgia for a better time and place, one we seemed to have once had but could now only imagine in our cowboy (and other sorts of) games. Play was for us a deeply nostalgic activity, manifesting our longing to be heroic and to be in a place where dreams were true. Not so much the play itself, but the desire that play enacted was what we need to attend to.

Nostalgia is not a genre; it is a feeling. Nostalgia is desire. Like parody, which is not a feeling but a mode of intertextual reference that is difficult to avoid, nostalgia slips into much of the cultural production aimed at children. Both childhood itself and the past that it so often invokes appear attractive, even romantic. Winnie-the-Pooh and his friends dwell among the untrodden ways beside the springs of a happy river, and the thought of Christopher Robin experiencing a strange fit of passion that will take him from the Hundred Acre Wood to a school somewhere beyond this charmed place leaves us with a tinge of melancholy. Oh, that those good times would come again, and alas how piquant the sadness when we grudgingly accept that they will not.

Nostalgia, then, may be a feeling that keeps us from turning to face the future, a conservative yearning for that which has passed, the escape from the here and now that my students keep wanting to find in children's literature itself. Or it may be a reminder that what we experienced when we were young was a version of what William Blake termed the Vales of Har, a place of confinement and half-truths that cannot offer fulfillment until we are able to look back on it from the outside. Nostalgia may keep us confined or it may allow us to see how far we've come from confinement. Mementos from the past can keep memory fixated on the past or they can allow memory to keep recreating and rethinking that past. The past can be, no doubt, an alluring place, but we must live in the present. Some of Alan Garner's work considers mementos of the past in this nostaglic/anti-nostalgic manner; see for example the plates in *The Owl Service* or the axe head in *Red Shift*.

 , "Nostalgia is a sentiment of loss and displacement, but it is also a romance with one's own fantasy" (Boym, xiii). The word *nostalgia* derives from the Greek words *nostos* and *algia*, the first signifying a return home and the second meaning longing. A longing to return home to his wife was what Odysseus felt as he paced the shoreline on Calypso's island every morning after his night with the lovely lady not his wife. All night long he slept in the arms of the beautiful Calypso. In the morning, he wept and longed to return to the wife, who was patiently waiting for him by her loom. Of course we know he does return home to patient Penelope, but Tennyson gives us a clue as to the efficacy of nostalgia satisfied when he imagines Odysseus restless for travel and adventure as he sits by his "still hearth" and contemplates his homeland's "barren crags." Tennyson here gives us nostalgia's dark side: "How dull it is to pause, to make an end, / To rust unburnished, not to shine in use!" (57–58). Nostalgia posits a place of unchanging purity and innocence, a home where we were protected and cared for, a time when everything seemed made for us rather than set against us. William Blake's *Songs of Innocence* evokes this time and place with a precision that underscores its tenuousness and ambiguity. To look to the past nostalgically is to imagine a future better than the present we now have. It may also be to imagine a future that returns us to ways of life left behind.

 Let's glance at the ways of life left behind. Most often nostalgia evokes a longing for what we perceive are past glories, and this longing may become so strong as to render us ill, incapable of directing ourselves to tasks at hand. This is how the Swiss doctor Johannes Hofer interpreted nostalgia when he wrote about it (and in the process named it) in 1688. Nostalgia was a debilitating sickness that manifested itself in soldiers who longed to return to their homelands. During the American Civil War, "the American military doctor Theodore Calhoun conceived of nostalgia as a shameful disease that revealed a lack of manliness and unprogressive attitudes" (Boym, 6). We have come a long way since then, of course, and where once nostalgia was a matter of health, it is now a political and economic matter. Today nostalgia sells and nostalgia curries votes. And far from being unmanly, nostalgia evokes a notion of manhood that draws on the image of the man as strong and independent and capable of controlling his environment. Feminist critics have for some time noted the male nostalgia for a time when men ruled the roost. In this sense, nostalgia is a conservative, even reactionary emotion. And the cowboy is about as nostalgic—and hence reactionary—a vision of manhood as we could look for.

As Jane Kramer puts it, the first American cowboy was most likely a rustler, and it took the twentieth century and "the imagination of Easterners to produce a proper cowboy—a cowboy whom children could idolize, and grown men, chafing at their own domesticated competence, hold as a model of some profoundly masculine truth" (19). Kramer refers to the cowboy as "Rousseau's Émile with a six-gun" (20). The man she writes about, a Texas cowboy Henry Blanton, who worked on a ranch in the 1970s, grew up mimicking the cowboys he saw in the movies, Joel McCrea, John Wayne, and Gary Cooper (108). She calls Henry Blanton the "last cowboy," but we know the allure of the west, and its lonely male on horseback keeps drawing young men to mimic the stoic silences, the rugged individualism, and the self-conscious amble of the cowboy hero. Nostalgia can and does have a distinctly masculine identity, one that presents the image of a man as in control, front and centre, as an ideal devoutly to be restored, if only those pesky women would understand just how urgent it is that a man do what a man's gotta do.

The B Western

As strange as it may seem, the landscape of the western and the cowboy who inhabits this landscape evoke home, that home ever so far away in the palm of your hand. Most of us know that quintessential cowboy song, "Home on the Range."

> Home, home on the range
> Where the deer and the antelope play
> Where seldom is heard a discouraging word
> And the skies are not cloudy all day.

Animals frisking in play, upbeat talk whenever talk occurs, and blue skies from one long horizon to the other. Home here is what a character in John Ford's *The Searchers* (1956) says the hard-bitten land of the west (Texas, in this film) will become: "a fine good place to be." Something ever more is about to be, and when it is—when that being comes into existence— we will have an ontological comfort zone. The nostalgia of and for the west and the westerner is a deeply conservative force that perceives the past as a place of beauty and rightness—the way things are supposed to be, when men were men and women liked it that way. The title of Roy Rogers's first film as a star gives us the sense of home in the west: *Under Western Stars* (1938). Similar titles appear frequently in lists of the B western. *Under Arizona Skies* (1946), *Stars over Arizona* (1937), *Under California Stars* (1948), *Under Fiesta Stars* (1941), *Under Montana Skies* (1930), and *Under Nevada Skies* (1946) are just a few. Direct evocation of "home" appears in many titles. Here's a sample: *Home in Oklahoma* (1946), *Home in San Antone* (1949), *Home in Wyomin'* (1942), *Home on the Prairie* (1939), *Home on the Range* (1946). The title that says it all is *Homesteaders of Paradise Valley* (1947). Since some actors appear in several of these films, we can conclude that Roy or Gene or Rocky or any number of other western stars are at home anywhere out west. Home is the lone prairie where the buffalo roam and the cowboy rides free from family and the restraints of work. No wonder nostalgia gets a bad rap when it dwells on such reactionary masculinity. The western is all about the past as a lost Atlantis where men rode free, especially free of the constraints imposed both by women and by institutions of any kind (marriage or government or business or religion or whatever). And the willingness of screenwriters and directors to locate this lost Atlantis of the west in modern times is an indication that they wish their viewers—many of them boys from about eight to twelve or fourteen years of age—to believe that what appears lost is not lost entirely. Young cowpokes can emulate their heroes by seeing the films, buying the gear and other cowboy stuff, and playing cowboy games.

The past, then, is nowhere more alluringly presented than in the western, a genre that sets out to give us the past as engrossing and romantic. Sometimes it actually presents the past as present—in westerns set in modern times with automobiles and airplanes and factories and gangsters from the city. "When the truth becomes legend, print the legend," as a character puts it in John Ford's *The Man Who Shot Liberty Valance* (1962). The call of the west is a siren song difficult, if not impossible, for some men (and some women) to resist. Many studies of the genre take a self-consciously autobiographical perspective. Jane Tompkins begins her study of the western with the confession "I love Westerns" (3). Martin Pumphrey admits that his interest in westerns is not entirely academic; he tells us he grew up "playing cowboy" and following the exploits of the Cisco Kid, the Lone Ranger, Cheyenne, and Matt Dillon (51). A similar tone appears in Mike Dibb's study of the director Budd Boetticher (161). And the many popular studies of the series western by writers such as Bobby Copeland, James Robert Parrish, Alan G. Barbour, James Horwitz, and Buck Rainey are unashamedly nostalgic; these writers look back fondly, at times even mawkishly, at the Saturday-matinee western icons of their childhood. Their nostalgia is restorative, in Boym's terms. These writers, and others like them, attempt to keep the past alive by holding festivals in which they showcase both the films and the stars from their youth; they wear the clothes they associate with their cowboy heroes; they write reminiscences; they collect western memorabilia; they decorate their homes and automobiles with western paraphernalia; they maintain websites devoted to their cowboy heroes; and they travel to places that hold memories of the old west and its Hollywood connections.

Take for example James Horwitz's *They Went Thataway* (1976). Horwitz begins his search for the heroes of his childhood with a chapter titled "The Front Row Kid." He evokes the enthusiasm with which kids of my generation adored the cowboys. He says these cowboys "put a man-sized boot print on your brain at a time when there were still very few tracks up there to mark the fact that anyone had passed that way. And they left, every Saturday, a pretty clear trail to follow, a trail that gave hope of full days and fantasies and the promise of one day becoming man enough to fit your own footstep into that boot print, to make your own trails" (7). He goes on to describe how for "Front Row Kids and small-town boys, every glorious day was full of shouting and shooting and thundering hoofbeats, barroom brawls and jailbreaks, stampedes and stagecoach journeys through the Badlands and the Indian Territory and daydream cowtowns of our back yard" (9). He then recounts his pilgrimage out west, where every man young or old ought to go, seeking those old western heroes, and he describes his meeting with several familiar figures, including Charles Starrett, Russell Hayden, Sunset Carson, and Gene Autry. His book is an elegy for the old cowboy stars. He concludes that his trip down memory lane amounts to "standing over a dead body and talking about it," and he confesses to "more than a touch of melancholy" (278).

Doug Nye, author of *Those Six-Gun Heroes* (1982), posted an article on the website The State in June 2003 titled, "My heroes have always been cowboys." This short article begins with an anecdote from Nye's childhood and ends with a return to this anecdote. He tells us that "the

Western has always remained especially meaningful to me. Perhaps that fondness for the genre was first stirred when my dad thought enough of a movie cowboy to wake me up that night so long ago [to listen to Roy Rogers on the radio]." He calls that experience "magical," and he ends with the observation that "for some of us, the magic has never died."

Nostalgia and melancholy go together like stagecoach and horses or like Hoppy and the Bar-20. We can see this in the many websites devoted to the cowboy heroes. Here is a sample: Charles H. Dudley's "Hoppy" and the Bar-20 Ranch-Hands, the unofficial website for William "Hopalong Cassidy" Boyd; Charles C. Chaney's Favorite B-Western Performers from the 1930s; Jim Moore's The Hero Is a Man on a Horse; Bob Callaghan's Horse Opera; Brian's Drive-In Theater; and Cow-Boy.com. Joe Konnyu's CowboyPal: Home of the Silver Screen Cowboys is one of two essential websites for these cowboys and their films. Here the visitor can listen to old-time radio, see clips from a Zorro serial, chat with other interested visitors, and access other sites with western themes. However, by far the best of the websites is Chuck Anderson's The Old Corral. This is a massive site with information on everything you would want to know about old B westerns and their stars. Seventy-seven articles trace the careers of eighty western stars; another eight cover the Cowboy Trio series; five articles give the history of the Lone Ranger on film; eight outline other series such as the Durango Kid, Red Ryder, and Cisco Kid series; other articles cover subjects such as musical groups, sidekicks, child actors, villains, stunt people, comic books, and gun-belt trivia. Here too the visitor can find links to sites that describe movie locations (Lone Pine, Corriganville, and so on). The Old Corral is a labour of love and likely one of the Internet's most impressive sites. It is also unabashedly nostalgic. Here is what Chuck Anderson has to say about his site's purpose:

> The Old Corral website is dedicated to those wonderful cowboy heroes, heroines, sidekicks, heavies, and supporting players that rode the silver screen from the 1930s through the early 1950s in B westerns and cowboy cliffhangers. My goal is to simply rekindle memories of those great silver screen adventures, and to provide information, critique and education on the actors, actresses and films of the genre.

The Old Corral succeeds masterfully in its enterprise and is rightly seen as a "comprehensive history" of the B western. It is, quite simply, indispensable.

Rekindling memories can, of course, have more than one purpose, just as nostalgia can have more than one manifestation. As recently as 2003, Thomas S. Engeman writes in defence of cowboy culture, pointing out that various American presidents (Jackson, Harrison, Lincoln) "invoked their vigorous frontier origins in order to increase their democratic stature." He also mentions Teddy Roosevelt, Ronald Reagan, and George W. Bush as presidents who "continue to embrace the cowboy way." Engeman defends this "cowboy way" in a world in which the frontier has not yet disappeared. He says the United States "continually encounters frontiers contested by the enemies of democracy," but "the American knight-hero restores public confidence" and ensures "the return of democratic law and order" ("In Defense of Cowboy Culture," http://www.claremont. org/publications/crb/id.1036/article_detail.asp). Here is nostalgia turned back into aggression and a love for the paths of glory. More recently, John Tirman has argued that America needs to redefine its frontier myth: "If the world is essentially regarded as a font of anti-American terrorism or rivalry, as a social, political, and physical wilderness to be tamed, then we will be battling in the diminishing space our old habits have forced us into. That frontier is closing. The daunting but necessary task of redefining our horizons is upon us" (40). Tirman goes back to John Winthrop, a seventeenth-century divine, for a possible model for such a redefinition. We might begin closer to home with the silver screen cowboys. The B western tries to draw the frontier myth into contemporary times by placing Roy Rogers or Gene Autry or any of the others in mid-twentieth-century contexts. Past glories need not be past, they seem to say.

More recent western movies too have shown this yearning for past glories; take for example such paeans to the early western films and western heroes as *Hearts of the West* (1975), *Barbarosa* (1982), *Rustler's Rhapsody* (1985), *¡Three Amigos!* (1986), and *Sunset* (1988). The many attempts of Hollywood to produce revisionist westerns—from *The Wild Bunch* (1969) to *Unforgiven* (1992), from *The Ballad of Little Jo* (1993) to *The Jack Bull* (1999)—have been unable to avoid presenting the Old West as a place redolent of romance and adventure. As I write, the most recent example is Kevin Costner's 2003 film *Open Range*, in which the continuing apology for righteous violence in the face of tyranny and greed finds expression. The female lead in this film (Annette Bening) is willing to overlook the hero's penchant for killing people because he does so only when provoked by the ugliness of foreign greed and aggression. The good cowboy enacts good violence, and we laud him for this. And so the cowboy and the western landscape continue to occupy a place in advertisements for clothing, cars, cologne, beer, and even headache remedies. Our culture seems tenaciously attached to the cowboy as a figure whose attractions are distinctly nostalgic. But this subject is not singular; as we have seen, nostalgia comes in several varieties and may serve several purposes.

First, we need to make a distinction between the films themselves and their nostalgia for a time and place when justice, honour, and manhood were respected and successful, and the study of these films today, half a century after the last one was made. The first point to make about nostalgia generally is that it imagines a time and place and people who exist only in imaginative space. As we know, the good old days were seldom as good as we insist on imagining them to have been. And most of us realize that such bad men of the west as Jesse James, William Bonney, or John Wesley Hardin were hardly the men of honour they appear to be when played on screen by the likes of Tyrone Power, Johnny Mack Brown, Robert Taylor, or Rock Hudson. In the B westerns that are my focus, Billy the Kid and Jesse James can come in the guise of Roy Rogers or Don "Red" Barry or Bob Steele or Buster Crabbe or Sunset Carson. These westerns unabashedly turn history into fantasy. Films such as Gene Autry's *The Phantom Empire* (1935) and Tim McCoy's *Ghost Patrol* (1936) are out-and-out science fiction, and as such they indicate just how fantastic Poverty Row's version of the west was.

The historical backdrop to these films may be anywhere from the mid-nineteenth century, when Texas was trying to make it on its own, to the days of the Civil War, or from Reconstruction to the turn of the century to the First World War to the Depression to the Second World War. Time seems not to matter. The cowboy heroes wear the same clothes, have the same ivory-handled pistols, tooled boots, decoratively-stitched trousers, and embroidered shirts whether they are helping Texas become a state or helping the United States government fight foreign spies working for either the fascists or the communists. These cowboys ride horses even when the bad guys have taken to trucks, cars, and sometimes even airplanes. And the heroes' horses—with such dramatic and dashing names as Silver, Tarzan, Raider, White Flash, Trigger, KoKo, Black Jack, Topper, Rush, Silver Bullet—just about always travel faster than the trucks, cars, and planes that the baddies use for their getaway. Heigh-ho, Silver, away! Horse and rider never seem to reach the end of the trail; they just keep on catching villains no matter how sophisticated the villains become, and they do so in the time-honoured manner of the cowboy with his six-guns and his horse.

From the point of view of nostalgia, the past invades the present. Roy Rogers and Gene Autry and other B western stars made films with contemporary settings, but the plots always involved bad guys trying to swindle honest people or rob banks or rustle cattle or steal water or somehow avoid the law. And the hero always rides a horse, sports fancy hardware, and plays the cowboy to perfection. These films even manage to romanticize the United States' imperialist tendencies. In Gene Autry's *Round-up Time in Texas* (1937), Gene and his buddies ignore the title of the movie and travel to South Africa to deal with diamond thieves and tap the bonanza for themselves, and in *Law of the Pampas* (1939), Hopalong Cassidy and his friends travel to a generic South America (somewhere across the Andes from Chile), where they too deal with bad guys and generally sort things out for the people there. Hoppy's young sidekick, Lucky Jenkins (Russell Hayden), remarks that the Andes look like "our" Rockies, and he insists on calling his Spanish *compañero* Ferdie instead of Ferdinand, although Ferdinand repeatedly asks him not to do so. We have the American cowboy laying claim to South America and diminishing its people. Perhaps one of the strangest of such films is *Kansas Terrors* (1939), the action of which does not take place in Kansas. No, this film sees two members of the Three Mesquiteers travel to a small, unnamed Caribbean island, where they help a band of rebels and their leader against the island's cruel ruler. After ousting the dictator, the two Americans return home taking with them the rebel leader, who now becomes a member of the group, which can justifiably carry the name the Three Mesquiteers.

Such a political use of nostalgia, the championing of the country and values from which the myth of the cowboy derives, is a recurring feature of the B western. In many cases, the villain represents big business or corrupt government, but in many other cases the villain is distinctly foreign. When these films are not criticizing the forces of big money and greed that trample the rights of the small rancher and local small business person, they reflect the arrogance of American imperialism and at the same time the paranoia of American isolationism. Villains are often Mexicans, Native Americans, German spies, French Canadians, or unspecified foreign nationals. When they appear in these westerns, black people are often treated as comic buffoons, as was often the case in Hollywood films of the 1930s and '40s. Lincoln Theodore Monroe Andrews Perry (a.k.a. Stepin Fetchit), Fred Toones (a.k.a. Snowflake), and Erville Alderson provide the antics (often uncredited) in such films as *Wild Horse* (1931), *Haunted Gold* (1932), *Hair-Trigger Casey* (1936), *Two-Gun Sheriff* (1941), and *Haunted Ranch* (1943). The attitude to the Other, then, reflects either the paranoia of nationalism at its worst or a no-longer-palatable paternalism toward those considered hardly capable of taking care of themselves (Native Americans, African Americans, Chinese Americans). The films' nostalgia for the time when might was right and so was white (a phrase that occurs with some frequency in films of the 1930s and '40s is "That's mighty white of you") reveals the dark side of nostalgia, its complicit connection with a reactionary political agenda.

An examination of the B western films' nostalgic look at the past is made complex by the effect of nostalgia on the viewer of these films. A genuine interest in the B western is likely to contain its own nostalgia, especially for those who grew up watching these films either at the local cinema or on TV. The websites I mentioned earlier are the creations of men of my generation. I was what Horwitz calls a front row kid. In the 1950s it was easy to be a front row kid because westerns were everywhere, and certainly they were a staple of prime-time television. In 1959, the year of greatest concentration of westerns on television, thirty-two westerns aired each week in prime time (Yoggy, 218). In 1954, my parents took me to the Canadian National Exhibition, in Toronto, where I saw Roy Rogers, Trigger, and the whole entourage from the TV program *The Roy Rogers Show*. I, and many of the kids I played with, lived and breathed the cowboy life, vicariously of course. We put no distance between ourselves and our heroes. We were those heroes in some deeply psychological way. For me, the identification with the cowboy provided a complex cover and compensation for a troubled home life. To enter the world of the cowboy was to escape the anxiety of home. In addition, the belief in right and in a masculine honour that would defeat all villainous activity was comforting. In an important way, Gene and Roy and Hoppy and Lash and the rest were ego-ideals, Ideal-I's that reflected our fantasies of capable manhood. In the films, these heroes were often father figures, but not to me. My father was the terror; I was the hero. The hero was I in fantasy.

I recount this mini-history of my childhood devotion to the cowboy in order to make clear that I come to the subject carried on the breezes of nostalgia. Memory allows me to reflect that not only was I a fan of the cowboy but that that fact must continue to colour my view of both the past and the westerns I recall loving with a passion. The question is: Ought I to view these films and their stars dispassionately? How can I be certain that the values of masculine honour, independence, and aggression are ones I can look upon critically? Vigilante justice, paternalism toward minorities that easily becomes xenophobia and racism, sexism, love of the gun: these are some of the values communicated by the B western. How does nostalgia influence the way we understand paternalism, sexism, and so on?

The following passage—the opening to J. Brim Crow and Jack H. Smith's celebration of the B western, *The Cowboy and the Kid* (1988)—is a clear expression of the nostalgia many men of my generation feel for the B western. The authors begin by asserting that their book "is a book of memories." They go on to describe the content of their book:

> In these pages you will be transported back to those days when you sat in the darkened Bijou or Rialto or whatever it was called in your town and enjoyed a pure American art form, the Western. . . . To two generations, the Saturday Matinee was more than entertainment. It was a place where kids learned things like honesty and honor and fair play, all the while thinking they were just having a good time. It was a time to be remembered and cherished. It was a time that will not come our way again. (xv)

Learning things while having a good time reminds me of learning things while messing about in boats. The nostalgia for a time and place when people were young and lived without the burdens of responsibility, when people were prior to the clash of sex and needed only a few good companions (usually of the same sex) to make life satisfying, when people felt attached in deeply satisfying ways to their homes, whether those homes were enclosed spaces or wide-open landscapes, is of course the reflection of a desire for pastoral, for that which never was but perhaps is evermore about to be.

William Empson long ago, in *Some Versions of Pastoral* (1935), made the connection between pastoral and children, remarking that as urbanization and industrialization closed off pastoral spaces, the values invested in such spaces transferred to children. Perhaps the most defiant vision of pastoral we have is J.M. Barrie's *Peter Pan* (1904), in which Peter and his Lost Boys inhabit the island of Neverland, where they can play cowboys and Indians to their hearts' content. Nostalgia does not so much remember the past as it *"uses the past"* (Davis 10), and Peter and his group are too young to remember the past anyway. They can use it only for their games. For reasons that are clear, nostalgia is an emotion more likely to be felt by adults than by children. But even children remember, however deeply the memory lodges in their unconscious minds, when the mother tended to their every need and desire. The cowboy films are versions of *Peter Pan* in that they deliver ostensibly grown-up boys who play their games of cowboys and Indians and yearn for mothers they can never have.

I'll offer just one example of what I mean, using the film *Fuzzy Settles Down* (1944), one of the series in which Buster Crabbe plays Billy Carson (a variant of Billy the Kid). In this film, Billy's sidekick, Fuzzy Q. Jones (Al St. John), decides to purchase a newspaper in Carson City. The previous owner was murdered because he printed warnings concerning law and order in an attempt to intimidate the local bad men. We never learn much about the bad guys except that in the first scene they rob the bank, and we know that their leader is Lafe Barlowe (Charles King). Fuzzy asks the former editor's daughter to stay on and help with the business. Billy thinks settling down is downright silly, and he laughs at his friend's foolishness. Throughout the film, Billy exhibits an immaturity that irritates the young woman, Edith Martin (Patty McCarthy). And yet Billy and Edith find each other attractive. Billy accompanies Edith home on more than one occasion, and when she thanks him for seeing her home, he says she need not thank him since he was going that way anyway. Clearly, Billy has a mature man's interest in this young woman; however, like a young boy, he cannot admit this and at the end of the film he rides off in the usual heroic fashion. To underline the attractions of independence and a life without women, Fuzzy gives the newspaper back to Edith and hurries to catch up with Billy. The life of a cowboy is away from women, away from towns, away from the settled life. Billy lives a life of adventure—and what is this adventure but a form of play?

Stretching the world of play from childhood into adulthood can have deleterious effects. In the recent film *Down in the Valley* (2005), we see a young man, Harlan (Edward Norton), who has absorbed the ways of the Hollywood cowboy so deeply that they have skewered his sense of reality. His attempts to live the life of the cowboy result in tragedy. We do not know what films Harlan has seen. All we know is that he comes from southern California but tells people he is from the Dakotas. His speech, his mannerisms, his clothes, and his two-gun holster set with its Colt .45s inform us of the fantasy he has grown up with. Another recent film, *Elephant* (2003), deals with a school shooting reminiscent of the Columbine High School shootings that took place in Colorado in April 1999. I am not suggesting that B western films are somehow directly responsible for Columbine or other violent acts over the past decade or two. I am, however, suggesting that the fantasies the B western films presented to my generation live on, mutated, perhaps, and less innocent. But to think that such fantasies—because they were "innocent" back then—contain a vision not only worth preserving but worth emulating is to perpetuate immaturity. We need to understand the past and its fantasies, not repeat them.

Playing with guns—paintball and computer games and fast-draw contests and rifle ranges—perpetuate the cowboy's play. I lived the adventures when I was eight and ten years old, but looking back now I worry that playing with guns has captured so many. It is time to refashion our nostalgia. It is time to reflect on the cowboy and his friendly gun.

Arms and the Man
The Friendly Gun

Shoot low, they might be crawlin'.
—Monte Hale

I have few pictures of myself as a boy, but one of these, taken in 1954, shows a family gathering in which I am front and centre (figure 4.1). Behind me are my parents, my sister, my maternal grandparents, and an aunt. I am nine years old. Everyone in the photograph stands and smiles; everyone is inactive, everyone but me. I have my shoulders slightly hunched and my head moves forward and down over my chest. In my right hand is a toy pistol, and my left hand is about to draw a second pistol from its holster. These guns indicate my desire to play the cowboy. I'm wearing two toy six-guns, and I'm drawing and aiming at the camera. I am enacting a fantasy by playing cowboy right there while my family appears oblivious to the guns as if these are everyday items. Of course, they were. When I was a boy, I played cowboys just about every day of the week, and my family got used to hearing me make shooting sounds and clip-clop sounds as I rode my imaginary horse outside and inside the house and shot my toy pistols left and right. Another photograph taken at the same family outing shows more clearly than this one my gun belt with its silver decorations. I suspect this gun and holster set was new, although my memory is blank on this point. What is clear is just how pleased I was with the gun, how proudly I wore the holster, and how engaged I was in performing the quick draw. I was, of course, emulating the cowboy heroes I saw in the movies (at the time this photograph was taken, we did not have television).

Figure 4.1 The McGillis family in 1954. The author, in the foreground, demonstrates his prodigious fast-draw technique.

Pictures such as this one are not rare. A survey of personal websites will turn up any number of photographs from the 1950s in which little boys, and sometimes little girls, appear dressed up in cowboy costume and wearing pistols or holding toy rifles. What is noticeable about my picture is that I do not have the cowboy accoutrements—hat, boots, necktie or scarf, shirt, or any of the other cowboy paraphernalia that one could buy back then. I assure you that I coveted these items. I desperately wanted a hat, especially one like Roy Rogers wore, white with a low crown that had two circles pressed into it. It had distinctive blocking no other cowboy hat had. I pleaded with my mother for a hat like Roy's or for any authentic-looking cowboy hat, but to no avail. Then one summer an aunt and uncle went on holiday to Mexico, and when they returned they brought me a hat, an elaborately decorated Mexican sombrero with tassels dangling around the rim. I happened to be staying at the cottage of a friend when my aunt and uncle returned. The whole family came to the cottage to deliver the fancy sombrero to me, and they did so with much pride and a bit of fanfare. As for me, I took one look at that Mexican hat with its sissy tassels and, once I had it in my hands, began to pull each tassel off with determined yanks. My mother was mortified; the others were surprised. My mother took me to the bunkhouse to teach me a lesson. That was as close as I got to having a real cowboy hat.

The fact that I have pistols, however, and none of the other gear, signifies the importance of those pistols. Pistols were the most important
part of a cowboy's gear. What any self-respecting boy of that time wanted
first and foremost was a gun, or as many guns as possible, all resembling
the ones we saw in the cowboy movies. We loved to pretend to shoot,
and we would use anything to represent a gun—from the toy guns like the
one in the photograph to sticks we pretended were rifles and even to our
extended forefingers and cocked thumbs. Obviously, we did not think
much about the significance of the gun. To us, it was just a friendly part
of our fantasies and games. It was a combination of fashion accessory, toy,
baton, tool, and firearm. It was any number of things except something
that actually could kill another person. We were aware that real guns fired
bullets and that bullets were potentially lethal; however, the heroes we
watched on celluloid more often than not used their guns to shoot the
guns from the hands of villains. They could do this no matter how they
were positioned vis-à-vis the villain. It did not matter if they fired from the
side of their adversary or whether they shot straight on. It did not matter
how far away they were from their adversary. Their sure aim always
ensured that only the villain's gun received the impact and no ricochet
ever penetrated flesh. When a villain dropped his pistol and grabbed his
arm as if shot, no blood appeared, and his hand or arm functioned normally
again within seconds. When men—villains or the nameless members of
a sheriff's posse—did receive a mortal wound, the impact of the bullet
rarely left a tear in clothing or a hole in flesh or blood seeping through
cloth. If a cowboy received a bullet in the chest, he nearly always fell forward rather than backward, as if the impact of the bullet had had no effect.

Perhaps the defining moment in the movies of that era came in George
Stevens's *Shane* (1953, the year before this photograph was taken), when
the gunfighter Shane (Alan Ladd) gives the boy, Joey (Brandon de Wilde),
a shooting lesson. Shane tells Joey's mother (Jean Arthur) that a gun is a
tool that a man must use with skill and care. *Shane* presents openly what
western films had been communicating without self-consciousness for the
previous twenty years and more. The gun is a man's best friend. Use it well
and it will repay you with satisfaction. The gun is, as we have so often
heard, a symbol of manhood. Indeed, the measure of a man is indicated both
by how he wears a gun and how he shoots it. The man demonstrates complete control over the gun by various tricks he performs, twirling one or
two pistols at once, tossing the gun in the air in nifty arcs, and displaying
a lightning draw and unerring marksmanship. A series of publicity pho-
togrpahs showing Johnny Mack Brown demonstrating his dexterity with

a pistol to an admiring young man and woman illustrates the cowboy's mastery of the gun. Four of the photos in this series appear on the Joe Bowman wesite (www.joebowman.com/browntribute.html), and all five are available on the Old Time Radio Catalog website (www.otrcat.com/star-western-theater-p-1037.html).

At least one B western, *Starlight over Texas* (1938), made an attempt to address directly the significance of the gun. In this mishmash of a film, Tex Norman (Tex Ritter) roams the Mexican border dealing with rustlers and stagecoach robbers and generally setting to rights various dastardly goings-on perpetrated by a gang of villains. The film opens with a stagecoach robbery, then cuts to Tex riding along singing merrily about starlight over Texas, and then cuts to Tex's finding an apparently abandoned stagecoach. Hiding in the bushes is a Mexican family—grandmother, mother, and son. The young son is Ramon Ruiz (Salvatore Damino), and he has an interest in guns. Later in the film, at a fiesta held at the governor's hacienda, Ramon sees Tex without his guns and asks where they are. Without answering the question, Tex asks Ramon if he likes guns, and of course the boy says he does. Tex launches into a speech: "Guns are a lot like human beings. They get all sorts of ideas. Sometimes they feel good, they're happy, they want to show off, so they break bottles or shoot out the lights." At other times they "say nothing," they just "listen and watch, like soldiers on sentry duty." Sometimes, he says, they want to see people dance (a reference to an earlier scene in the film). And finally there are times when they are "dangerous when mad," and they "spit out death." "That's all I know about guns," he concludes as he walks away from Ramon.

Tex's explanation is not very helpful. He never does answer Ramon's question, and what he says just confuses things. From Tex we learn that guns are as unpredictable as human beings—and as predictable. They are toys and playthings; they are, like soldiers, protective and visible signs of order; they serve to control as when they force someone to dance; and they are lethal, spitting out death. What Ramon does not learn is whether guns are good or bad, whether they are necessary, or whether they have uses on specific occasions or in specific contexts. Should everyone have a gun? Should Ramon pursue his interest in guns? The boy hears nothing that could either temper his interest in guns or teach him something valuable about them. And unlike Shane, Tex never tries to teach Ramon about the proper use of the gun or how to use one. Ramon, and boys who see this film, will most likely find Tex's lecture tantalizing, like the gun itself. The gun is a paradox: toy, plaything, military equipment, carrier of death, and romantic accessory of the cowboy hero.

Ramon and the rest of the boys for whom he serves as focalizer want Tex to wear his guns, not to talk about them. Guns are a feature of performance. Several films have the hero performing trick shooting in a travelling medicine show. Performance indicates both skill and capability; guns are a feature of the man's capable performance. They signify the connection between performance in the sense of acting and performance in the sense of carrying out a role unconsciously, learning to transform performance as role-playing into being. But guns remain somehow free from performance because they are unpredictable, dangerous, and empowering; they can support law and order and they can break laws and foment disorder. They are most often in the hands of men rather than women. They testify to the power of the male hero, and most boys find the allure of the male hero difficult, if not impossible, to resist. And in the B western, we see guns carried by young boys (and sometimes young girls). Prompted by the western movies, children like myself eagerly included guns in their fantasies of control and power. We desired to incorporate ourselves into the performance fantasy of the gun.

The B western, however, remains largely silent on the issue of guns and kids, although if the number of films in which kids carry and use guns is any indication, we can conclude that the idea of kids learning to use guns is thoroughly acceptable in the ideology these films communicate. Take for example *Gunsmoke Ranch* (1937), a Three Mesquiteers film that begins with shots of floods and desolation—scenes that are reminders of the Depression. Later, a crooked land dealer offers "free" land (forty-acre ranches) in Arizona and free passage to the west. We see three bus-like vehicles travelling through a rocky western landscape, where they spook the horses of the Three Mesquiteers. Stony (Robert Livingston) has eyes for one of the passengers, Marion (Jean Carmen), who is travelling with her father and younger brother, Jimmy (Sammy McKim). One scene has Jimmy, brandishing a Winchester, pretending to ambush the Three Mesquiteers, and Tucson says, "Guns weren't made for children to play with."

"How's he going to be a westerner if he doesn't learn to shoot?" Lullaby retorts.

Stony says from now on Jimmy will have to use a slingshot, and later in the film Jimmy uses his slingshot to hit a bad guy in the face before the bad guy can shoot at the Mesquiteers. The message is mixed here. Jimmy shouldn't play with guns; on the other hand, he needs to learn to shoot. So he substitutes the gun with a slingshot, a weapon more obviously a toy than the Winchester. Yet this toy serves a serious purpose in thwarting the villains. I think the confusing message here is that the shooting object—gun or slingshot—is a toy that serves the purpose of training the boy to be a bigger boy. Clearly, as the photograph of my family suggests, the gun is a toy prized by young boys. What made the pistol so attractive a toy? Obviously, the pistol and the holster in which it rested were a significant part of what defined our cowboy heroes. The hero wore an elaborately tooled gun belt, often with two holsters. His six-shooters were fancy too, sporting white handles and gleaming with buffed silver. The villain, on the other hand, often wore a battered and undecorated gun belt with an unattractive holster that contained an undistinguished pistol with dark handles and a uniformly dark barrel. The hero's gun-and-holster set was meant to catch the eye. It signified neatness, efficiency, wealth, style, and individuality; the villain's set communicated opposing qualities: sloppiness, inattention to detail, poverty, conformity, and plainness moving to ugliness. Less charitably, we might say that the hero's gun and holster were meant for show, whereas the villain's were meant for use. However, we could never leave the cinema without knowing that style and use went together when it came to the hero's repertoire. Style defined the man. He looked good, and he could use his guns efficiently. He was a deadly shot.

The appearance of the gun belt and guns was of prime importance. This is true from the earliest years of the western, even in the silent film period, when contrasting styles are visible even among the heroes themselves. William S. Hart was the taciturn, granite-faced hero who wore what were supposed to be realistic range clothes and whose gun belt and pistol, although not without evidence of craft in their design, were relatively plain. Tom Mix, on the other hand, wore flashy clothes—"the black (or white) ten-gallon hat, the silk shirt and the round-top boots" to complement his impressive six-shooters (Nye 1982, 7). In the 1920s, the contrast between hero and villain sharpens considerably as cowboys such as Buck Jones, Ken Maynard, and Fred Thomson adopt a style closer to that of Tom Mix than to William S. Hart. As we move through the 1930s to the 1950s, the emphasis on intricately crafted leather and steel with silver and pearl adornment increases. The cowboy's hardware, along with his clothing, becomes more obviously the costume that marks his special quality of authority. Near the beginning of her book on the western, Jane Tompkins remarks that when the men she talks to "speak of their youthful afternoons at the movies," they have "a certain ruminative tone in their voices." She goes on to say that they pronounce names such as Roy Rogers, Gene Autry, and Lash LaRue as if they were "words to a prayer whose meaning they have forgotten" (15). And these cowboy heroes with their flashy clothes and hardware are akin to holy figures. They are conveyors of truth and models of behaviour. The gun is their sceptre, their lightning bolt, and their hammer of Thor. The gun wins the west, tames towns, guarantees freedom, liberty, and justice.

A publicity photograph of Ray "Crash" Corrigan holding his resplendent gun belt against an equally lavish saddle clearly indicates how important the look of the gun and its holster is. See the Corrigan page on Brian's Drive-In website: www.briansdriveintheater.com/westerns.html. In this picture we see the cleric with his objects of office. Only a special person could wear such special accoutrements. The carefully tooled workmanship on belt and guns reminds us that these are works of art, to be admired for their aesthetic appeal. The deadly use to which such objects may be put is less evident than their beauty. These are works of art, worthy to be worn by a chosen man—a cleric or perhaps an artist. The cowboy is an artist-hero, as much admired for how he looks, and for his style, as for what he does. His guns signify in a complex manner; they suggest the man capable of action and control, a man who wields weapons of destruction and who wields these weapons with the knowledge of a scientist. He knows how they work and how to gauge distance and wind velocity and light and movement so that he can shoot a target that is still or moving, near or far away. He appears capable of shooting accurately from impossible angles and from impossible positions and from a galloping or even rearing horse. His unerring shooting also reminds us that the cowboy is an artist of the gun. The gun does his talking for him; they are "singing guns," as the title of a film with Vaughn Monroe expresses it (1950). *Guns and Guitars*, a 1936 film with Gene Autry, connects guns and music in its title, and we know the popularity of the singing cowboy from the mid-1930s to the mid-1950s. The cowboy's words could take the form of bullets or musical notes. For young boys, this figure is something of a messiah whose words can accomplish deeds just as much as his fists and guns can (see figures 4.3 and 4.4).

Looking again at the guns, holsters, and cartridge-holding belt that Ray Corrigan displays, we can see clearly the aesthetic importance of the gun. The gun takes its place as part of the total costume from distinctive hat (usually white), to embroidered shirt and trousers to handsomely worked boots. The saddle across which Corrigan spreads the gun belt reminds us that the cowboy comes with a horse, and his costume and gear (saddles, rope, guns, and so on) typify him as a latter-day knight, a mid-twentieth-century Lancelot. All that gear is weighty, materially and

Figure 4.3 Monte Hale—in bib shirt, pressed trousers, and white stetson—bearing arms. Note the leather holsters, white-handled silver revolvers, and the powder horn. Source: Mr. Monte Hale.

symbolically. I think that Roy Rogers captures both senses when he describes the gear he and Dale Evans used:

> Dale and I dressed pretty fancy, but our outfits were nothing compared to what Trigger wore. Trig's best saddles were made by Edward H. Bohlin, whom people used to call the Michelangelo of saddlecraft. . . . Eddie Bohlin's saddles were covered with the most intricate silver and gold work and some of them weighed up to a hundred and fifty pounds each.

Figure 4.3 Monte Hale with horse. The fine decorative work on saddle and bridle, the stylized flowers on Monte Hale's shirt, and the ornate belt buckle, gun belt, and pistol combine to create an eye-catching bouquet of western motifs. Source: Mr. Monte Hale.

He also made gun belts, holsters, belt buckles, chaps, and spurs, and he did some of the most beautiful gun engraving you ever saw. To this day, I still like to wear my Bohlin belt buckles. . . . But I'll tell you one thing he made I don't wear much: the silver-trimmed *buscadero* gunbelt and twin holsters that used to be part of my King of the Cowboys outfit. For fun recently, I strapped that big rig on, and I couldn't believe how much it weighs! I swear I can hardly stand up in it, much less do a running leap onto Trigger. (161–62)

The hero's guns are weighty. And note the jaunty tone Roy adopts, and the broad smile on Ray's face in the photograph. Guns are good friends; they make one smile.

The friendly gun is an aspect of the gun as toy. As a thing to play with, the gun is friendly. The sense of the gun as a toy is apparent in the B western. In *The Fighting Champ* (1932), with Bob Steele, the gun is clearly connected with another type of boys' play—boxing. Early in the film, Brick Loring (Bob Steele) stops the robbery of a stagecoach and rescues the passengers. The two passengers are boxing champion Spike Sullivan (Kit Guard) and his manager, Nifty (George Chesboro). Both are impressed with Brick's skill with his six-shooter, and Sullivan remarks that "if he is as nifty with his mitts as he is with that cap gun," he must be a good boxer. Cap guns are, of course, what I am carrying in the photograph that I began with in this chapter. And in the films, the gun is about as lethal as a cap gun. Take for example, *Bar Z Badmen* (1937), in which Johnny Mack Brown plays a young smart aleck who likes nothing better than shooting up his hometown. In the opening scene, Johnny and his friends ride into town and shoot up the Chinese laundry, the clothing store, and the saloon. Johnny finds himself in front of a judge to account for his actions. He accepts exile rather than a term in jail as his punishment, and as he leaves the courtroom he fires another shot to demonstrate his lack of remorse.

Often in these films, when the hero or villain uses his guns to shoot at people, no one is seriously wounded, but when someone receives a mortal wound from a bullet fired by our hero or anyone else, he falls without fanfare or blood or sound. And he reappears in the next film. Actors such as Charles King or Bob Kortman or John Merton or any number of other familiar faces reappear in film after film, playing similar characters, many of whom die in similar ways but then get up for the next film. The films work in much the same way as boys' cowboy games worked. When we played cowboys, we often received mortal wounds that kept us down for a few seconds, and then we jumped up to prepare for the next shootout. We enjoyed what Leslie Fiedler called "good clean violence" (1972, 273).

The opening of the Mesquiteers' films draws attention to the friendly gun. The first films in the series—most of them with Robert Livingston as Stony Brook, Ray Corrigan as Tucson Smith, and Max Terhune as Lullaby Joslin—begin by introducing each of the Mesquiteers. First Stony, then Tucson, and finally Lullaby; each of them smiles in turn at the camera in a gesture of welcome to the audience. These are happy-go-lucky fellows, and they invite us to play along. As I pointed out earlier, the films with John Wayne as Stony open with a direct appeal to the friendly gun. These friendly fellows use their guns as toys; part of their appeal comes in the direct way in which they draw, twirl, and point their weapons at us: it's the same way we draw and point our toy pistols at our friends when we play our cowboy games. The actions mimic the quick draw and remind us that these cowboys are proficient with their guns, fast on the draw, and accurate in their aim. The opening of Republic Studios' Red Ryder films in the 1940s is similar in its accent on the friendly gun. As the film credits begin to roll, we see a large book, which nearly fills the screen. From this book emerge Red Ryder and Little Beaver on horseback from the left. Red pulls one of his two guns and begins shooting left and right, apparently in random fashion, as if he and Little Beaver were surrounded by unseen bad guys. Red's random firing is just the sort of thing we did in our cowboy games. For examples of what I describe here, see *Conquest of Cheyenne* (1946), with Wild Bill Elliott as Red, and *Santa Fe Uprising* (1946), with Alan "Rocky" Lane as Red.

It was precisely actions such as this that gave rise to my desire as a child for a set of toy pistols that looked as much like the real thing as possible. Or we wanted Winchesters that replicated the ones our heroes used. To capitalize on this youthful covetousness, the Daisy Manufacturing Company launched a series of ad campaigns in which the toy guns they sold were described as the "spittin' image" of the ones actually used in the Old West (as seen on film). The gun was the *objet a* that activated our fantasies. With it, we could feel as if our fantasies had a basis in actuality. The gun was protection from our own fears; it completed the fantasy of competence and control. With a gun in our hands or in our holsters, we need not fear diminishment or lack or impotence. The gun, like so much else in the world of the B western, had its auto-erotic significance. Our fantasies of control or competence managed our desire; in other words, these fantasies formed a barrier to the terror of the real. Fantasy always does this; it teaches us how to desire. If we manage our fantasies well, we have no difficulty dealing with reality. The important thing is to remain conscious of what is fantasy and what is not.

The desire to own guns like the ones worn and used by our heroes had as much to do with marketing as with character formation or socialization or the learning of useful skills. In fact, it had everything to do with marketing. As Tom Diaz notes in *Making a Killing:* "The entertainment media . . . often serve the interests of the gun industry, intentionally or not, by portraying the use of firearms as an effective and acceptable means to solve disputes" (4). Along with the gun press and gun industry, the entertainment media have "helped create and maintain the unique U.S. gun culture, within which the firearm is less a utilitarian tool than an icon, so laden with implicit value that its hold over its devotees approaches the mystical" (50). As Diaz goes on to say, the gun embodies "a complex of values that includes manliness (defined in warrior terms), individual liberty (as against the state), self-reliance (as against everyone else), and the administration of peremptory justice by ad hoc personal means (shooting 'bad' people)" (50). The gun as iconic object seems to me clear in the B western.

The gun still has this "mystical" aura about it, as Jane Tompkins points out in her account of a trip to the Buffalo Bill Museum in Denver, Colorado, where in June 1988 she saw guns galore. Any number of websites champion the gun as the foundation upon which American liberty rests. As children, we (the boys I played with and I) lusted after guns. Guns occupied much of our waking lives, our games and fantasies, and perhaps our dreams. I can recall the passion I expended vainly trying to convince my mother to buy me a Red Ryder BB gun and secretly playing with my father's shotguns when no one was around to stop me. The gun was something every real man should have in order to accomplish his work as provider and protector. We felt we needed guns to prove something of our character as males. And this is precisely what the marketplace wanted us to feel. Consumer items often appear to us as necessities; marketers present them to us as objects of desire. I could give umpteen examples, but one will do. A TV commercial for Charmin toilet tissue that showed Mr. Whipple going into orgasmic reaction whenever he squeezed the Charmin. The message is that with Charmin bathroom tissue, desire—a desire connected to bodily necessity—finds satisfaction. The combining of the erotic with the impolite is evident in depictions of the gun as well. If we have desires, then these require satisfying and satisfying safely. Desire demands control. The marketplace is the supplier of that which is necessary to satisfy and control desire.

Mention of the Red Ryder BB gun should remind us of how direct the connection is between the B western hero and the gun as commodity. Fred Harman's Red Ryder character, who appeared first in the comics in 1938, appeared in films played by B western stars Don "Red" Barry, "Wild Bill" Elliott, Allan "Rocky" Lane, and Jim Bannon. The Daisy Rifle company used the Red Ryder figure to sell its BB guns to youngsters as early as 1939. Daisy presented the BB rifle as an object of desire, and it did so by presenting the rifle to us as both a toy and an icon of western myth. To depict the gun as an iconic object is to render it an object of desire. In a way, the gun became for us a fetish object. The gun as fetish works in both a Marxist and a Freudian manner. As commodity, the gun is an object "endowed with life," with a mysterious value above and beyond its rational worth (Marx, 52–53). As symbol, the gun serves as a calming assurance of the absent penis (see Freud 1981). In both Marxist and Freudian senses, the fetish is a substitute for something we desire but do not (cannot) have.

Our desire for the gun was, of course, our desire for something Imaginary. I take this term from Jacques Lacan (1988) and use it to suggest that the gun was that which we desired as an object of power. It represented what we wanted, as males, to be. As an object, the gun exists as something we imagine will satisfy us; its existence is more imaginary than real. We saw it in films, and the films served as a replacement for the mirror in which we first became aware of an Other, a person outside ourselves, an Other that was both alien and familiar. That Other becomes the Ideal-I, the person we want to be. Paradoxically, we are that Other, just as we are not that Other. As children, we were our cowboy heroes, just as we could never be those heroes. The gun was both object and subject in that it represented something separate, desirable, and in a real way unattainable, while at the same time it was an extension of ourselves. We wore it on the hip and pulled it to show skill and aggression. To be blunt and rather obvious, I point out that the gun was visible evidence of our phallic power, or at least our desire for phallic power. In other words, a company such as Daisy appealed to male desire; it understood male fantasies of potency. With the gun, we could not only connect ourselves to a phallic potency but could also become men while remaining boys. The gun is as much a symbol of boyhood—a lack of maturity and full development—as it is any other kind of symbol.

And so we have a complex connection between a consumer item and the male psyche. This consumer item, the gun, is rare in its longevity. As Diaz points out in *Making a Killing*, the gun industry must find ways of marketing a product that does not wear out the way most consumer items wear out. Fridges, cars, computers, watches, and so on wear out. We purchase perhaps several over the course of our lives. A gun, however, may last a lifetime or more. Such durability in a consumer product is hardly conducive to big profits, so the gun industry seeks to expand its market and convince potential buyers to buy more than one gun. Why not encourage everyone in the family to own a gun? Guns serve various purposes, after all. There are recreational guns, guns for hunting, guns for protection and home safety, and guns for display. One way to create a vigorous market for guns is for the industry to tap the youth market. Get them young and keep them buying guns for life. The Daisy Manufacturing Company has reached out to children for decades, especially in its line of BB rifles. What I suggest is that the entertainment industry was complicit with gun manufacturers as early as the 1930s and '40s. Cowboys wore fancy guns and gave their names to a range of toy pistols and rifles. As kids, we wanted Hopalong Cassidy pistols, Roy Rogers pistols, Red Ryder BB guns, and so on. The connection between the films and other forms of popular culture where guns might be advertised is clear. Most cowboy heroes had their own line of comic books, in which we saw Roy or Johnny or Gene shoot just as efficiently as they did in their films. The comics gave advertising space to Daisy, and the importance of the Red Ryder BB gun is pivotal. The idea is that the boy learns to fetishize the gun as an *objet petit a*, something of an extension of himself and something that fills a lack. The small object stands in for that which was lost, the Real that we wish restored but which actually delivers death and chaos—the Real we think we remember can never be restored. The child sets out to obtain as many toy guns and cap pistols as he can. He moves on or graduates to the BB gun, which serves as the transition to more adult guns. The man can never have too many guns. For Lacan, the *objet a* "is the signifier of desire" (Sarup, 98). The gun is a substitute for something missing. In Freudian thought, what is missing is the female penis that Freud argues "the little boy once believed in and—for reasons familiar to us—does not want to give up" (1981, 352). In Lacanian language, what is missing is desire itself, which can be signified but never achieved. Desire is empty precisely because it is impossibly full. The gun signifies desire, and the man's relation to his gun is the relation to the *objet a*—that is, a relationship that covers over lack and inadequacy and incompleteness. Carrying a gun, the man can feel complete, strong, and confident while all the time remaining unfulfilled.

The *objet a* signifies desire in its expansive sense, whereas the fetish object signifies sexual desire. For Freud, the fetish is "a token of triumph over the threat of castration and a protection against it" (1981, 353). The desire for the woman's penis or for the continuing belief that the woman (the mother, of course) has a penis, finds a nicely ambiguous symbol in the gun. As fetish, the gun is both desirable and dangerous, both mysterious and familiar, both a part of one's own body and a part of someone else's. No wonder the cowboy is so powerful a figure. He represents a masculinity of control, an erotic mastery, and the gun testifies to this mastery.

I am trying to make the connection between the psychoanalytic significance of the gun as phallus, the object that carries the man to control of the Other and carries out the law of the father, and the gun as an aspect of the market economy. In the context of the marketplace, the gun remains a fetish object, just as all consumer items become fetishes. Unlike a TV or a washing machine or toilet tissue, however, the gun is lethal. Selling guns sometimes means identifying the lethal nature of guns and sometimes disguising their lethality. The image of the gun in the B western movies works on the gun as attractive object of desire. Everything about the gun accentuates the genital region of the male body. The glittering belt-and-holster set worn by many of the cowboy heroes draws attention to the male genital region, and the double effect of the pants' belt and the gun belt works similarly to attract the eye to the waist. The six-gun itself is obviously phallic in design, and the cocking of the hammer carries with it a resonance that fits with a discourse of sexuality. Perhaps the best examples of the gun as phallus occur in Hoot Gibson's westerns. Gibson had a wryness none of the other cowboys had, as if he instinctively knew the implications of the gun. He often did not wear a gun-and-holster set; instead, he would shove his pistol inside his pants, front and centre, making the phallic connection as explicit as one could ask for. In at least one film, *Boiling Point* (1932), he carries his pistol in a pocket in his chaps and in doing so offers an answer to Mae West's famous question "Is that a gun in your pocket or are you just glad to see me?" We know that sometimes a gun is just a gun, but often it signifies something more.

If the gun as fetish disguises and defeats castration anxiety, then it also points (literally) to the Other who must succumb to the potent male phallus. The gun is all about control and repression. He who wields the gun is he who dominates and makes others do as he wishes. Teddy Roosevelt's "big stick" carries with it a resonance that conjures up Rough Riders and guns and the Old West. Looked at this way, the connection made by the National Rifle Association and other gun groups in the United States between the gun and fundamental freedoms of the American citizen is terribly misguided. The gun represents the opposite of freedom; it represents repression and control.

A particularly pertinent example of the gun as a friendly controller appears in *Powdersmoke Range* (1935), a Three Mequiteers film based on William Colt MacDonald's novel of the same title. In both the book and the film, Tucson has a shootout with Sundown Saunders but does not wish to kill Saunders. To ensure that his bullets only wound his adversary, Tucson replaces his .45-calibre pistols with what the book describes as a "single action .32-20, on a forty-five frame" (1997, 192). The smaller gun, so we are asked to believe, will prove gentler. Tucson will win the duel without fatally wounding his adversary. Saunders will receive a mere flesh wound, as a sort of spanking, will see the error of his ways, and will become friends with the man he was trying to kill. Tucson intends to shoot the man into goodness.

We can see why the gun has to be friendly. To make repression and control acceptable, those who wish to dominate a social group must make their control attractive. The title of William Wyler's 1956 film, *Friendly Persuasion*, expresses what I am trying to articulate about the gun. (The film is about pacifism, however.) Guns are friends of the family, and even women and children use them. Take for example William Witney's *The Trail of Robin Hood* (1950), with Roy Rogers. One scene in this film, about the growing and selling of Christmas trees, presents a skeet-shooting competition, billed as a turkey shoot. The competitors are vying for a prize turkey that will become the main dish at someone's Christmas dinner. Taking part in the shooting is Sis McGonigle (Carol Nugent), the sister of Roy's sidekick, Splinters (Gordon Jones). Sis is a young girl, probably on the verge of puberty. She is the clever one in the McGonigle family; Splinters is a handyman and bricoleur who often needs Sis's assistance. At the turkey shoot, Sis wins the prize turkey. But she refuses to have it killed for Christmas dinner. This sequence in the film presents the gun as an object for sport shooting, and such sport can be played by the quite young, even the quite young female. Young males, on the other hand, are allowed to use the gun for the manly purpose of shooting bad guys. In *Riders of Pasco Basin* (1940), with Johnny Mack Brown, a young boy, son of the local newspaper editor whom the bad guys murder, uses a rifle to fatally shoot his father's killer.

But the gun represents something even more deeply imbedded in the psyche than the mixture of control and repression. In the Ken Maynard film *Arizona Terror* (1931), Ken's gun is a sign of his origins. His gun was made in Yuma and sports two notches on its grip. For those who see this gun, the identity of its owner is readily apparent. Similarly, in the Trail Blazers feature *Death Valley Rangers* (1943), Bob Steele has distinctive guns that identify him to the bad guys. In other words, the gun comes to represent its owner; it is its owner. Gun and man are inseparable. When we were young we identified our heroes with their style, and one aspect of their style was the look of their guns and the manner in which they wore them. Cowboys such as "Wild Bill" Elliott and Rex Allen wore their pistol handles forward in their holsters, reversing the usual way cowboys carried their pistols. Most heroes wore distinctive gun belts, the most obvious being those worn by Buck Jones and Dennis Moore (a.k.a. Denny Meadows). This connection between the hero and his gun becomes more direct and obvious as the B western gave way to the TV western. Among the TV western heroes were several who used distinctive guns: Shotgun Slade (Scott Brady) "carried a unique custom-made, two-in-one double-barreled shotgun that he preferred instead of a normal six-gun" (Jackson 1994, 141); Wyatt Earp (Hugh O'Brien) wore a long-barrelled pistol known as the Buntline Special; Christopher Colt (Wayde Preston) "wore a pair of Colt .45 single-action army revolvers" (ibid., 98); Johnny Ringo (Don Durant) wore a pistol known as the "Le Mat Special," which could fire the usual six bullets plus one shotgun shell; and Josh Randall (Steve McQueen) used "a custom-made .30-.40-calibre sawed-off Winchester carbine" known as his "Mare's Leg" (ibid., 130). We could extend this list with Yancy Derringer, Lucas McCain, Johnny Yuma, and the Lone Ranger with his silver bullets.

The complicity of these films and later of the TV series in the marketing of guns to American youth works to embolden the gun industry in its targeting of the young as potential consumers of their products. Daisy Manufacturing has always targeted youth, as the picture that decorates the Daisy Museum website indicates (figure 4.5). We see a young lad carrying a Daisy BB gun. He wears modern but rural clothing and he stands tall above a rural landscape that has a rail fence on the lower left. Most of the background of the picture shows big sky with fluffy cirrus clouds, among which we discern figures from the frontier past. The picture is redolent of nostalgia for days gone by, open spaces, and a time when the male—man or boy—could roam the open country with gun in hand. The gun industry continues to invoke the west, the frontier, and the cowboy in its effort to market firearms. But now this industry moves from the relatively innocuous BB air rifle to assault guns and machine guns. Consider the cover of Feather Industries 1991 product catalogue (figure 4.6). A father and son stand in a landscape similar to the one in the Daisy picture—rolling foothills with mountain peaks just visible on the horizon reminding us of open spaces, freedom, the west, and, yes, the cowboy. In the foreground, the father has apparently just placed in his son's arms a machine gun. The son cradles this weapon and smiles. Behind the two figures is a table upon which we can see at least one other weapon. Father and son share the pleasures of shooting.

The gun industry's appeal to the youth market has intensified over the years. Advertisements in magazines such as *Guns & Ammo, Machine*

Figure 4.5 An image that appears on the history page of the Daisy Manufacturing Company's website (http://daisy.com/history.html) and, in a variant in which the western landscape is replaced by a waving American flag, on the site's splash page (http://www.daisy.com). Since 1939 Daisy has marketed its Red Ryder BB rifle to boys.

Figure 4.6 The front cover of Feather Industries' product catalogue, 1991. Father, son, and machine gun share a moment of togetherness.

Gun News, and *Gun World* clearly identify boys in their early teenage years as consumers. So too do gun catalogues, as the Feather Industries catalogue illustrates. The 1992 Smith & Wesson catalogue contains what Greg Cahill terms "a feel-good ad." Cahill describes the ad as portraying "a father and preteen son resting against a boulder in a piney wood and enjoying a little quality time while junior takes aim with a .45-calibre pistol. The emphasis is on the rite of passage and nostalgia." Cahill goes on to quote from this ad: "Seems like only yesterday that your father brought you here for the first time. . . . Those sure were the good times—just you, dad, and his Smith & Wesson."

The most disturbing example of gun advertising appears on the back cover of a 1990 number of *Machine Gun News* (figure 4.7). This cover contains an advertisement for Fleming Firearms with the caption "Short Butts from Fleming Firearms" (see Cahill). The accompanying photograph shows a young blond girl (Cahill says she is two years old) wearing a bathing suit. Her body is in profile and she turns her head to the camera and flashes a broad smile. Her pose is suggestive, and the suggestion is the stronger

Figure 4.7 The back cover of *Machine Gun News*, from an issue of 1990.

because of the automatic weapon she carries in her hands at waist level. Behind her is a wall lined with a variety of assault machine guns. Whatever the message Fleming Firearms thinks it is passing on to those who might gaze on this photograph, the notion that guns are friendly—the stuff of, dare I say it, white childhood innocence—is clear in the connection of female infancy with firearms. I write this paragraph on the day a fourteen-year-old student carried three handguns to school in Red Lion, Pennsylvania, and shot his school principal and himself (24 April 2003).

As early as 1932, in a film called *Come On, Tarzan*, we hear the cowboy hero, Ken Maynard, assert: "Gun glory is the language of the west." *Gun Glory* is also the title of a 1957 western starring Stewart Granger. Maynard speaks of gun glory as the language, the speech, of the west. The good cowboy lets his guns do the talking for him. Tex Ritter, as itinerant lawyer Tex Haines in *Dead or Alive* (1941), wears his law books on his hips. The connection between the gun and language brings us back to iconic representations of Christ as the Harrower of Hell, with a sword emerging from his mouth. Our sense of language as deed finds definition. Force is language, the only language for certain situations. This is the argument, and we continue to hear it in the discourse of war. "Wanted

Dead or Alive" has taken on renewed currency in the years since 2001, and the troops are on the march to carry the language of force in several areas of the world.   Gun glory pretty well articulates the sense of the gun I experienced when I was a boy. I can recall the joy I took in playing cowboy and making shooting sounds as I brandished whatever served for a gun—a toy, a stick, an extended finger. And I recall, with something of a shiver, playing with my father's shotguns when no one else was home. Later, a friend lent me one of his family's .22-calibre rifles and took me into the country to shoot gophers. And then we had family days shooting at targets as impressive as tin cans and trees. I think perhaps the moment I became aware of the difference between the innocuous shooting in the cowboy movies and the shooting of real guns (the difference between reel and real guns) came one day when I was with my family at my grandfather's cottage (not the grandfather in the photograph that opens this chapter) and a few of us were shooting my grandfather's pistol. Here was my first opportunity to shoot a gun that resembled the weapons most favoured by my cowboy heroes. They rarely used Winchesters, preferring handguns. In the movies, their six-shooters were capable of shooting accurately over long distances, far longer than any Colt .45 could actually reach. But the fantasy aspect of these movies did not register with us; we accepted what the cowboy did as somehow real. And then I shot my grandfather's pistol. The noise was not the most surprising thing; the most surprising thing was the kick of the gun in my hand. It just about bucked out of my grip. The bullet flew somewhere close to ninety degrees into the air, I imagine. The shock of the discharge worked its way into my imagination and the realization of the power and deadliness of this gun became clear.

And so what to conclude about the gun? Gun glory remains intact on film. The look of the gun, and the cowboy's efficiency with the gun, are impressive to me even now. And I can find fun in the filmic rendition of the shootout, with perhaps some measure of satisfaction working its way through my psyche. However, when I hear one of these cowboy heroes utter a line such as the one Carleton Young delivers in *Billy the Kid's Fighting Pals* (1941)—"Old Colonel Colt makes 'em all the same size"— I am reminded of the kind of thinking that results in a book such as *More Guns, Less Crime: Understanding Crime and Gun Control Laws*, by John R. Lott, Jr. (2000). Lott's title succinctly and accurately expresses his thesis. I am reminded of how often in the westerns that are my subject the hero is a man not connected to law enforcement; he is a normal citizen. In other words, the vigilante aspect of the hero is significant. And Lott's argument fits neatly into the world view of vigilantism. He argues strenuously for the passing of legislation that permits citizens to carry concealed handguns because such legislation "deters violent crimes" (160). Without such legislation, and without the issuing of as many permits that allow concealed handguns as possible, "ordinary citizens are sitting ducks, waiting to be victimized" (197). We are back to the code of the west where gun glory is the order of the day.

I continue to find enjoyment in films that contain guns, heroes, and shooting. Clearly, the male psyche finds pleasure in fantasies of control and power. Clearly too such fantasies all too readily translate into reality. Children seem to have a capacity to filter fantasies, and we need to develop this capacity, not leave it behind. To bring the capacities of childhood into adulthood—this is the task. And we know that all children, like all adults, do not have this capacity. What the cowboy heroes that I take as my subject offer is a clear-cut fantasy. Their guns, like their clothes and their saddles and their exploits and their ability to carry out superhuman actions, remind us that they are the Imaginary, impossible ideals that have life only in the world of play and pretend. They are not real and we drag them into reality at our peril. They tell us everything about capable manhood and nothing about being men in a complex and dangerous world where a capacity for violence can only perpetuate the agony and horror of real wounds, bloodshed, and needless death.

But let me end on a rather more moderate note. Remember that Red Ryder BB rifle I so desperately wanted when I was ten years old. It so happens that there exists a film that examines this precise desire. The film is *A Christmas Story* (1983). It is not a B western but a film about a boy's fascination with the cowboy heroes of B westerns and his resulting desire for a Red Ryder BB rifle. The film is set in the 1950s. It opens with the main character, the boy Ralphie (Peter Billingsley), on his bed reading a western comic book, and on the back cover of this comic is an advertisement for a Red Ryder BB rifle. Ralphie fairly drools over this advertisement; he wants nothing more than a Red Ryder BB gun, the Grail of Christmas presents. In one of the film's daydream sequences, Ralphie sees himself dressed in flashy cowboy clothes, carrying his rifle, and shooting masked bad guys (seven of them) who try to invade his house. His mother and his teacher warn him that such guns will put his eye out. My mother told me the same thing. Eventually, Ralphie receives the precious gift from his father, who explains that he had one when he was a boy. Clutching the rifle, Ralphie races outside in his galoshes and pyjamas. His shot ricochets off a piece of metal and hits him near the eye, breaking his glasses. In the confrontation that follows, the film sides with Ralphie and his dad when Ralphie fools his mother into thinking the damage resulted from a falling icicle. The boy gets his gun, the father relives his youth, the American family continues its love affair with Red Ryder, cowboys, and guns. Plus ça change ...

Give Me My Boots and Saddles
Camp Cowboy

If Tom Mix got out of his grave and saw my clothes, he'd get back in again.
—Nudie Cohn, qtd. in George-Warren and Freedman, 99

When we were kids, we were acutely aware of the clothes our heroes wore. And I'll note at the outset that makers of films and marketers of clothing were acutely aware of our awareness. Heroes represented money in the bank for manufacturers, wholesalers, and retailers of cowboy clothing for kids. And by clothing, I include everything from shirts and trousers to boots, hats, scarves, vests, detachable cuffs, and even chaps. Kids could go to bed wearing Hopalong Cassidy or Roy Rogers pyjamas. Everything our heroes wore caught our eyes (not that we ever saw them wearing pyjamas), and what caught our eyes we looked for in mail-order catalogues from Sears and Eaton's and asked for as presents for Christmas and birthdays. Remember that Roy Rogers stetson with the distinctive blocking that I coveted. If we were lucky, our parents would buy us not only that but the whole outfit; if we were unlucky, we could pretend we had the things we desired. Even those of us who never received cowboy boots or a real cowboy hat or vests and trousers could usually convince our mothers, at least once in a while, to buy us what passed for a cowboy shirt. I can recall wanting a shirt like the one Eddie Dean wore in the B westerns. The shirt I have in mind was serviceable and stylish, not too flashy and yet distinctively patterned. It had smile pockets with arrow trim and a dark yoke and dark cuffs. I remember this shirt as my choice among many memorable shirts worn by my heroes because it suggested neither a uniform nor a garment for special occasions. After all, I did not unequivocally like all the shirts the cowboys wore. I had, for example, an ambivalent relationship with fringe. The shirt I wanted looked plain enough that I might hope that my mother could afford to buy one and would agree to do so. The Eddie Dean shirt was my choice, but it certainly was not the only shirt or item of clothing that caught my attention.

Like my friends, I wanted "to occupy these characters." I use the words of my friend Nancy Stewart, who commented in a note to me that the "whole 'clothes make the man' or the performance. . . . It is almost like drag." We'll consider this idea later. For now, I notice that each of the cowboy heroes had a distinctive sartorial style, and their distinctive wardrobe became more pronounced as the years moved on. Clearly, those responsible for cowboy wardrobe understood that clothes make the man. Cowboy clothes were important as indicators of the cowboy's special status, his almost holy function as protector, mediator, and intercessor. These clothes also drew attention to the hero's body. Shirts and trousers tended to fit tightly. Rarely did we see our heroes without their shirts, but their clothing nevertheless accentuated their physiques. Among other things, these clothes signalled sex appeal, but the sex appeal invested in cowboy apparel is richly ambiguous. The use of cowboy style for purposes of camp, and to draw attention to androgynous and gay masculinities, reminds us that the masculinity of the cowboy heroes was not one-dimensional. The hegemonic masculinity of the soldier, the GI Joe, was not the masculinity of the cowboys I admired.

In the early days, cowboys such as Buck Jones, Tim McCoy, and Ken Maynard, who all began their careers in the silent film era, wore neat but not too flashy clothes. Buck Jones wore a distinctive frontier shirt with lace-up front at the neck instead of buttons; his trousers of choice were durable denim, and his hat was of the ten-gallon type, usually white. Tim McCoy favoured a more severe and gentlemanly appearance. He often wore a gambler's coat (later associated with the television character Maverick) that allowed him to be taken for either a professional gambler or a preacher (a person often referred to as a *sky pilot* in these films). McCoy dressed in black, reminding us of the hero's association with death. As for Ken Maynard, he was usually neat, wearing tight-fitting shirts tastefully embroidered with smile pockets and piping. Maynard also wore tight trousers that showed stitching across the buttocks and down the side of the leg, effectively drawing attention to this cowboy's ample posterior.

Other cowboy heroes of the 1930s—including Bob Steele, Bob Baker, Fred Scott, Johnny Mack Brown—dressed neatly but not especially flamboyantly. One cowboy, Hoot Gibson, stands out for his drab clothing, which was likely closer to a real cowboy's garb than anything worn by the other B movie cowboy stars of the day. Villains and extras typically wore real working clothes, clothes that most likely did not come from studio wardrobes and were the clothes they wore off the set as well.

By the mid-1930s a change began to appear in the clothing worn by the heroes, most obviously in the clothing worn by Gene Autry and Hopalong Cassidy (William Boyd). Both began their B western film careers in 1935. Autry's clothes were similar to those worn by Ken Maynard, although he came as more of a package, dressed to complement his horse, Champion, who had a heavily decorated saddle and a bridle distinctive for the small pistols that dangled by each side of Champion's mouth. With Autry, we were on the way to Roy Rogers, who, after Autry enlisted in the Army Air Corps in 1942, became Republic Studios' most popular western star. With Rogers, flamboyance blossomed. But before Roy Rogers came on the scene, we had Paramount Studios' only B western star, Hopalong Cassidy.

Hoppy dressed in black, from his high-topped hat to his boots, which he wore outside his black trousers. Hoppy's only concessions to colour were his necktie, which was reminiscent of a Boy Scout necktie, his pearl-handled pistols, the white trim around the top of his boots, and his white horse, Topper. Once in a while Hoppy would wear a light-coloured shirt, and less often appear in disguise wearing an easterner's suit, as he does in *Hoppy's Holiday* (1947), or even an Arabian outfit complete with Ghutra and Agal, as he does in *Outlaws of the Desert* (1941). Mostly, however, Hoppy was the man in black, and his familiar dress became a sort of uniform. Hoppy's clothing represented Hoppy's character: stern but straight, neat even when dusty from the range, efficient and dependable, predictable and unambiguous. The appearance of the hero in a readily identifiable outfit became common, and a few more heroes in black arrived on the scene: the Durango Kid (Charles Starrett), Lash LaRue, and Zorro the most prominent of these. The Lone Ranger provided a variation on the theme, appearing in a soft-blue outfit, except for his white hat. Red Ryder, played by four actors over the years, also had a standard outfit. Trademark outfits are, perhaps, easier to market than plain, functional work clothes.

The standard outfits worn by Hoppy, Red Ryder, Lash LaRue, and the Lone Ranger connected these heroes with the superheroes of the comics and radio, characters such as Superman, Batman, and the Shadow. Like the comic book super heroes, the Lone Ranger, the Durango Kid, and Zorro had faithful sidekicks and concealed identities. The outfits worn by the heroes served the purpose of reminding us just how out-of-the-ordinary these men were. The solid colours—black or red or blue—carried weight as colours of goodness or death or swiftness. It is no accident that the cowboys wore more colourful and elaborate outfits as their comic books increased in popularity. The graphic form of the comic accentuates the performance aspect of the characters. The cowboys performed masculinity, and their costumes were as much a part of their messages as were the plots in which they found themselves performing.

These films were small morality plays, and the cowboy heroes had to look the part of the stern lawgiver. But their distinctive clothing easily serves a fetishistic purpose. The single-colour look of Tim McCoy, Hoppy, the Lone Ranger, the Durango Kid, or Lash LaRue reminds us of the phallic power these heroes represent. The films begin with a crisis, often involving a woman in trouble. The hero enters and thrusts himself into the action until things explode in a gunfight that settles the crisis. Then the hero withdraws until the next crisis in the next film. Sex, whenever it surfaces in these films, does so in order for the hero to display control and celibacy. An example appears in *Death Valley Rangers* (1943), a Trail Blazers film. (The Trail Blazers series, from Monogram Studies, was one of the era's several trio series—films starring three heroes, as in the Three Mequiteers films. The Trail Blazers series comprised eight films produced in 1943 and 1944.) *Death Valley Rangers* has a scene in a restaurant in which our three heroes (Hoot Gibson, Bob Steele, Ken Maynard) are shown relaxed and kibitzing. Steele has eyes for a young beauty (daughter of Forrest Taylor, the captain of the Rangers), and for this the other two give him a hard time. Bob clearly thinks of settling down with this young woman. At the end of the film, Ken and Hoot draw Bob away from a life of domesticity. Ken and Hoot are older and wiser than the young whippersnapper Bob, and they know where true freedom for the male resides—and it is not within the confines of marriage.

The neatly dressed cowboys represent phallic power, the law of the father. In other words, the hero ensures a continuation of symbolic action, the only action possible in the world we inhabit after we leave infancy. Phallic power, paradoxically, maintains its strength through a fantasy of continuation: foreplay that cannot end in climax but is prolonged in an ongoing ride to further justice and order. The heroes in these films repeat the same actions over and over. They exhibit obsessive-compulsive behaviour that keeps them from settling into domestic life.

Nowhere is the call to celibacy and prolonged foreplay more obvious than in the Hopalong Cassidy films in which Hoppy's young sidekick, Lucky Jenkins (played by Russell Hayden and later Rand Brooks), falls for a young woman, often an eminently eligible young woman. In some films the young man clearly desires to stay with the woman, but his mentor, Hoppy, registers disapproval, perhaps even jealousy, and at the end of each film Lucky rides off with his male companions. Women are attractive to young Lucky and they clearly activate his libido. In one sense, then, he never gets lucky. In another, he is lucky precisely because he never gets lucky. The luck this man has takes the form of an older man who "saves" him from himself—from the restrictions of domesticity—and turns him back to the open range. The pattern is set early in the series. For example, in *Trail Dust* (1936), Hoppy's young sidekick, here named Johnny (Jimmy Ellison), falls for an attractive young woman (Gwynne Shipman). Hoppy and his band of trail herders have come to this woman's aid. At the end of the film, Johnny plans to stay with her; Windy (George "Gabby" Hayes) has a wound and needs to convalesce, so he plans to stay behind, too. To make matters worse, all of Hoppy's men are about to abandon him. Hoppy sulks and says he wishes Johnny and Windy would come with him, but these two say goodbye and seem set for a new life away from the range. Hoppy rides away with his head bent and pouting, but the guys suddenly come to their senses and ride after him. The film ends with a shot of Johnny, Windy, and Hoppy together, Hoppy with a broad smile on his face. The homosocial world remains integral to the vision of these films.

As Eve Kosofsky Sedgwick has noted, "much of the most useful recent writing about patriarchal structures suggests that 'obligatory heterosexuality' is built into male-dominated kinship systems" (1985, 3). Sedgwick sees a "continuum between 'men-loving-men' and 'men-promoting-the-interests-of-men'" (3). An interesting B western that flirts with men-loving-men but reverts to men-promoting-the-interests-of-men is *The Crooked Trail* (1936), a Johnny Mack Brown film that may offer more in its title than a first impression might indicate. In this film, Jim Blake (Johnny Mack Brown) saves Harve Tarlton (John Merton) from dying in the desert. The two men forge a friendship as they work their gold stake. We see them behaving as young men do, kidding each other, horsing around, and living intimately in their cabin. Jim has not only saved Harve's life, he has also saved him from a life of profligacy and crime. Their work together forging for gold is successful and they have a good life together. Then a young woman, Helen Carter (Lucile Browne), arrives on the scene.

Jim gives his affection to her and the two of them get married. Harve grows jealous. He steals money from Helen's father, abducts Helen, and pressures her to marry him; he does this not because he has any interest in the woman but because he wants to hurt Jim for transferring his affections. Of course Jim rides to the rescue and the two men square off in a gunfight. Harve proves his love for Jim in the climactic shootout. The relationship between men in this film comes as close to expressing love between two men as any B western I have seen. (The big-budget film *Warlock*, released in 1959, explores a similar relationship between Clay Blaisedell [Henry Fonda] and Tom Morgan [Anthony Quinn]. *The Crooked Trail* is a precursor to *Warlock*.)

In the cowboy films that are my subject, men live together, work together, eat together, fight together, kibitz together, compete for women together, and even get into the same bed together (this happens in the Hopalong Cassidy films, for example). But no one would accuse (the operative word here) these men of homosexuality. The irony is that such men refuse the enforced heterosexuality of marriage and domesticity and at the same time remain staunchly and independently heterosexual. Any hint of homosexuality attaches instead to the bad guys or in some cases the swishy sidekick. In *The Crooked Trail*, the hero has no idea that Harve has the kind of affection that might lead to an act of desperation (his abduction of Helen), and the viewer can rest easy on Harve's account: from the beginning of the film Harve has given evidence of his immitigable badness. When we first see him, he is escaping from jail and commits murder. His affections are as crooked as his morals.

Instead of accepting a heterosexual relationship and the domesticity that goes with it, Johnny in *Trail Dust*—and, in later Hopalong Cassidy films, Lucky—rides off with the older man, whose clothing reminds us of the fetish. According to Freud, the fetish has a paradoxical function both as a sign of "triumph over the threat of castration and a protection against it" (1981, 353). It is, Freud says, that which saves a man "from becoming a homosexual" (353–54), because it endows women with that which makes them acceptable. As Marjorie Garber suggests, the fetish signals lack and also the "covering over" (121) of lack. Garber connects the fetish with nostalgia for that which has been lost—the mother or, in Lacanian terms, the Real. When Hoppy, Johnny, and Windy ride away to another adventure, they are entering that Real that will serve them as holding space until they return to the Reel for another foray into protection and danger.

The fetish offers protection from the male fear of castration, from the disempowering life of hearth and home and helpmate. The fetish also reminds us of displacement and disguise. The fetish covers over fears of inadequacy and failure. With the fetish in hand, so to speak, we can continue to feel in control and hence free from bothersome restrictions. It's a kid thing, really. The fetish is a sign of dependence disguised as independence, of immaturity masquerading as maturity. The fetish also signals ambiguity. What kind of man goes around wearing the kind of clothes Hoppy wears, or wearing a mask like the Durango Kid or the Lone Ranger? Perhaps an even more pointed question is: What kind of man dresses in black, wears his hat at a jaunty angle, has high-heeled boots, and sports a fifteen-foot bullwhip looped over one of his pistols? With Lash LaRue, we have the fetish turned parodic.

The potential for parody is evident in all these characters, as the films *Rustler's Rhapsody* (1985) or *¡Three Amigos!* (1986) show. Early television shows such as *Your Show of Shows* (1950–54) or *The Ernie Kovacs Show* (1952–53) regularly parodied the western. But the B western parodied itself with characters such as Lash LaRue. Lash looked and spoke like Humphrey Bogart. Often he played a character named Cheyenne Davis, and he travelled with a grizzled old sidekick named Fuzzy Q. Jones (Al St. John). The Lash LaRue films were among the most cheaply made, but they were popular nonetheless. Lash was the King of the Bullwhip. At least one other cowboy, Whip Wilson, used the whip as his signature weapon, but Lash claimed top billing. What Lash had that Whip did not have was panache—due in part, no doubt, to that black outfit. He *wore* his masculinity, as did most of these cowboys. He was a cocky fellow, and his all-black outfit emphasized his efficiency and ambiguity. Lash looked and talked as if he could be a bad guy, and that whip reminded us of his snappy snake-like quality. Often, Lash was a lawman travelling under cover, but he never had the appearance of a straight-arrow man of peace or of a man who could ever settle into domesticity. Compared to Steve (sometimes Steve Norman, sometimes Steve Sanders, sometimes Steve Brent, and sometimes other Steves), the alter ego of the Durango Kid, Lash was a dark figure, capable of things unimaginable. His clothes and whip remind us of fetishes and of sado-masochism.

As good an example of Lash's potential for sadism as we could ask for is available in *The Law of the Lash* (1947). This film is noteworthy for the psychological manipulation Lash carries out on the villain, Lefty (Lee Roberts). Knowing that Lash has seen evidence (a woman's rings) that will incriminate him in a stagecoach holdup, Lefty tries to ambush Lash. But Lash uses his bullwhip to subdue Lefty. Lash and Fuzzy then keep Lefty isolated in a cabin. Ostensibly, he is in the cabin to recuperate from the wounds Lash inflicted on him, but he knows that in reality he is a prisoner. Lefty begins to go stir-crazy watching Fuzzy whittle a piece of wood and listening to the incessant ticking of the clock. "Can't you do anything but whittle? Can't that clock do anything but tick? Three days of whittlin' and tickin'," Lefty moans. Lash eventually lets Lefty go, but Lefty has to walk to town. On the way, Lefty struggles to decide what to do. We hear his voice as a voice-over—an extremely rare device in these films—as he agonizes over his fate and the best thing for him to do. He throws the incriminating rings away, but shortly after he does this Lash rides up and returns them to him. Lash is playing mind games with Lefty, and the villain is losing his grip. Lash uses him to ferret out the main villain, a man called Decker (Jack O'Shea). Decker too falls victim to the lash.

Sado-masochism is deeply embedded in the male psyche, and we can locate it in all these western heroes. Lash makes the connection visible with his whip, his rakish hat, and his swagger. His typical stance has him standing with his hat at a raffish angle and his hands on his hips in a defiant and commanding pose. It is difficult to take this guy seriously, although I know that as a kid I admired Lash's complete competence and what I can only call his cocksure style. Lash LaRue and Whip Wilson, as their names indicate, were exaggerations of the law of the father. They took control and maintained it with their willingness to whip the bad guys into submission. Whereas the bullwhip in the A western was a weapon chosen by the villain (see *The Kentuckian*, 1955, or *Bullwhip*, 1958), in the B westerns of Lash LaRue and Whip Wilson the whip was the hero's sexy object of choice. He preferred to lash his adversary into submission rather than shoot him. The whip is even friendlier than the gun. It penetrates without killing. Like the gun, the whip represents the phallus, that object which in the Lacanian view motivates and allows for desire.

In their article "The Fantasy of Authenticity in Western Costume," Jane Marie Gaines and Charlotte Cornelia Herzog remark on the sado-masochistic aspect of cowboy clothing:

> Undeniable in the Westerner's costume is the supernaturalism of the favourite props of the Victorian fetishist, with the functionality of whips and spurred boots having been demonstrated in countless incidents in thousands of narratives of survival. . . . The high-heeled boot had its origin in the need to dig heels into the ground to secure the wrangler in the process of roping steers, but has its flip erotic side in the exquisite torture of the sado-masochist's fantasy. The cowboy chaps had their essen-

tial function in their protection of the front part of the leg but took flight
in fantasy as they framed the crotch area, going on to enter the realm of
the baroque in the extreme bat-winged chap or the sheepskin of the
angora goat-hide chap with silver-concho trim as seen on Tom Mix and
other showmen cowboys. (178)

Costumes became so elaborate that designers such as Nathan Turk, Nudie
Cohn, and Rodeo Ben were thought of as artists, and Nudie's creations
of stylish chaps were dubbed the Sistine Chaps. Nudie Cohn called himself King of the Cowboy Couturiers and Dior of the Sagebrush (Chapman). When Gaines and Herzog speak of the baroque quality of western
costume, they mean that the elaborate western costume has a camp quality and therefore easily passes into parody.

Lash LaRue, with his bullwhip and black clothing, indicates the tendency of the B western to parody itself. One of the most obviously parodic elements of these films and their heroes is the clothing they wear.
Even more easily parodied than the outfits of Lash and the Durango Kid
or the Lone Ranger or Hoppy are the garish outfits often worn by the
likes of Rex Allen, Monte Hale, or Roy Rogers. These cowboys wore outfits designed by the likes of Turk, Cohn, and Rodeo Ben. Turk began
designing and making clothing for cowboys in the 1920s and Nudie Cohn
worked for him and in the late 1940s opened his own business. Rodeo Ben
designed the first Wrangler jeans (see Beard and Arndt). These three,
along with others who came a bit later, fashioned the elaborately decorated shirts with fringe and embroidery and even rhinestones that the
cowboys wore for publicity photographs and personal appearances. Gene
Autry asserts that he "never wore glitter," but that he did dress "in loud,
colorful cowboy clothes" (qtd. in Bull, 38). Roy Rogers tells us that the
glittery shirts he wore for personal appearances allowed fans in all sections of an arena to see their hero (*Happy Trails*, 160). In Rogers's films,
the usual formula has him dressed in relatively plain checked shirts for
most of the action and then in fancier duds in the brief denouement. The
gaudy shirts, pants, and boots created by designers such as Nudie Cohn
became more baroque over the years, and they passed from the film cowboys to the singers of country music—people such as Buck Owens, Hank
Williams, Hank Snow, and more recently Gram Parsons, Dwight Yokum,
and Marty Stuart. The designs fit the man: Roy Rogers had shirts with his
dog Bullet embroidered on them, and we can see shirts with cacti, wagon
wheels, musical notes, donkeys, steers, Indian heads, and so on. Among
the most outrageous designs is one Nudie did for a jacket of Gram Parsons: it shows a pattern of marijuana leaves.

Figure 5.1 Dale Evans with Roy Rogers, both in western fancy dress. Publicity photo, 1955. Source: The official Roy Rogers–Dale Evans Website:www.royrogers.com/lane -index.html. Used with permission.

That such costumes have potential for camp should be obvious. The gay community picked up on this potential in its adoption of cowboy fashion; and in taking as its own the flamboyance of certain cowboy fashions, the gay community encourages us to consider again those duds worn by Roy and Gene and the others. Just what are we supposed to make of the fine clothes that would never have been found in the wardrobe of any real range cowboy and yet adorned the bodies of our heroes? These shirts are a sort of tattooing, drawing attention to the bodies of those who wear them. The world of fashion might refer to these shirts as unisex. They suggest androgyny, as any number of photographs of Roy Rogers and Dale Evans, both looking spiffy in their embroidered and fringed shirts, remind us (see figure 5.1). A review of the many photographs of western clothes in Holly George-Warren and Michelle Freedman's *How the West Was Worn* or in Debby Bull's *Hillbilly Hollywood* will illustrate the androgynous aspect of western wear. For example, Carl and Pearl Butler, husband and wife country and western singers of the 1960s and 1970s, wear the same blue rhinesone-decorated outfits in a photograph included in *Hillbilly Hollywood* (61).The clothes bespeak queerness. They remind us of cross-dressing and drag. They are fetishistic, and herein lies their intricacy. The fetish, according to Freud, belongs to the male psyche, and its function is precisely to ensure navigation into heterosexuality. For all the flirtation with the gay and queer, the man in fancy cowboy duds traverses a sexual territory that is resolutely heterosexual. The clothes bespeak a confidence that castration, either the mother's or the man's, cannot wound him who wears such finery. The clothes are a defence against castration.

The clothing is, without doubt, the stuff of camp. Camp, however, poses a problem because of its inextricable connection with homosexuality—specifically male homosexuality. Richard Dyer asserts that "camping about . . . is just about the only style, language and culture that is distinctively and unambiguously gay male" (49). He goes on to say that "something happens to camp when taken over by straights: it loses its cutting edge, its identification with the gay experience, its distance from the straight sexual world-view" (60). Straight camp, according to Dyer, differs from gay camp in that it is less critical of dominant patriarchal values; it is more ambiguous and even complicit with the norms of conventional straight society. Dyer offers the example of John Wayne. Gay camp refuses to accept Wayne as "an embodiment of what it 'really' means to be a man," whereas straight camp "puts a different emphasis":

> The authority, power and roughness of the Wayne image are still dear to
> the straight imagination, but they have been criticized heavily enough in
> recent years (by gays and camp among others) for there to be embar-
> rassment about directly accepting or endorsing such qualities. Camp
> allows straight audiences to reject the style of John Wayne; but because
> it is so pleasant to laugh, it also allows for a certain wistful affection for

him to linger on. However, affection for John Wayne can only be in reality affection for that way of being a man. (60)

Dyer's argument about defusing camp's critical stance toward "the straight
sexual world-view" has its counterpart in queer studies. Writers such as
David M. Halperin and Eve Kosofsky Sedgwick argue that appropriation
of "queer" by straight writers "dematerializes" queerness (Sedgwick, 8;
see also Halperin, 112–13).

Although the force of such articles is impressive, I suspect that any
liberatory politics must reject such an argument. Dyer sees straight camp
as nostalgia rather than critical distance. However, I think it is possible
to have affection for that which one does not accept as reality. We can
have reactionary nostalgia and constructive nostalgia. The capable manhood of figures such as John Wayne or the cowboy heroes I am writing
about offers satisfying fantasies of "what it 'really' means to be a man."
But the point is that they are fantasies, and boyish fantasies at that. To
assume such fantasies are to be mimicked by "real" men is to confuse reality with fantasy. And the space between affection and acceptance is crucial, since this is the space for reflection and criticism. The cowboys are
short-sighted, insular, anti-social (for all their protection of social values), anarchic, and immature. To see them as camp figures is to enjoy
them for their artifice and to set them at a distance from any notions of
manhood we might wish to emulate. They are fun precisely because we
do not and cannot take them seriously. They are what Susan Sontag calls
naive camp: "Pure camp is always naïve" (282).

Camp cowboys were our heroes. Camp is, among other things, what
Sontag refers to as "failed seriousness" (283). But I don't think that camp
intends seriousness. This is not to say that seriousness is not possible with
camp, just that camp parades as frivolous. The privileging of style over
content or *comment* might seem at first to be antipathetic to the traditional thrust of that which the culture produces for children—books or
films that privilege comment or content over style. Transparency often
triumphs in literature for children, since children are not (supposedly)
informed enough to negotiate irony or sophisticated coding. If this were
true of cultural production for children historically, and I am not sure
that it was, then it may no longer be the case. Books such as *The Stinky
Cheese Man* (1992) or *Fungus the Bogeyman* (1977) or even *The Cat in
the Hat* (1957) might give us examples of camp. Or for young adults we
might cite books by Francesca Lia Block, with their campy hip-
ster/slinkster characters. As for films, *Toy Story* (1995) and its sequel

and many of Disney's animated features offer instances of camp (see Mallan and McGillis). Camp is elusive, but we would be wrong to dismiss its relevance to child culture. Children may have an affinity for camp precisely because camp

> is perky and self-conscious, self-aware and maybe naïve. Camp is mercurial and difficult to pin down. Camp is polymorphous and perhaps even perverse.
>
> Camp aesthetics disrupt or invert many Modernists' aesthetic attributes, such as beauty, value, and taste, by inviting a different kind of apprehension and consumption. Words such as "kitsch," "bad taste," "mocking," and "nostalgia" emerge in discussions of camp aesthetics. There is a certain hipness that surrounds camp and other signifiers of queer culture, such as fetishwear, body piercing, lesbian chic, and drag. Beauty and value diminish in importance as audacity and energy come to the fore. A camp aesthetic delights in impertinence. It likes to challenge rather than satisfy. Its satisfactions derive from a sort of *jouissance* of acceptance. (Mallan and McGillis, 3)

Camp champions difference, and it prompts a creative response.

But how do we identify camp? Costume and gesture can be very campy. This we know from the gay community. But what makes a costume or a gesture camp? When Gilles and Pierre photograph themselves in studded shirts and with guns in their hands, they signal camp, but when Marty Stuart wears rhinestones and embroidered jackets he signals affinity with a certain Grand Ole Opry tradition of country performance. Is the latter camp? Camp is grandly stylish and it can be nostalgic. It yearns for that which both seems a past ideal but never was, and also for that which is yet to come into being. Camp tests the limits of possibility. It inhabits the region of make-believe and pretend. Camp is both something inherent in the object and something in the eye of the beholder. The B western is camp for some and decidedly not camp for others. Camp nostalgia is unlike another kind of nostalgia that seeks to recreate or return to the past. Camp nostalgia does not so much revere the past as see it as a challenge to the status quo. Camp has fun with the past while utilizing it for reflective purposes.

We recall that many of the B westerns either are self-reflective, having plots that involve filmmaking (for example, Gene Autry's *Shooting High*, 1940, and Monte Hale's *Out California Way*, 1946) or heroes who are performers. The singing cowboy is obviously a performer, but other stars such as Johnny Mack Brown, John Wayne, and Ken Maynard play characters who perform trick shooting or rope tricks in medicine shows. The medicine show makes frequent appearances in these films. Max Terhune is a ventriloquist, and he has his dummy, Elmer. Gene Autry's films often cast him as a radio performer, as do the films of Jimmy Wakeley and Roy Rogers.

And performance in the sense of conscious play-acting is a theme in the many films in which the hero wears a disguise—whether the permanent disguise of a Durango Kid or a Lone Ranger or the occasional disguise of a Tim McCoy when he pretends to be a Mexican (*Code of the Cactus*, 1930) or a Hoppy when he pretends to be an eastern dude (*Sunset Trail*, 1939). Good guys are always going under cover or infiltrating the bad guy's gang, pretending to be someone other than who they really are. I especially like *Riding Avenger* (1936), in which the plainly dressed Hoot Gibson spends most of the film disguised as the flashily dressed Morning Glory Kid. The parody here draws attention both to Gibson's usual plain style and to the sartorial flash of his fellow western stars. We might go so far as to say that the overriding theme of the B western is performance and pretend. Even characters who play themselves—and B western stars do play characters named Roy Rogers, Gene Autry, Rex Allen, Rocky Lane—signal performance in their recognizable costumes. Others, such as Hopalong Cassidy, the Lone Ranger, the Cisco Kid, and the Durango Kid, become inextricably connected to the men who play these characters: William Boyd, Clayton Moore, Duncan Renaldo, and Charles Starrett. Other actors played both the Lone Ranger and the Cisco Kid, but we remember only Clayton Moore and Duncan Renaldo in these parts. Charles Starrett starred in countless B westerns from the mid-1930s to the 1950s, but we remember him as the Durango Kid, a character he played in sixty-four of his 131 western films for Columbia between 1935 and 1952. Camp style makes sure we connect costume, character, and actor. The camp aspect of the B western hero asserts his masculinity "in an even more exaggerated way than if [he were] playing it straight" (Mallan and McGillis, 5). In camp, performance becomes conscious and conscious performance means self-control. The hailing of unconscious, unreflective performance finds itself challenged in camp.

We know that these films not only had an audience of kids but that they sought this audience. Gene Autry has pointed out that his audience comprised mostly women and children (see Stanfield, 111), and by the time the B western movies morphed into television, their appeal to kids became direct. When I was a boy, I watched *Cowboy Corner* with host Danny B, a daily showing of movies with Bob Steele, Lash LaRue, and the rest that was broadcast, on the only channel we received, just as I got home from school. The program clearly was meant to appeal to children such as myself. TV shows starring Hopalong Cassidy, Roy Rogers, and Gene Autry contained segments, either at the beginning (*The Roy Rogers Show*) or at the end (*Hopalong Cassidy*), in which the star spoke directly to kids. Early reviews of the serial western indicate that kids formed an important segment of the audience. *Weekly Variety* (4 December 1942) asserts that Republic's *Thundering Trails* is "calculated to hypo juvenile blood pressure." The same paper (31 August 1936) assures readers that "Kids will like" what they see in another Republic film, *Ghost Town Gold* (see also Buscombe, 35ff.).

If the audience for these films consisted largely of kids, we might ask why the cowboys slid so easily into parody and camp. One answer relates to children's affinity for parody and camp performance. Children are capable of taking something seriously and seeing it as silly at the same time. Children know the difference between fantasy and reality and are willing to allow fantasy to parade as reality for the period of pretend in which they submit to the pull of fantasy. To put this another way, kids like to dress in costume and to pretend to be other people, and I suspect that they are fully aware that their heroes are doing the same—that is, dressing up and pretending to be guys who can accomplish impossible deeds of horsemanship and marksmanship. Gene and Roy and Hoppy dress up and pretend to be heroes of the range. It scarcely matters whether Hoppy can ride well or not (he cannot); the films are nothing more than make-believe. Camp simply foregrounds make-believe. The first few Hopalong Cassidy films, in the mid-1930s, have Hoppy appearing dusty from the trail, but by the early 1940s the dust has disappeared and Hoppy never looks as if he has spent time driving cattle or mending fences. It is well known that when the hero fights, his hat usually stays on his head as if it was glued in place. (The hat often disguises the stunt person performing the fight or the daring leap.) The films are not shy of signalling their elements of pretend. Let's pretend to be cowboys and wear outlandish costumes with perfectly shaped hats, shiny pistols, glittery belts and boots, and clean, well-pressed shirts and trousers. Children can delight in all this finery as an aspect of performance and play.

Knowing how any viewer reacts to what she or he sees is not easy. But most of us can remember identifying with our heroes on the screen. What we need to recognize is what *identify* means. Christian Metz has posited a theory of cinema viewing based on Lacan's "mirror stage"—that moment in an infant's life when she first sees herself in a mirror. This is the moment the infant becomes aware of something other than herself. She is suddenly aware that she does not exist in the world alone but shares the world with another—in this case, that Other is herself, her reflected image. For Lacan, the child experiences the Imaginary, an idealized vision of himself as the Other he would like to be. Metz takes the cinema to be a Lacanian mirror, except that the spectator does not see himself reflected in the mirror/screen. Instead, he sees other objects of various types and sizes. But positioned as he is in line with the projector's beam, the viewer is in a way the creator and perceiver of the film he watches. In other words, the viewer sees himself on the screen and yet does not. Here's how Metz puts this:

> In order to understand the fiction film, I must both "take myself" for the character (= an imaginary procedure) so that he benefits, by analogical projection, from all the schemata of intelligence that I have within me, and not take myself for him (= the return to the real) so that the fiction can be established as such (= as symbolic): this is *seeming-real*. (57; italics in original)

Even a child viewer has this double perspective. He pretends that what he sees is actually happening and yet he knows it is not. He is both his cowboy hero and not his cowboy hero. The act of viewing the screen is quite literally a projection: both a mechanical projection and a psychoanalytic one. The projection itself is a performance in the sense that it carries out a function.

But performance is one thing and camp performance is another. The camp performance steadies our gaze on the mirror itself. Camp performance keeps us in touch with the fact that we are looking at a mirror, that what we are looking at is Imaginary, artificial, unnatural, a constructed and framed image. The exaggerated quality of camp—its flirtation with queerness, its call to ironic reading rather than naïve acceptance, its insistence on performance as exaggerated gesture—deliver what Pamela Robertson calls "guilty pleasures." We can take pleasure in something a little bit transgressive. Our relationship with camp texts differs from our relationship with other kinds of texts. For one thing, camp is to a great extent in the eye of the beholder rather than something inherent in the text itself. This subjective aspect of camp is especially apparent in texts for children. What adults might take as camp, children might take seriously, and I suppose the reverse is true as well. But camp does inhabit children's texts. In fact, the camp aspect of children's texts is crucial; camp ensures detachment. When we encounter camp, we live outdoors, as it were, removed from commonality and conformity. We are, strange as it may seem, good Scouts. Camp dares to be different. Camp is as camp does. Camp is pleasurable precisely because it flaunts itself audaciously. We know that camp experience is related to queer experience. Indeed, camp is queer. Robertson argues that camp is a "queer discourse . . . because it enables not only gay men, but also heterosexual and lesbian women, and perhaps heterosexual men, to express their discomfort with and alienation from the normative gender and sex roles assigned to them by straight culture" (9–10). The cowboy's refusal to settle down with wife and children signals his discomfort with the normative gender roles of straight culture. But, as Robertson and others have argued, neither that which is queer nor that which is camp is necessarily gay or anti-straight (see Robertson, 10; Bordo, 165). Think of both camp and queer as offering a liminal zone in which spectators may try on identities, in which they may reflect and experiment.

If the camp ground is a liminal space, a space removed from normalcy, then when we inhabit this space, we have open to us the opportunity for passage. The films I am examining provide youngsters with rites of passage, after all. Many of the films have child characters, often but not always males, and these children clearly learn aspects of identity and character from the heroes who enter their lives and then depart at the end. *Shane* is probably the best-known example, although the B western offers many others. *Trigger, Jr.* (1950) tells the story of young Larry, a boy afraid of horses, afraid of animals generally, and downright afraid of life. Roy Rogers comes along with Trigger and Trigger, Jr., and the three of them help Larry, both through example and encouragement, to overcome his fears and to carry out a heroic action by riding Trigger, Jr., and getting help for his ailing grandfather. By the end of the film, Larry has acquired confidence, but he has a lot of growing still to do. We see him riding a pony, not a full-sized horse like Trigger, Jr.

What camp and queer deliver is ambiguity, a deliberate confusion of easy categories. Children are themselves campy. Children enjoy dressing up, cross-dressing, and parading in costume; they like artifice and flamboyance. And they appreciate camp when they encounter it in others. I suspect we find examples of camp even in the literature aimed at the very young: *Where the Wild Things Are*, and Maurice Sendak's work generally, is camp; Van Allsburg and Raschka and Seuss all have their campy moments. Roy Rogers and the other B western cowboys are decidedly camp. The elaborately tooled boots, the large and loud spurs, the shirts with fringe and embroidery, the chaps, the gun belts, the scarves, the stitched pants, and the huge hats are the stuff of extravagance. Charles Starrett's scarf, if I can take just one example, was extremely long. Apparently, this scarf was a piece of silk cut from a nightgown worn by Rita Hayworth. Starrett remarked: "It always blew beautifully in the breeze" (Old Corral, http://www.b.-westerns.com). This cowboy comes draped in part of a woman's nightgown! What does this say about gender? At the very least, we have here a reminder of the fetish, cross-dressing, and ambiguous manhood. We also have the stuff of camp.

From the perspective of gender construction, camp has a positive role to play. Let me return to my own childhood and reflect upon my entry into masculine culture. Like many small boys, I had heroes in both cinema and sports, and the cowboy has obvious affinities with the sports hero. Indeed, today, rodeo counts as a sporting event. Both the cowboy and the athlete engage in what are, or were, typically masculine activities—activities that demand bodily discipline and strength along with agility and sound judgment. Both wear an identifiable outfit or costume. Both often have catchy nicknames. And both may be a part of a team, usually the most important part of a team, the sports hero with his teammates and the cowboy with his sidekick (or sidekicks, since often the cowboy is part of a trio). These men—cowboys or sportsmen—are leaders. These men are role models for the young. At first blush, they present versions of hegemonic masculinity—the kind of all-male human being that conventional evocations of John Wayne or Michael Jordan suggest. This man is courageous, efficient and skilled, smart, handsome, selfless, and judicious. He is in control. Confronted with this man, women swoon and small boys cheer. He is the man Joey Starrett sees in the gunfighter Shane. He commands respect.

But as role models, the cowboy and the sportsman have their differences. The hegemonic male is unlikely to turn up in company wearing fringe and glitter (Dennis Rodman is perhaps the exception that proves the rule). The fringe that dangles from buckskin shirts, the kind worn by TV's Wild Bill Hickok (Guy Madison) or by Davey Crockett (John Wayne) in *The Alamo* (1960), is acceptable wear for a manly man, but the flouncy glitter and fringe of shirts worn by Rex Allen or Roy Rogers is another matter all together. These duds are queer, or at least camp, which amounts to much the same thing. These clothes have an androgynous quality; women sometimes wear clothes like these. The clothes do not necessarily signify homosexuality. No one, I think, would call Roy Rogers or Gene

Autry gay, although characters in at least two films—*Midnight Cowboy* (1969) and *Repo Man* (1984)—refer to John Wayne as a "faggot" (see Russo, 81). But I am prepared to call Gene and Roy queer. These guys present an image of masculinity that has a visible feminine side. Their love of finery suggests a man who lives for more than the hardness of the trail. These guys have an eye for beauty, even over-the-top beauty. In short, these guys know style when they see it. And they are not above adopting style for style's sake. These are camp cowboys. The self-conscious assumption of a costume, the flaunting of the masquerade, signals immaturity. Camp is a guilty pleasure because it subverts the norms of straight living, and also because it keeps us loving childhood. The time when we could dress up without fearing that others would categorize us is the time of childhood. To love that time is to fall into what James Kincaid has called "child loving." The campy cowboy is eternally boyish, resistant to growing up.

I suspect I knew this even when I was a boy. Obviously, the cowboy's clothes made an impression on me and on boys like me. We wanted to dress like our heroes. But as I indicated at the outset of this chapter, I had an ambivalent relationship with certain of the cowboy clothes. I wasn't entirely certain of all that fringe and glitter. Better to have the more modest shirts worn when Roy or Rex were chasing bad guys, the checked cotton shirts or denim shirts that served as their workaday wear, than the gaudy fringed affairs they wore for publicity pictures and on their personal appearances.

The excessively decorated shirts such as the one we see Rex wearing on the cover of his comic book are meant to attract the eye (figure 5.2). They communicate a complex of masculine traits: neatness, wealth, cleanliness, self-confidence, and strangely enough, the natural; this shirt and many like it depict animals or plants or images that remind us of the west and its association with nature as opposed to what Huck Finn calls "sivilization." Allen's shirt has stylized profiles of horses' heads and horseshoes decorating the yoke, smaller horseshoes on the collar, and an abstract design on the sleeves. Instead of buttons, this shirt has the frontier-shirt lacing. Below the yoke, the garment is covered with long gold fringe. Fringe hangs from the outside of the sleeves. The shirt has masculine images complemented with feminine colour and fringe. (The gold fringe reminds me of the gold jewellery worn by many a macho man these days.) It has the whiff of cross-dressing, and it reminds us of the fetish. Marjorie Garber suggests that the "concept of 'normal' sexuality,

Figure 5.2 Rex Allen, resplendent on the cover of his Dell comic book, No. 30 (September–November 1958). Source: The Grand Comics Database Project, www.comics.org/details.lasso?id=112306.

that is to say, of heterosexuality, is founded on the naturalizing of the fetish. And this in turn is dependent upon an economics of display intrinsic both to fetishism and to theatrical representation" (119). The paradox is that the very process of "naturalizing" is unnatural. Rex's shirt unnaturalizes by drawing attention to itself as costume, display, pretend, performance. As long as the cowboy wears his costume, he remains home on the range, but once he trades his glitter and fringe for workaday clothes, he resigns himself to the drab utilitarian and domestic role of the father and labourer.

No one in the world I inhabit on a daily basis wears a shirt like the one we see Rex Allen wearing on the cover of the Dell comic. Once a year in the city where I live, Calgary, Alberta, people (both men and women) dress up in country clothes for the Calgary Stampede. But even then shirts like Rex Allen's are rare to non-existent. The point is that when the people of my city wear clothing that might aspire to the campy hipness of Rex Allen's shirt, they are quite consciously inhabiting an Imaginary. They perform. They partake in the carnival spirit. And the salutary effect of performance, either on the part of the cowboy heroes who are my subject or of Calgarians during the Stampede, is that it reminds us that whatever we do partakes of performance. We perform as gendered selves, and the gendered performances of cowboy heroes such as Rex Allen offer an Imaginary that is ambiguous, laced with finery not known in the repertoire of hegemonic masculinity.

Tall in the Saddle
Romance on the Range

Desires are already memories.
—Italo Calvino

What is a cowboy without a horse? Whatever he is, he is incomplete. Cowboy and horse not only complement each other, they allow each other to function in proper western fashion. When I was young I had visions of myself riding tall in the saddle. The Bates family lived across the street from where I lived, and the Bates family had a small corral at the back of their house in which they kept a horse for Mr. Bates's employer, a local oil man named Soper who, as it happened, owned and operated the local movie theatre. My sister and I often took carrots and apples to the corral to feed the horse, but we were never allowed to ride it (I can no longer recall if the horse was a stallion, mare, or gelding). I never did learn to ride a horse. But this did not keep me from pretending to ride. I had a makeshift saddle made with a belt and pillow draped over the iron frame at the foot of my bed, and I would spend evenings pretending I was galloping after some desperado who needed catching. The image in my head was of the recurrent close tracking shots of my heroes riding their horses, sometimes riding and shooting. This is the image that opened both *The Roy Rogers Show* and *The Lone Ranger* TV show, and it was one of the distinctive features of early Ken Maynard movies. Most B westerns, especially as the form became more clearly aimed at kids in the 1940s and '50s, use the tracking shot to accentuate the heroic image of horse and rider. As Jenni Calder has noted, speaking of western fiction: "If the hero is on a horse he is halfway towards convincing the reader of an irresistible manliness" (103). And if the hero is on a galloping horse and maybe firing a pistol, he is three-quarters of the way to convincing the viewer of an irresistible manliness.

The hero, whether a cowboy or Robin Hood or a knight such as St. George, rides a horse. Even more modern heroes have horses, although these horses may be of a distinctly different shape. The hero on motorcycle is familiar in many films, from *The Wild One* (1953) with Marlon Brando, to *Terminator 2: Judgment Day* (1991), with Arnold Schwarzenegger. The spaceship too may serve as a horse stand-in, as we remember from *Star Trek* or even more explicitly in the short-lived TV series from Joss Whedon, *Firefly* (2002). In a pinch, a car can stand in for the horse as well, as we see in *The Fast and the Furious* (2001) and its sequels and in several James Bond films. *Son of Paleface* (1952) poked fun at the horse-and-hero dyad when the B western was still in vogue; at the end of this film, which has Roy Rogers starring along with Bob Hope, Hope's Jeep rears in imitation of Trigger's famous pose. The relationship between horse and rider is usually quite simple: the horse is an extension of the rider, a symbol of his power and status. David's famous painting *Napoleon at St. Bernard* (1800; see figure 6.1) expresses this symbolic connection between hero and horse, and it provides the source of an iconic image that has since been replicated by most of the cowboy heroes.

This pose, with horse and rider rearing back and up suggests victory, power, strength, bravery, control, and confidence; this is the heroic pose par excellence. The difference between the portrait of Napoleon and that of Roy Rogers and Trigger is that most viewers of these images will know both horse and rider in the one and only the rider in the other. Who knows the name of Napoleon's horse? But the cowboy often meets the viewer as rider-with-horse: Roy and Trigger, Gene Autry and Champion, Hopalong Cassidy and Topper, the Lone Ranger and Silver, Tex Ritter and White Flash, Ken Maynard and Tarzan, the Durango Kid and Raider, Rocky Lane and Black Jack, Rex Allen and KoKo, Buster Crabbe and Falcon, and so on. H.F. Hintz provides a comprehensive list of the cowboys and their horses in *Horses in the Movies* (1979). Hintz associates the horses with the B westerns' appeal to children, and he asserts that these films with their famous horses "helped teach youngsters to respect and love animals and the principles of fair play" (13). In other words, he wants us to think of the "horse heroes" as separate from their "masters." But with duos such as the ones I list above, we are surely meant to think of them

Figure 6.1 *Napoleon at St. Bernard* (1800), the iconic horse-and-rider image, by Jacques-Louis David (1748–1825). Source: Neo-Classicism and French Revolution http://www .bc.edu/bc_org/avp/car/his/CoreArt/net/neocl_dav_stber.html.
Figure 6.2 Roy Rogers, at ease and in control, on a rearing Trigger. Publicity photo ca. 1944. Source: Happy Trails Highway, http://www.happytrailshighway.com.

as symbiotic. Trigger is "the Smartest Horse in the Movies" because Roy Rogers is "King of the Cowboys." Champion is the "World's Wonder Horse" because Gene Autry is the "World's Greatest Cowboy." KoKo is "the Miracle Horse of the Movies" and Rex Allen is "the Arizona Cowboy." It does not matter that at least five horses played Champion in Autry's films or that Hoppy rode several Toppers. What matters is the imaginary connection between one horse and one hero. The special horse only emphasized the special qualities of the hero. And the special colouring of the horse (so often either white or palomino) allowed the viewer to recognize the hero among a pack of riders or in the distance (Calder, 97). Even those cowboy heroes who did not ride a horse as famous as Trigger or Champion rode horses the viewer could easily pick out from among many horses, and often these were white. Kermit Maynard, lesser-known brother of Ken, rides a white stallion in *Rough Riding Rhythm* (1937), and this horse performs dramatically when Kermit whistles.

Trigger, like most of the horses associated with the heroes, was a stallion. The male hero rides a male horse, just as he associates with male sidekicks. He rides a horse of a distinctive colour, often white, sometimes black or palomino. Only one B western hero, the Cisco Kid, rides

Figure 6.3 Publicity photo in which Monte Hale serenades his horse, reminding us of the cowboy's first love. The horse appears to be suitably impressed, and Mr. Hale appears splendidly attired—in stetson and flower-embroidered shirt, with a neckerchief that echoes the red of the embroidery. Source: Mr. Monte Hale.

a pinto, and this is significant. The pinto is often the horse of choice of children, women, or Native Americans. Roy Rogers takes a pinto as a present to his chosen girl in *Springtime in the Sierras* (1947). Most pintos are smaller than the stallions the heroes ride; the pinto is a horse for less-than-manly characters, and the only hero who rides a pinto happens to be Mexican. Most bad guys ride indistinguishable bays (brown horse with black mane). Only the hero rides a thick-necked, distinctively coloured stallion. And this horse and this man need only each other for company and companionship. The world of a cowboy is largely, if not entirely, an all-male world. Men and stallions without women and mares reinforce the parthenogenetic implications of the cowboy's world.

We used to make jokes about the cowboy and his horse, jokes that turned on the cowboy's choice to stay with his horse and leave the woman behind. Such jokes contain an important point: the cowboy does have an intimate relationship with his horse. This intimacy is implicit in the many films in which the hero chooses to leave town and a woman to spend days and nights on the open range with his horse. A film such as *The Golden Stallion* (1949) makes what is implicit explicit. In this film, Roy Rogers's horse Trigger is convicted of murder and sentenced to death. What happens is that bad guys are smuggling diamonds across the Mexican border, hiding them in the specially fashioned horseshoe worn by a tame palomino mare that runs with a herd of wild horses. Trigger gets a crush on the palomino mare. When one of the bad guys appears to threaten the mare, Trigger kills him. Poor gallant Trigger finds himself summarily tried and convicted of murder. Roy comes to his rescue by taking the blame; he receives a five-year prison sentence, during which time Trigger, Jr., appears on the scene back at the ranch. Trigger, Jr., eventually reveals the smuggling plot and saves the day. The film turns on the relationship between Trigger and Roy. Trigger's philandering— which we must assume resulted in Trigger, Jr.—lands Roy in jail. Trigger's brief fling with unfaithfulness has dire consequences. We might guess that Trigger's libidinous behaviour results in Roy's incarceration, because Roy, not Trigger, needs chastening. The man must learn self-discipline. He must learn to master his libido. He must, in short, move beyond the pleasure principle.

The scene in which Trigger receives the death penalty and Roy comes to his rescue receives high praise from no less discerning a critic than Quentin Tarantino: "I love this scene. . . . It's a really tough scene, a tough, tough scene. But it's not the kind of scene you expect, all right. The emotion is right out there. But if you buy it, and I totally buy it, then it can make you cry" (Lyman, 2). This is one tough scene, made to make tough guys like Tarantino cry. Rick Lyman, the reporter who watched *The Golden Stallion* with Tarantino, appears to agree when he describes the scene and notes that a close-up of Rogers communicates a subtle shift in Rogers's feelings: "Somehow, fear, regret and calculation all begin to wash out of his eyes even though his face doesn't move a muscle. He drops his head, a decision made" (2). Tarantino and Lyman react to the emotional intimacy between man and horse, an intimacy conveyed not in words or even deeds but rather in a simple look and a lowering of the head that mask an ineffable depth of feeling. This is masculine expression of feeling at its most exquisite, a form of expression that communicates in its very refusal to speak or register pain. When Roy drops his head, we know the depth of his feeling. This is a quiet gesture repeated by many cowboys, perhaps most powerfully in Ford's *The Searchers* (1956), when Ethan Edwards (John Wayne) looks through the doorway of his brother's burned-out home, sees the body of the woman whose name he has just called, and drops his head. We do not need to hear Edwards or Rogers speak their pain. Indeed, it is unlikely that either character possesses the language equal to it.

In the case of *The Golden Stallion*, Roy and Trigger are the two most important characters in the film. Tarantino notes:

> Roy and Trigger are best friends. Trigger is not just his best horse; he's his best friend. You know, in some movies, a cowboy might go to jail to save his best friend from being shot down dead. Well, Trigger is Roy's best friend. It's the easiest leap to have him do that here, yet it's so powerful and so unexpected. What's great is that you buy it, you absolutely buy it, and I don't know that I really would buy it from anybody else but Roy and Trigger. (3)

Roy spends his five years in prison, at hard labour. As Lyman notes, "Tarantino finds it odd that this is so moving to him." He quotes Tarantino's assessment of Rogers's character:

> Nowadays, Roy Rogers seems almost too good, but you buy it from him somehow. I find myself being moved by his common decency. Life's events and other people's actions have no effect on him and his heart. He didn't save Trigger to become a bitter man; he did it because it was what he had to do. His code is his code. The whole world can change, and it doesn't change his code. (5)

The code of manly behaviour includes the principle of loyalty to one's friends and the truth that a cowboy has no better friend than his horse. As Hintz suggests, films that focus on horses "teach youngsters to respect and love animals and the principles of fair play" (13). They may do this, but while they are communicating a love of animals, they are connecting masculinity with the animal in man.

In *The Unknown Ranger* (1936), with Bob Baker, a wild stallion (later called Pal and looking like Trigger) fights the bad guys' stallion. Later, Pal is captured and the bad guys and good guys vie for him; the one who rides him successfully gets to keep him. They draw cards and the two good guys lose and must attempt to ride the stallion after the two bad guys. Both bad guys (played by Bob Kortman and Harry Woods) are thrown. Bob Baker's pal, Chuckler (a rough, unshaven Hal Taliaferro, who appears in earlier films as Wally Wales), also gets bucked off, after one of the bad guys spooks the horse. Pal is never broken. Nevertheless, late in the film, when only this horse is available, Bob rides him to chase down the baddies, who are trying to get away with the ranch horses and cows. The connection between horse and rider, their wild and powerful expression of will, is clear in this film. The good guy can ride Pal because Pal instinctively accepts him as companion and master and because the good guy is wild at heart.

The horse draws attention to the body. Horses are beautiful to look at and so are horse and rider together. I recall the description of the "great draught-horses" in D.H. Lawrence's story "The Horse Dealer's Daughter" (1922), "swinging their great rounded haunches sumptuously." In the story, an onlooker, Joe, feels as if the "horses were almost like his own body." In the films, the horses are mostly well groomed—even the wild mustangs appear well cared for. Their coats are short, and they often gleam as they gallop. Even the sound they make is pleasing. The horse is a metonymy for the cowboy. If we feel some reluctance to gaze on the cowboy's body, we can always gaze at his horse. And the horse is invariably a stallion, even if in fact the horse who plays the cowboy's friend is a gelding (e.g., Tim Holt's horse, Duke). Energy and potency are the attributes of the horse, as much as intelligence. The man, like the horse, must combine sensibility, reason, and strength. And he must also be sexy. The sensuousness of horseflesh is one feature of these films. The camera catches the smooth and well-groomed coat of the animals and the flexing of their muscles as they gallop. Much screen time in these fifty- or sixty-minute features consists of shots of riding, either villains chasing stagecoaches, posses chasing villains, villains and good guys riding to or from town, heroes chasing villains, or folks out for a ride. *Rough Riding Rhythm*, which I mention above, is a loosely connected series of scenes of riding. The emphasis, however, is on the cowboy hero and his steed. The two of them communicate a mind–body connection that suggests the man must combine the powers of reason with the physical beauty, power, and grace of a well-toned body. If we cannot see the hero without a shirt, then we can see his horse. If the hero's muscles remain hidden under a fancy shirt and long trousers and chaps, then his horse can reveal the body in all its sensuous beauty.

In a way, the horse reflects manhood itself. Take for example another Roy Rogers film, *My Pal Trigger* (1946). Roy plays an itinerant horse dealer and seller of fancy leather goods. He owns a mare called Lady, and he wants to have a palomino stallion, Sovereign, owned by rancher Gabby Kendrick (George "Gabby" Hayes), sire a colt with Lady. But Gabby is cantankerous and unwilling to negotiate. Roy is kicked out of Kendrick's party, held at a club owned by Brett Scoville (Jack Holt). That same night, Lady and Sovereign, who has been taken from Gabby's ranch by two of Scoville's men, Hunter and Carson (Roy Barcroft and Leroy Mason), run away together and mate. In the morning, a wild black stallion comes to Roy's corral and fights Sovereign. Scoville and his two henchmen watch the action from a hillside, and after a few minutes Scoville shoots and kills Sovereign. Roy hears the shot. He shoots once at the three riders. Roy is accused of killing Sovereign and Gabby becomes even more cantankerous, seeing Roy as a horse murderer and generally as a low-down skunk. Roy is arrested and a trial ensues. Roy needs $1000 for bail. A seedy lawyer (played by an uncredited Ted Adams) offers to provide the bail money, but for a price that amounts to everything Roy owns, including the horse Lady. Roy mortgages all his belongings to make bail. Then he flees on Lady. We follow his wanderings all winter. In late winter Lady foals. Roy has to fight to keep her in a barn while she delivers the newborn that will be Trigger. We follow Roy as he raises the colt over the next year or so. One day, young Trigger is caught in an animal trap. A cougar appears. The cougar and Lady fight. Roy arrives to shoot the cougar, and then he is forced to shoot Lady, who is seriously injured. Finally Roy returns to Gabby's ranch to give Trigger to Gabby (as replacement for Sovereign) and to turn himself in. He wants to clear things up. Gabby refuses the "half-breed" horse. Roy gives himself up to the law. During his stint in prison, his belongings—including Trigger—are auctioned off.

Through a bit of chicanery, Trigger ends up the property of the club owner, Scoville. Roy pays his debts with the proceeds of the auction and is a free man. Scoville hires him to train Trigger. Then Scoville manoeuvres Gabby into a bet that his horses can beat Gabby's in a race. Gabby has a large gambling debt held by Scoville. The bet is that if Gabby wins, his debts are cancelled; and if Scoville wins, he gets Gabby's ranch. Gabby does not know that Scoville now owns Trigger. The two men make a side bet that we hear about at the end of the film. Roy learns that Dale (Dale Evans), Gabby's niece, was responsible for getting him out of jail. He also learns of Scoville's duplicity, and he feels compromised about the race because he is supposed to ride Trigger. We are now to believe that Trigger will not perform for anyone but Roy. Complicating matters is the fact that Dale is to race Gabby's horse. During the race Roy helps Dale win and thereby saves the day for Gabby. All gets sorted out, and, because of the side bet we heard about earlier, Gabby now owns Trigger. In a gesture of forgiveness, Gabby gives Trigger to Roy.

In other words, one father (Gabby) gives a son (Trigger) to Roy, who has been father to Trigger all along. We could say the film is about ownership and the conferring of ownership, but more pointedly the film is about fathers and the fathers' siring of sons. Roy sires Trigger. The viewer may not make the connection between the stallion that is responsible for Trigger's conception, Sovereign, and Roy Rogers, King of the Cowboys, but the connection lives in the allusion to royalty. Roy is not only the main male here, the king of cowboys; he is also the author, the creator of the story itself. The film uses a voice-over with Roy as narrator. He tells us the story of how he came to own Trigger, and tells us too that the "hardest thing [he] ever had to do" was to shoot Lady after her fight with the cougar. The shooting of Lady leaves Roy as Trigger's only surviving "parent." Roy is the capable man who does not need a woman. He can survive independently, outside civilization, and he can raise a son by himself. We see a montage of scenes in which Roy teaches Trigger a variety of tricks, including the famous pose of horse and rider rearing and reaching for the sky. This pose suggests the inseparability of man and horse. It intensifies our understanding of the trust between horse and rider. Trigger grows to prove his worth and nobility. We know he can win the race. That he does not win is a sign of the generosity and self-sacrificing nature of his father and master. In one sense, Trigger represents, as sons do, the father's libidinal energies, his continuing potency. That Roy masters Trigger and holds him from winning the race only proves that Roy has mastered his own libidinal energy. Body and mind are fully integrated. We might notice that in *My Pal Trigger* Roy wears a greater number of fancy shirts than he does, perhaps, in any other film. Yet none of these shirts has the gaudy fringe of Nudie Cohn's more outrageous creations. Roy's are fancy but tasteful shirts that draw attention to him and to his body and its agility.

This focus on the body is a feature of these westerns. It is apparent in the various spectacular mounts that the hero executes in so many of these films. In *Rough Riding Rhythm* (1937), for example, Kermit Maynard leaps into the saddle without using the stirrup, or he hops into the stirrup in a fluid motion—something Roy Rogers perfects and many of the other cowboys use (bad guys, sidekicks, and other characters never mount in this way). He swings easily into the saddle even as his horse begins to gallop. One set piece has Kermit on the roof of a barn. From there, he throws a rope over a beam that extends from another building, and using this rope he swings through the air to land gracefully on his white horse. Horse and rider then gallop away from their would-be captors. We see this kind of acrobatic daring in film after film. Perhaps the most effective of such mounts is the running mount. The rider takes hold of the saddle horn as the horse begins to gallop, swings his legs forward so that he is holding on at the side of the horse in full flight, then allows his feet to come to the ground, where they hit the earth and follow through back, up over the horse's back and down into the stirrups. Pony Express riders often appear before us using this style of running mount (see for example, *Winds of the Wasteland*, 1936, or *Pony Post*, 1940). When we recall how often characters refer to women as horses (usually fillies), and the various uses of the word *mount* itself, the sexual connotations of the horse are difficult to ignore.

The sexuality I flirt with here is that innocent sexuality of so many children's books, especially those from the nineteenth and early-twentieth centuries. Perhaps the best expression of what I am getting at appears in Kenneth Grahame's *The Wind in the Willows* (1908). In this book, as in so many of the B westerns, a contrast exists between the horse and the automobile. Even the dust created by horse and machine make a contrast. The motor car "flung an enveloping cloud of dust that blinded and enwrapped [Ratty, Mole, and Toad] utterly" (36), whereas the horse kicks up dust that smells "rich and satisfying" (32). The horse conjures up romance, that sense of connectedness that delivers a satisfyingly sensual feeling. In Grahame's River Bank world, nature expresses romance: the various flowers—loosestrife, willow herb, comfrey, and dog rose—are like ladies waiting for "the shepherd-boy for the nymphs to woo." One last flower is "the knight for whom the ladies waited at the window, the prince that was to kiss the sleeping summer back to life and love." This flower is the "meadow-sweet" (45). Clearly, romance is invested in natural things. Grahame's vision is pastoral, and so too is the vision of the westerns. In Gene Autry's *Springtime in the Rockies* (1937), the name of the ranch owner for whom Autry works is Knight. The plot turns on the familiar conflict between cows and sheep, and the very presence of sheep reminds us of pastoral. As in traditional pastoral, this film focuses on country living, relaxation, and courtship. Gene and his boss, Sandra Knight (Polly Rowles), have a romance that one of Sandra's girlfriends says ought to take place in the sunset in order to intensify the charm. The film highlights the western landscape as a place of harmony, song, and, in a word, romance. This is the romance—innocent, fun, infused with pastoral ease—that we might associate with the forests of Arden. The western is a form of pastoral romance, but this one is self-conscious in its evocation of this form of narrative.

The word *romance* turns up in several B western titles—*Romance on the Range* (1942), *Romance Rides the Range* (1936), *Romance of the Rockies* (1937), *Romance of the West* (1946)—and it carries both formal and thematic implications. The formal aspect of romance consists of the heroic plots in which a special man, sometimes with the help of other people, restores the unity of the human and the natural that has been rent asunder by villains who rustle cattle or hoard water or poach game or steal horses or waste land for railroads or dams or their own satisfaction.

Thematically, romance raises the topic of sex. *Romance on the Range*, for example, tells the story of a western ranch owned by an eastern lady, Miss Stewart (Sally Payne), who has never seen the place she owns. The film begins with a gang of baddies who steal fur from traplines. These furs are what keep the lady in New York wealthy, and she is not happy to learn that her business is suffering because of thievery. Meanwhile, the thieves kill one of the ranch hands. The ranch foreman (Roy Rogers) vows to catch the murderer. The stage is set for Miss Stewart to travel west and meet foreman Roy. Romance, then, refers to the adventure that ensues as the hero-sets-things to rights and also to the sparks that fly between the lady and her cowboy. The film ends with a song that pointedly undermines the romance between man and woman and underlines the romance of the range. The two senses of romance—as the free-dom-stifling connection between man and woman and as the untram-melled freedom of the open range—inhabit the phrase "romance rides the range." We hear the ranch hands singing that a cowboy's life is "full and free" but that he says "goodbye to his liberty" when "romance rides the range." In this rare instance in the B western, the film ends by show-ing both the triumph of romance in its evocation of heterosexual love and the self-destructive nature of romance. Romance is both life-affirm-ing and life-restricting.

But when the cowboy remains with his horse, as he usually does in these films, romance as freedom from restraint can thrive. It thrives as both the vision of unity between the human and the natural and as a narcissistic onanism. As human and natural unity, the connectedness of man and horse suggests, as Jane Tompkins points out, "that horses fulfill a longing for a different *kind* of existence. Antimodern, antiurban, and antitechnological, they stand for an existence without cars and telephones and electricity" (93; italics in original). In *Colt Comrades* (1943), a con man (Earle Hodgson) swindles Hopalong Cassidy's sidekick, California Carlson (Andy Clyde) by selling him drilling equipment so he can find oil on the property in which Hoppy and his friends have an interest. Hoppy and Lucky are more interested in cattle than they are in oil, but the ranch is in dire straits because of a lack of water for the cattle. California spends much of the film sitting in a hammock and forcing Earle to do the drilling for oil. Hoppy and the others ride around with the cattle and eventually get framed as cattle thieves just as they are getting the other ranchers organized against the villain who is hoarding the local water. Just when matters look darkest for the good guys, water instead of oil comes through California's well. The ranch with its cattle will survive, and the need for oil evaporates. A slightly later film, *Conquest of Cheyenne* (1946), depicts a successful drilling for oil on another hard-pressed ranch. We might assume the film is forward-looking, but the hero, Red Ryder (Wild Bill Elliott), finds the newfangled contraptions— automobiles and oil rigs with their greasy engines—confusing. In the end, he remains with his horse and small sidekick, Little Beaver (Bobby Blake). They do not depend upon such unnatural machinery.

Romance, then, reflects the ancient notion of the triumph of the human. In romance, the hero never really comes to rest; he continues a journey that will end in some vision of human "fraternity" (Frye, 173). George Stevens's *Shane* provides a good example. Here the mysterious stranger rides from the high country to the valley, where homesteaders try to eke an existence against the harshness of nature and the greed of a land baron. The stranger assists the homesteaders in their struggle to make the valley a home, and then he returns to the high country that is the source of myth. Many B westerns use some variation of this mythic story. A close parallel is *Homesteaders of Paradise Valley* (1947), with Allan "Rocky" Lane as Red Ryder. The structure of this film is common to virtually all the Rough Riders series that star Buck Jones as Buck Roberts, Tim McCoy as Tim McCall, and Raymond Hatton as Sandy Hopkins; at the end of each film the Rough Riders go their separate ways—Roberts to Arizona, McCall to Wyoming, Hopkins to Texas. A similar structure is evident in those films with mysterious masked heroes, such as the Durango Kid and the

Lone Ranger. The series of Johnny Mack Brown films for Monogram Pictures (beginning in 1943), in which he rides alongside Sandy Hopkins (again played by Raymond Hatton), deliver this mythic plot as well. The myth presents a hero—who may be a composite, as in the Rough Riders films—alone in the sense of unattached to any material reality we see in the film.

The three cowboy lawmen in the Rough Riders series claim to have homes in Arizona, Wyoming, and Texas, but we rarely see these homes. The first entry in this series, *Arizona Bound* (1941), opens with a shot of someone paring the calluses on his feet. This is a character named Bunion (Horace Murphy), who works at the Buck Roberts ranch. Buck says he feels settled and comfortable, but as soon as he receives a telegram from Bat Madison (like Charlie in the *Charlie's Angels* television show, Madison never appears in the films) asking him to take on another adventure, Buck wastes no time in leaving his ranch. And at film's end Tim McCall makes it clear that the three pals need the life of adventure to give their lives meaning. Like Tennyson's Ulysses, these three representatives of the western hero are "strong in will / To strive, to seek, to find and not to yield" (ll. 69–70). They "cannot rest from travel" (l. 6). The clue to the "mythic" and decidedly loose nature of the heroes' ties to home lies in the ongoing gag from film to film about Sandy Hopkins's impending marriage down in Texas. The other two make fun of Sandy's existence under the continual threat of marriage, effectively signalling their own single lives and the freedom that the single life allows.

Jane Tompkins beautifully evokes the "homey" connection between the man and his horse:

> The sense of comradery and peaceful coexistence between man and horse should, perhaps, modify our sense of the endings of many Westerns. When the hero has to leave town at the end of the story and gets back on his horse and rides into the desert, he is not unaccommodated. The saddle he sits on is large and comfortable, and usually ornamented; to it are appended all sorts of gear—canteens, rifles, ropes, knives, bags of food, blankets, articles of clothing. There is a homeyness about all this equipment, so neatly stowed. The saddle leather creaks companionably, the bridle and spurs jingle. The clip-clop of the hooves beat out a pleasant rhythm. The horse is the hero's home on the range, a mobile home to be sure, but better than a real house or a real trailer because it is alive, someone to talk to, to count on when the going gets tough. When he leaves the girl at the end of the movie, the hero isn't going off into the wild blue yonder all by himself; he is coming home to his horse, and together they are going to seek new adventures. (97)

But Tompkins allows her enthusiasm to carry her away. At least in the B western (and probably in westerns generally), life on the range may appear comfortable, but a strange disconnection underlies it. When cowboys gather round a campfire, for example, it's far from clear where their frying pans and bedrolls and coffee pots and food and changes of clothes come from. Nor is it clear how, when our hero rides into town with nary a sign of luggage, he appears in a later scene in a different set of clothes, sometimes for purposes of disguise. The cowboy's self-sufficiency has something fantastical about it.

Self-sufficiency is the fantasy of manhood. The cowboy needs no one but his horse and perhaps a sidekick or two to share the trail with. The freedom the cowboy and his horse experience is, however, double-edged. On one hand it allows for the realization of full independence, but on the other it entails the near-masochistic self-discipline of a man willing to push his body to the limit, willing to do without the comforts of home, willing to do without pleasure in any conventional sense. The cowboy's mastery of the horse is a self-mastery. The horse's obedience is the cowboy's own submission to repression. This signature of repression works in both the big-budget westerns and the B westerns. Where the two kinds of westerns differ is in the friendship between hero and horse. This friendship signals the comforts of the homosocial group. The man is best when he is among equals, and the most equal is his horse. The horse, in other words, is the cowboy's Imaginary, that other self that is his best self.

A film that makes this clear is David Miller's *Lonely Are the Brave* (1962), in which man and horse live and die together in a world that has passed them by. We travel Lacanian territory here, and its intricacies indicate both the comforts of the Imaginary and its impossibility. Time and again, the western sets up the cowboy and his horse in binary opposition to ranch families, bankers and towns, oil derricks, automobiles, trains, airplanes, and all that entails progress and industrial society. I'll offer two examples. The first is arguably the most bizarre western ever made: *The Phantom Empire*, with Gene Autry in his first starring role (1935). This twelve-chapter serial pits Gene and his horse, Champion, against the threatening forces of an underground futuristic empire called Murania. Muranians have robots and death rays, but such scientific wonders are no match for the Wonder Horse and his redoubtable rider.

My second example, *Riders of the Black Hills* (1938), begins with a montage of shots of various horse races interspersed with newspaper headlines: Black Knight wins at Saratoga, Black Knight wins the derby (Kentucky), and so on. Then a cut takes us to a train travelling through the dark. The next cut takes us inside a boxcar, where we see Black Knight, his jockey, his trainer, and the black actor Fred Toones, known here as Snowflake. The action begins when a gang of robbers stops the train and kidnaps Black Knight. Another cut takes us to a scene in which the Three Mesquiteers round up a herd of mustangs and capture the lead stallion. A scene follows in which Stony (Robert Livingston) breaks this stallion and the Mesquiteers decide to call this impressive horse Mesquite. Mesquite looks just like Black Knight. The names Mesquite and Black Knight might remind us that the three cowboy heroes known as the Three Mesquiteers have the energy and natural nobility of wild mustang stallions coupled with the honour and heroism of medieval crusaders.

The film's plot concerns the plan of Black Knight's owner, Mrs. Garth (Maude Eburne), to fund a children's hospital with the money Black Knight wins. When her horse is stolen, she fears she will fall into penury. During the hunt for the kidnapped horse, a fumbling Sheriff Brown (Roscoe Ates) arrests the Three Mesquiteers because the horse they are leading (Mesquite) resembles Black Knight. Our heroes end up in jail, where we see them two to a bunk—Stony and Tucson in the lower bunk and Lullaby and his dummy Elmer in the upper. Lullaby uses a trick with handcuffs to fool the sheriff, get the keys to the cell, and then escape with his two buddies. Black Knight is still with the kidnappers, however, and the big race is about to take place. Stony concocts the idea of having Mesquite take the place of Black Knight in the race. This plan meets with approval, but Mesquite (now performing the part of Black Knight) will run only when he hears a gun, so Lullaby has to shoot to get him started. Black Knight/Mesquite wins the race, but the bad guys discover that Black Knight is really Mesquite, so they try to blackmail the wealthy family by threatening to reveal that the horse that won the race was a ringer. The Three Mesquiteers ride to the rescue. The confusion between the two horses clarifies, and the bad guys receive their comeuppance. Throughout, Stony's infatuation with Mrs. Garth's niece, Joyce (Ann Evers), is apparent, though she is the fiancée of Mrs. Garth's lawyer, Frank Melton (Don Weston), the head bad guy. At one point, Tucson ridicules the impetuous Stony by calling him Casanova Brooke. But once Mrs. Garth's affairs are in order and her horse is restored to her, Tucson makes Stony come home. The final scene has Snowflake talking to the camera, saying what special fellows the Three Mesquiteers are. They are special because they are free from the kinds of restrictions Snowflake must endure.

The irony in *Riders of the Black Hills* resides in the two horses, Black Knight and Mesquite. Black Knight is a racehorse, coddled by his trainer and owner and made to race for a living. Mesquite, on the other hand, is a wild horse, broken to the saddle by a cowboy. Mesquite can run as fast as Black Knight, although he needs the prompting of a gunshot. The symbolic value of the horse as libidinous energy, free to roam at will, does not fit easily with either Black Knight or Mesquite. The irony is the irony of manhood manifest in the B western. The hero, like the horse, represents freedom, and at the same time he represents restraint. The hero's anarchic spirit inevitably breaks under the requirements of law and responsibility. But as long as horse and rider continue to look attractive, the irony can remain subdued and satisfyingly unobtrusive. The attractions of the cowboy and his horse appeal to our specular imagination; they are the Imaginary. And we recall that the Imaginary, in Lacan's tripartite division of the psyche, exists between the Real and the Symbolic. More than the Real or the Symbolic, the Imaginary depends upon lack (see Metz, 58–68). We yearn for the condition of the rider and horse rearing in triumphant freedom even as we inhabit a symbolic universe that demands that we deliver ourselves to the greater good of duty and social conformity. The sexual ripple apparent in the love between a man and his horse—like the transgressive sexual hints in the homosocial environment generally and in those campy clothes specifically—leads back to the safety of heterosexuality and group identity.

White Hats and White Heroes

Who Is That Other Guy?

That's mighty white of you.
—sentiment heard in many B westerns

G rowing up in a small town in eastern Ontario, I had little opportunity to see people who did not reflect my own ethnic and racial background. The town had a few stores owned by people with names such as Wiseman and Smolkin, and a restaurant or two owned by the Ings and the Wongs, but generally the town was pretty much like the one described by Roch Carrier in his story "The Sorcerer" (1979). In that story, the arrival of a black man in a small Quebec village sends the wife of the restaurant owner screaming down the street in fear. Racial and ethnic Others were less than real; they were not part of quotidian reality; we experienced such strangers as decorative, a sort of Imaginary Other that provided the dominant group (white people like myself) with convenient outlets for fun. Candies came in the shape of little black people. Toys included a range of "Indian" objects such as canoes, tomahawks, and feathered headbands. Our parents could purchase ashtrays and knickknacks in the shape of black people. The music we enjoyed contained a strong inflection of blackness. The racial Other was a presence even in a community such as the one in which I grew up, although this presence served only a decorative purpose. In decorating our lives, the racial Other served the more important purpose of reinforcing our sense of the normalcy and rightness of whiteness. The shirts worn by the cowboy heroes often sported embroidered patterns that demonstrated the decorative function of the Other (profiles of Native Americans, tomahawks, feathers, and so on). So too did the films in which these cowboy heroes starred. When I use the word *decorate*, I signal how normalcy worked for those of my generation who grew up white in small-town Canada. Whiteness was normal, so much so that we did not think about ourselves as racial beings. To be white was to be secure and comfortable and unthinking about race. White was normal to the point of invisibility. Thoughtlessness was also the condition of our sense of other races—Native Canadians or black people or people from Asia. We did not think about Otherness; we simply accepted it as an aspect of our lives that was comfortable and satisfying. The racial Other served to make our lives more colourful, as it were. And so *decorate* signifies here a form of racism unpleasant to look back on and not yet eradicated. We continue to have professional sports teams that decorate their uniforms with images of Otherness. What I am speaking about is a form of appropriation. It occurs when the dominant white culture thoughtlessly uses Otherness for its own pleasure. We can, I think, accuse the B western of doing precisely this.

Ghassan Hage calls the normalizing of whiteness the "White nation" fantasy; the fantasy stages desire and the desire here is for a nation that reflects the vision the dominant culture (in this instance the dominant racial group) has of itself. This vision is an ideal, an Imaginary, if you will, devoutly to be wished but not yet actualized. The ideal is a space in which we have the comforts of uniformity and control. Hage explains this fantasy as

> a space structured around a White culture, where Aboriginal people and non-White "ethnics" are merely national objects to be moved or removed according to a White national will. This White belief in one's mastery over the nation, whether in the form of a white multiculturalism or in the form of a White racism, is what I have called "White nation" fantasy. It is a fantasy of a nation governed by White people, a fantasy of White supremacy. (18)

The B western takes for granted whiteness as a norm.

Looking back at the western films I grew up with, I see a decorative presence of the Other. Films such as *The Red Rope* (1937) and *Jesse James at Bay* (1941) illustrate the decorative presence of the racial Other. *The Red Rope* opens with some comedic riffs on Lee Ching (an uncredited Willie Fung), the Chinese cook, who is baking cookies for the upcoming marriage of Tom Shaw (Bob Steele) and Betty Duncan (Lois January).

Betty's younger brother, Jimmy Duncan (Bobby Nelson), wants to take some of the newly baked cookies and Lee resists. The Chinese cook is a diversion, a bit of comic relief that adds flavour, as it were, to the film but nothing to the plot. The cook has a fear of the parson who is coming to marry Tom and Betty, although why he should have this fear remains unspoken. Clearly, he represents a pagan Other that can serve only to assist the white community as long as he remains anonymous and in the background. His anonymity extends even to the cast list, where he is conspicuously (at least today) absent.

Near the beginning of *Jesse James at Bay* is short scene in which a cowboy collects mail for Jesse. As this cowboy enters the store post office we can see in the background a Native American in full dress. We do not see this figure, who reminds me of a cigar store Indian, again; he serves only to decorate the scene. Also in this film, the main bad guy is a wealthy land speculator who has a black servant, Mose (an uncredited Charles R. Moore). Mose does little more than provide evidence that the villain can afford to have a black servant. As was the case with the Chinese cook in *The Red Rope*, the name of the black servant does not appear in the cast list. The racial Other remains an anonymous figure, serving to provide an important Imaginary Other to reinforce the whiteness of the dominant characters. In *Jesse James at Bay*, the Native American serves only to decorate the scene. We see a similar decorative appearance of Native Americans in *Springtime in the Rockies*. This film contains a scene at a community dance. The camera enters the dance hall through a doorway decorated with a lintel of feathers. Inside, the band is playing, and each musician wears a Native headdress and beaded buckskin clothing. These musicians are not Native American; they are playing Indian as part of their performance.

Consider also the Gene Autry film *Valley of Fire* (1951). Early in this film, in which Gene runs for mayor of Quartz City, we see a Chinese man scrubbing clothes in a barrel with a washboard while a Mexican points a pistol at him, presumably to keep him working. Here we have a hierarchy of races, and both are decorative in that neither serves the plot and neither interacts with each other or any other character in the film. That same year, the Roy Rogers film *South of Caliente* saw Dale Evans as Doris Stewart, who runs a racing stable with a number of black retainers. One of these is Willie (Willie Best in his final film). The bad guys murder Willie and a remorseful Doris remarks that Willie was "Dad's favourite." It seems that Willie is valued in much the same light as the horses on this ranch.

No line, however, is more telling than one spoken in the 1936 Hopalong Cassidy film *Three on the Trail*. During a romantic interlude in the film, young Johnny Nelson (James Ellison), Hoppy's sidekick, is out for a walk with Mary Stevens (Muriel Evans), the schoolteacher from the east. She expresses her fear of Indians, but Johnny comforts her with the information that he goes out every morning and "shoots a couple before breakfast." In a similar vein, in *The Frontiersman* (1938), Lucky Jenkins (Russell Hayden) tells the girl he is escorting on a buggy ride that they live near an Indian reservation but that she should not worry: "Every now and then young bucks come round and scalp and kill a few people and we have to run 'em back," he tells her. Comfortingly he adds: "Nothing very exciting ever happens here."

Silent but intense was the all-pervasive influence of whiteness. The world may contain a variety of peoples, but, for all we knew, the only people who mattered were reflections of ourselves. And we were, without doubt and without thought, white. We were also without blemish; normalcy was white and without visible disability. Disability often appears in these films in the form of a man in a wheelchair who invariably is a villain pretending to be disabled. Our heroes are the standard for normalcy. They are men devoutly to be emulated. The cliché that the cowboy hero wore a white hat and rode a white horse carried some truth as fact and a great deal of truth as metaphor. The three most popular cowboy heroes of the late 1940s and early '50s were Gene Autry, Roy Rogers, and Hopalong Cassidy. Gene and Roy wore the requisite white hat, although neither rode a white horse (Roy's palomino, Trigger, was of course a gesture toward whiteness). Both wore pistols with noticeably white handles. Hoppy, in contrast to Gene and Roy, wore black. But he rode a white horse and he sported a head of white hair that forcefully reminded us that underneath the outer black this guy was as white as they come. Good guys are white. Often in these movies we hear the phrase "That's mighty white of you," when one fellow thanks another for some kindness (e.g., *Boiling Point*, 1932; *Renegade Trail*, 1939; *False Colors*, 1943; *Corpus Christi Bandits*, 1945). White is the colour of value, and white means Anglo-Saxon male good-guy. The heroes are white and so too are the good sheriffs, most of the sidekicks, the kindly ranchers, good state governors, and other males who are on the side of right. And right means the good old-fashioned American values of order and independence and individuality and free enterprise. Those who are not white are representatives of villainy or else in need of paternal assistance and protection—women and children, harmless Mexicans or primitive native peoples, and, sometimes, Chinese or black people. But however we categorize characters who are not "white," they are the colonized, those who are in need of the paternal embrace of whiteness.

We can locate the colonial aspect of the B western in its treatment of minority characters and women and children. But a few of these films give us a direct view of American colonial activity: *Round-up Time in Texas* (1937), *Kansas Terrors* (1939), *Outlaws of the Desert* (1941), and *Law of the Pampas* (1939). In an earlier chapter I mentioned the "imperialist tendencies" in three of these four films. In each film, the cowboy hero and his companions sort out problems in foreign countries. In *Outlaws of the Desert*, Hopalong Cassidy and his sidekicks travel to "Arabia" to buy horses. There they meet conniving thieves and a dangerous desert sheik dubbed a "half-breed." They also meet the English-educated (read: good) Sheik Suleiman, played by Duncan Renaldo. Hoppy tells this sheik how to do away with his enemy by using an old Apache trick—pretend that everyone in camp is asleep and unaware and then catch the baddies as they attack. Hoppy proves to be smarter than the desert rats and, by implication, smarter than the Apaches from whom he stole (and therefore presumably was never victimized by) this trick. The references to a "half-breed" and the Apache equate the Bedouins of the desert with Native Americans, and both groups find their betters in the white man as exemplified by Hoppy.

Interestingly, Otherness in this film includes not only "Arabians" and Native Americans but also women. The connection between women and other minority groups dates back at least to the eighteenth century. In *Outlaws of the Desert*, Susan Grant (Jean Philips), the daughter of the wealthy rancher Charles Grant (Forrest Stanley), who accompanies Hoppy to Arabia, is headstrong and immature. In one scene, Hoppy's young sidekick Johnny (Brad King) spanks her, and Mr. Grant shakes Johnny's hand for dealing so well with his recalcitrant daughter. Nothing, however, exposes the film's equation of the female with the Other in its orientalist guise as well as the final scene. Here Hoppy's elderly sidkick, California, wears tin plates over his breast in mimicry of an exotic brassiere, and he attempts to perform an erotic Arabian dance. The film is as good an example of what Edward Said calls "orientalism" as we could find.

America's colonialist interests often turn toward Mexico in these films. One film may serve as an example: *Below the Border* (1942), from Monogram's Rough Riders series. In this film, the Rough Riders come to the aid of a Mexican rancher, Colonel José Garcia, and his daughter, Rosita (Linda Brent). The rancher is ill and unable to take care of his ranch. Rustlers are stealing his cattle, and the same gang steals the family jewels. Somehow the pun must surface when we reflect that the father is ill (i.e., emasculated). The gang blackmails Joe Collins (Dennis Moore), ranch hand and fiancé of Rosita, effectively emasculating him too. The gang's leader is Blackie Slade (Charles King), but the real boss of the outlaws is the local saloon owner, Scully (Roy Barcroft). As usual, the Rough Riders go under cover to ferret out the outlaws and their leader. Buck Roberts (Buck Jones) plays a crook on the lam named John Robbins, who is a fence for stolen goods. Tim McCall (Tim McCoy) masquerades as a cattle buyer. Sandy Hopkins (Raymond Hatton) mops the floor in Scully's saloon and generally skulks around.

Dennis Moore's character, Joe, is in love with Rosita, but he needs rehabilitation by the Rough Riders before he can be worthy of the girl. Of course the Rough Riders sort things out and restore order below the border. The ineffectiveness of the Mexican authorities is made clear in the scene in which Blackie Slade, a known criminal whose picture is on wanted posters on both sides of the border, speaks with a Mexican border guard without fear of being recognized. Things will go awry below the border until three good men from America arrive to straighten them out. At the end of the film, the Rough Riders return to their home turf, leaving Joe behind to marry Rosita. Mexicans are okay when they are beautiful or ill or in need of American assistance. With a reinvigorated Joe—no longer emasculated by the gang of villains, and a permanent fixture on the Mexican ranch—we can rest assured order will be maintained.

The message is always the same: real men are white and American. A remarkable scene in the otherwise unremarkable Johnny Mack Brown film *Rogue of the Range* (1936) will serve as a clear example of the inclusion of Otherness in these films. The plot has Johnny going under cover to catch a gang of stage robbers and their mysterious boss. Johnny plays Dan Doran, a gentlemanly bandit and happy-go-lucky character known as the Rogue of the Range. The word *rogue* is nice because it captures the Fiedlerian notion of the good bad boy. Dan confesses to a stage robbery in order to receive a prison sentence—something he needs in order to insinuate himself into the gang of bad guys. All along, he is working with Tom (Horace Murphy), the town sheriff. Early in the action, we watch as Dan saves a runaway carriage with a female driver named Stella (Lois January), a name that connects intertextually with *Stella Dallas*, first filmed in 1925. In the back of the wagon her father, an itinerant preacher, lies dead, but she does not know he has died. Dan does not wish to be the one to inform Stella of her father's death, so he passes the buck to the town doctor, and from then on Dan goes out of his way to help Stella without her knowing that he is her benefactor. His anonymous support tells us he is a good man, kind to women, and of course an upholder of the law. His attention to Stella's welfare tests the mettle of the other girl in Dan's life, the dance-hall girl Tess (Phyllis Hume), who loves Dan. Both Tess and the viewer of the film think Dan wishes to marry Stella; however, this is not the case. He really loves Tess, and he proposes to her at the end of the film.

The film contains nothing out of the ordinary. We have our hero, the two young women who serve as his possible love interest, a kindly sheriff, and bad guys. We do not have Native Americans or Mexicans or children or any other minority (aside from women) represented among the cast of characters. And because the film is so empty of Otherness, the scene that I examine below is all the more remarkable. It stands out as a reminder of how forcefully present Otherness is and how important the figure of the Other is to the meaning of the hero and his white masculinity. The hero could not be a hero without the presence of the Other. This Other is not necessarily a minority figure, although minorities offer the most visible presence of Otherness. To be Other is to be that which, by providing contrast, allows us to see the hero in all his whiteness. If the Other is a hypocrite, then the hero is honest; if the Other is a coward, then the hero is intrepid; if the Other is weak and vacillating, then the hero is strong and resolute. We could extend this list, but the point is that the Other is other than the hero. Often the chief villain in the B western is a pillar of the community—a successful lawyer, a well-dressed businessman, a gentleman rancher, or a politician. He is, in other words, a counterpart to the hero, who usually is a drifter, a man of the open range. The villain's ruffian henchmen are more visible examples of Otherness, often hirsute and scruffy, and sometimes racially coded as Indian or Mexican or French Canadian. Foreignness is a feature of Otherness, and films of the 1940s often present villains who are German. Xenophobia and patriotism ride the range. As Tom Sullivan puts it: "The standards of proper behavior suggested by the image of the cowboy were used to judge the behavior of others, women, or ... people from other countries or other cultures" (46).

Midway through *The Rogue of the Range*, an itinerant fabric salesman shows up. This man is obviously Jewish. He is a salesperson and speaks in a discernibly Eastern European accent. He has a beard and small cap. He passes by a café, the Golden Nugget (run by Tess and Stella), and smells breakfast cooking. He looks in through the window and sees Tess slicing ham. He twists his face in disgust and walks away but at the same time smacks his lips. But he can't resist. He returns to the café and asks for "some of that." Tess asks him if he is sure he wants what she is slicing, and he replies yes. Scene over. The joke is on Jews and pork. (One of the customers in the café actually asks for "some of that hog" to underline what is going on.)

This scene with the Jewish salesman is a throwaway. Its function is to add a bit of humour, to make a joke about ethnicity. The Jew is presented in stereotypical fashion as a retail salesperson. His accent places him as a foreigner in America. Most likely itinerant drummers did appear in western towns during the frontier period and perhaps even afterwards. But this character and this anecdote add nothing to the plot. The humour is nasty, presenting the Jew as a hypocrite. We know Jews are not supposed to eat pork, and we know this Jew knows he is not supposed to eat pork (the look on his face registers his disgust). But his hunger and the look of the meat and presumably the aroma emanating from the Golden Nugget enable him to overcome his scruples and beliefs. He allows desire to override principle; he could, after all, have ordered something other than bacon for breakfast.

We might leave the joke here, but the implications of what we see demand further consideration. If this man is a hypocrite, how can we trust him in business? We judge men by how they do business; this is clear in film after film. One of the most familiar villains in these films is the banker, the businessman par excellence. In fact, the banker is the villain in this film. The banker is, by association, as untrustworthy as the Jew. He is a moneylender, a usurer. He works his villainy by gaining the trust of others, and then he swindles them. He does not himself carry out the acts of robbery, but he controls them. He insinuates himself into the public trust and ensures that the public desires that which he has to offer. In *Rogue of the Range*, the only difference between the banker and the Jew is in degree of visibility. The Jew can hide neither his Jewishness nor his hypocrisy; the banker, however, eludes the eyes of the law until the hero uncovers him. In the case of the Jew, the camera does the uncovering. It places the viewer in a position of superiority over the Jew; we see how duplicitous he is. Like the hero, the viewer sees clearly: we see through artifice and hypocrisy. The viewer sees both the hero and the other characters that populate the screen, and these various characters, as Christian Metz has argued, are collectively the viewer's imaginary. Metz's Lacanian reading of the cinema allows us to see how the characters on the screen function as Imaginary Others. The bad guys and visible minorities are the Imaginary Others who confirm our own sense of superiority, our sense that we are important and right and secure. Otherness serves to convince us of the strength and security of our identity as white and strong and pure.

But this figure of the Other is unimaginable without that *other* Other: the good guy. The hero is our Imaginary, our Ideal-I. Heroes 'R' us. The catch is, of course, that the hero is us only in imaginary space. Film, like the unconscious, flashes before us like a moving mirror in which we see reflected visions of our desire—that which we desire to be and that which we desire not to be. The formulaic series western appealed to boys like me because our compulsion to repeat the experience of seeing the good guy chase the bad guy was necessary to our sense of ourselves; we required repetition of the experience because who we were was so elusive and out of reach. Maybe if we see one more cowboy catching one more bad guy, we will know for certain that we are the hero and that desire will be satisfied. Repeated viewing reflects the lure of desire, and each viewing can only leave us asking for more. Each viewing shows us that which we desire and consequently that which we lack.

Let me offer another example. In *Billy the Kid's Fighting Pals* (a.k.a. *Trigger Men*, 1941), one of the six films for PRC in which Bob Steele plays Billy the Kid, we have another throwaway scene in which the comical sidekick Fuzzy (Al St. John) tries to work a printing press. Fuzzy is inept and he gets printer's ink all over his face. In blackface he resembles the conventional Jim Crow image of the black man with big eyes and white lips. Seeing his black reflection in a mirror, Fuzzy gets a stick and smashes the mirror. Then, as he bends over the printing press, the villainous Badger (Charles King) and another bad guy enter the newspaper office. Fuzzy assumes a dialect and acts the part of a "darkie" (the villain uses the word). He tries to fool Badger and the other guy into thinking he is in fact a darkie. But the two bad guys see through the disguise and Fuzzy flees to the jail, where he manages to capture Badger, who had run after him with such speed that his momentum carries him straight into a cell. Billy arrives and calls Fuzzy "Uncle Tom" and "Mammy." The schtick turns on the cowardly black guy who runs from trouble and succeeds in spite of himself. The episode could have taken place without the blackface; the use of blackface is a gratuitous racial joke, not dissimilar to the joke about Jews in *The Rogue of the Range*. A similar thoughtless racism appears at the end of *Bury Me Not in the Lone Prairie* (1941) when Lem Fielding (Fuzzy Knight) inadvertently discharges his flintlock rifle and receives a face full of powder. When he sits up after falling, he appears in blackface and mutters: "Well, shut my mouth." There the film ends.

In *Billy the Kid's Fighting Pals*, just before Fuzzy works himself into blackface over the printing press, he complains that the first sheet he has printed is upside down. He adds, "Even a Chinaman couldn't read it." I am not sure of the logic behind this joke, but once again the film tosses off a racial slur. We are reminded that the film takes place, as so many of these films do, near the border with Mexico. The plot, such as it is, involves the banker having a tunnel to Mexico dug so he can smuggle stuff across the border; his intention is to own the whole town so he can do as he pleases. The allusion is to the megalomaniac dictator engaging in war in Europe at the time. The banker's desire to monopolize town business also reflects the American fear of Big Business—or what was then the American fear of Big Business. The bartender in the local saloon, a Mexican, turns out to be a law officer from below the border sent to investigate the smuggling operation. He has no part in catching the bad guys; his presence does little more than to underline the competence of the good white guys. Once again, the Mexicans benefit from American know-how and expertise.

The B western is, by definition, a narrative of imperialism—the settling and taming of the wild west. The hero confronts several types of Otherness—women, the racial Other, and the child. If the camera serves as our eye, and if what it sees is a projection of our desire, then the child who appears in so many of these films is clearly one aspect of the Imaginary Other we see reflected on the screen. Both boys and girls appear regularly as characters who either require the assistance of the hero or provide the hero with assistance. Obviously, the young boy or girl who comes to the aid of the hero is a function of the viewer's desire. Boys appear more often than girls in the role of helper, and, when they do assist the hero, they are indicators that the hero passes along his stalwart characteristics to the younger generation. If boys onscreen can ride and shoot and even outwit bad guys, then boys who view these films can fantasize that they too can do these things. If boys onscreen follow the hero's trail, then so too, in fantasy, can boys who watch the films. The hero serves as mentor and guide; this is why so many of the cowboy heroes had codes or rules to pass on to their young fans. But always the children in these films remain gathered into the fold of the hero's influence and protection. Those Three Mesquiteers films that contain orphanages—*Roarin' Lead* (1936), *Riders of the Black Hills* (1938; in which a children's hospital figures), *Heroes of the Saddle* (1940)—make it clear that children are vulnerable and weak. They require the tutelage and protection of men who represent the masculine values of order, justice, and the American way. These children, like the children who watch the films, are eager to accept the ground rules set out or represented by the older man who carries himself with authority and competence.

Sometimes children appear in films that express xenophobia, and when this happens the films reinforce the difference between white children who will form the next generation and the impurity that enters Western society with the arrival of the foreigner. Take *Tex Rides with the Boy Scouts* (1937), for example. Early in this film, Tex and one of his sidekicks, Stubby (Horace Murphy), ride to town, where Stubby takes his shirt to the Sing Fong Laundry. Stubby runs into difficulty with Sing Fong (Philip Ahn), who refuses to return Stubby's shirt unless he can produce his laundry ticket. Sing Fong is the stereotypical Chinese person who says such things as "No tickee, no washee." The Chinese laundry is also the place where the bad guy, Stark (Charlie King), comes to exchange his gold chip (not a nugget—a clue for Tex that Charlie is a member of the gang that robbed the train) for money. In other words, the laundry serves as a convenient fence for contraband: this place of business launders more than clothing. The Chinese fellow is obviously a usurer. He drives a hard bargain. He haggles with Stubby when Stubby tries to trade his watch fob for the gold chip (as a ruse to obtain the chip as evidence). Sing Fong wants cash as well as the watch fob. Stubby haggles and manages to reduce the price from $20 to $10. But we know that Stubby gets the raw end of the deal and that Sing Fong conducts his business in a less than completely honest manner.

Like Mexicans, Chinese people turn up as bad guys as in *Border Devils* (1932), in which the head bad guy appears to be a mysterious Chinese person who lurks behind a curtain to give his orders to the gang. But this inscrutable Asian is controlled by a white man who uses the Chinese man as a cover for his own nefarious ends. When foreign persons appear as bad guys, they serve as covers for the real source of villainy: the greed of American big-business interests as represented by Big Cattlemen, Big Bankers, Big Railroad Companies, Big Dam Builders, Big Politicians, Big Mine Owners, Big Philanthropists, and so on. As long as the ends of American imperialism are served by little businessmen—as represented by the cowboy hero who, ostensibly at least, holds certain abstract values in higher esteem than he does filthy lucre—we can laud American ingenuity and enterprise and independence. Once we are certain of the strength of the American hero, the foreign person comes under his patronage, as in *The Gay Buckaroo* (1932). In this film our hero, Hoot Gibson, has a Chinese cook who spouts Eastern wisdom as easily as Charlie Chan. Or the foreign person takes part in the entrepreneurial spirit of America by running a laundry or a restaurant (see *Carson City Kid*, 1940). In films such as *The Gay Buckaroo* and *Carson City Kid* we see the paternalistic side of the American masculine spirit. Here Chinese people come under the embrace of the American male, but in many westerns it is the black person, often played by black actors such as Fred Toones (a.k.a. "Snowflake") in *Riders of the Black Hills* (1938), *Haunted Ranch* (1943), and *Bells of San Angelo* (1947), or Blue Washington in *Parade of the West* (1930), *Haunted Gold* (1932), and *Smoking Guns* (1934). Interestingly, Washington does not appear among the list of players in any of these films in Phil Hardy's *The Western: The Complete Film Sourcebook* (1983), although in at least one of them, *Haunted Gold*, with John Wayne, he plays the hero's sidekick.

The inclusion of Chinese men, Mexicans, Native Americans, and black men in the B western reinforces stereotypes that define masculinity as white and American. Indeed, white and American become, tacitly, synonymous. The connection often made between the non-white person and white villainy works to suggest that any form of masculinity that deviates from the hegemonic variety exemplified by the hero must be foreign. Foreignness is any deviation from the normal American male who is strong, upright, honest, and, often, sexily sexless. The only exceptions to this rule of manliness are those "foreigners" who appeal to the hero's sense of protection and the comic sidekicks who are reminders that heroism can safely be parodied and that such parody is only a reminder that the hero is, after all, human.

Perhaps I can explain the point about villainy and foreignness with one example: *Renegades of Sonora* (1948). This film offers a yarn about a turn-of-the-century bad guy who attempts to reopen the Indian wars of a decade or so earlier. This bad man is Keeler (Roy Barcroft), and the film's opening scene shows Keeler and a henchman waiting to ambush two Indians, one wearing a full-feathered bonnet. Keeler shoots both Indians in cold blood and then loots their bodies to find a belt. This is a sacred Indian holy belt. Keeler informs his henchman that the Indians see this belt as their "idol." The henchman rides away with the belt and Keeler returns to his respectable job as a freight agent. He receives word that the henchman has been captured and the belt retrieved. Keeler wants war between Indian and white people, and so this news is not good, since the belt is being passed to the local Indian agent so he can convey it to the new chief (Keeler has killed the old chief). Cut to a lone rider, the courier, returning the belt. Four baddies appear and give chase, shooting all the while. Now our hero appears: Rocky Lane. Rocky shoots three of these guys, but the courier takes a bullet, too. He dies, but not before exacting a promise from Rocky to deliver the belt.

Rocky brings the belt to the town and to the Indian agency. There he gives the belt to a guy who is visibly nervous, continually touching his throat. Later we learn that Keeler once saved this guy from a hangman's noose. But for now Rocky notices nothing untoward. He gives the belt to this nervous man and leaves. An elderly cowhand named Nugget Clark (Eddie Waller) watches Rocky go, and then enters the agency and finds the dead body of the real Indian agent. Nugget fetches the sheriff and a chase ensues. The sheriff and posse go after Rocky, the presumed killer. Rocky can outwit them, but he does not do this, since he has no idea why they are chasing him. He is arrested and put in jail. After some palaver, he escapes and goes after the guy he gave the belt to (whom he has seen out the jail window). Once again, the sheriff and Nugget dutifully give chase. Rocky finally convinces Nugget to accompany him to the farm of the man Rocky is chasing. They go and are greeted by bullets. This greeting convinces the old cowhand that Rocky is on the level.

Rocky and his new friend Nugget go back to town to get the belt from Keeler, whom they now know to be the brains behind the whole thing. But Rocky has to tread carefully. He tells his friend to listen at the freight-shed window to hear Keeler implicate himself. Rocky enters, gets caught, successfully encourages Keeler to blabber, convinces Keeler to take him into the gang, but then Nugget is caught too and the jig is up. The villains tie up Rocky and friend and take them out to the country, where they plan to shoot them. While the two baddies debate which one should get Blackjack (Rocky's horse) after they kill Rocky, Blackjack unties Rocky. A fight ensues, fists fly, and Rocky gets the better of the baddies. The denouement quickly follows. Rocky and his friend, along with the sheriff and his men, round up Keeler, this after a fist fight between Rocky and Keeler. The Sheriff asks Rocky to stay and be Indian agent. He demurs (he's got to be on his driftin' way), but he suggests his old pal, Nugget, will make a good one. Rocky is on his way to Wyoming, where he says he will buy a spread and settle down. Not likely.

I have summarized the plot in detail to indicate the relative unimportance of the Indians in this film whose plot turns on the possession of a sacred Indian relic. They make but a brief appearance onscreen. And they are not the conventional savage Indians of so many early westerns. We are supposed to sympathize with them in their helplessness; they are childlike and ineffective in protecting themselves. As Sullivan asserts, Native Americans appear in the westerns "as savages or as children untutored in the ways of progress and civilization" (50). In *Renegades of Sonora,* they are children. Other films make the same point explicitly: *'Neath Arizona Skies* (1934) has a youthful John Wayne playing guardian to a young Indian girl who is heir to land rich with oil. Nothing, literally, is made of the Native American element in the plot, and we never learn why Wayne is helping the girl. The same plot device, in which an Indian child is protected by the hero, is used in the Red Ryder series, in the figure of Little Beaver. Most famous of all, of course, is Tonto, the faithful sidekick of the Lone Ranger. Tonto may be an adult, but he functions in much the same way as the child and other childlike Native Americans in so many of these films.

Sometimes Native Americans serve as figures of the mysterious primitive who practises arcane rites. Perhaps the most bizarre example of this occurs in *Hidden Valley* (1932), an early Bob Steele western. In this film, a lost tribe of Indians prays to the Goodyear blimp. Bob Harding (Bob Steele) is on an expedition with a professor. They look for a hidden valley in which a long-lost tribe of Indians is supposed to have opals and other gems. Right away we see that the expedition is not strictly anthropological. Their Indian guide (Artie Ortego, uncredited), fearing to enter the mysterious valley, leaves them soon after the film's beginning. Then they meet a prospector named McCord (V.L. Barnes). Bob goes off to get wood for a fire. Shots ring out. Bob returns to find the professor murdered. A nearby prospector thinks Bob is the murderer and hands him over to the law. At the trial, Bob is found guilty, but he crashes through a window and escapes the courthouse. Later, the sheriff reads letters he has received from people who claim to have spotted the fugitive as a stowaway on a boat, disguised as a "negra," and so on. The film also boasts the familiar brother-and-sister tandem—sis in love with the unjustly accused hero, and the brother who, despite his good intentions, falls in with criminals. A posse chases Bob, as do the bad guys. Bob flees and rides over a cliff. Later, Bob's horse goes down in the desert and he has to shoot it. The brother, meanwhile, who had departed to find the hidden valley on his own, finds it—only to be taken prisoner by a horde of whooping Indians, who prepare to make a human sacrifice of him. Bob finds a water hole, guarded by a deputy. He pretends to be out cold after falling off a cliff but comes alive and knocks the deputy out and takes the deputy's horse. Whereupon everyone ends up in Hidden Valley, including the girl, who has hitched a ride in an old friend's blimp (actually the Goodyear blimp). A rope ladder is dropped from the blimp, and Bob and the brother escape by climbing it. The Indians capture the four bad guys, and we can guess how they will be treated.

A similar presentation of Native people as primitives in the now pejorative sense appears in *Riders of the Whistling Skull* (1937). This film is about a search for a lost city, Luka Chukai, where our heroes find strange rites and walking mummies. The professors and the women who travel with them wear pith helmets, reminding us of so many pictures of African safaris. One of the anthropologists on the expedition, Professor Cleary (Earle Ross), calls the Native people "ignorant, dirty savages," and later Stony Brooke (Robert Livingston) finds what are supposedly Indian hieroglyphics, which, he remarks, signify a "cult of religious fanatics." Stony worries that these "fanatics" will carry out some ugly ritual with the captured white woman, Betty Marsh (Mary Russell). At one point, someone calls these Indians "Anastasias," a reminder of the Anasazi who disappeared in the American Southwest a couple of centuries ago. The main villains are a man named Rutledge (Roger Williams), a half-breed Indian agent and his Indian cohort (played by a white man, Yakima Canutt). The Native American actor Chief Thundercloud plays the Indians' high priest, and somewhere among the extras is Iron Eyes Cody, proving that Native Americans do indeed get to play Native Americans, sort of.

Another feature of the Natives in this film is their libidinous nature. One of the women anthropologists, Henrietta (Fern Emmett), remarks of a male specimen of Native people: "What a primitive masculine Indian." Clearly, her libido finds arousal in this "primitive" specimen, and she turns her attention to the much safer Lullaby Joslin (Max Terhune). Sex rarely rears its head in the B western, and when it does we can rest assured that it will appear only obliquely. The white male cowboy hero, as Fiedler noted about the American hero generally, is chaste and free of the taint of sex. Rarely do we see men without shirts in these westerns, except when they are boxing or when they are Natives on the warpath. The bare white male torso appears so seldom that it stands out when we do see it. And we see it in *Riders of the Whistling Skull*. Late in the film, Tucson Smith (Ray "Crash" Corrigan) uses a rope to climb down a cliff. An Indian cuts the rope above him and Tucson falls, tearing his shirt; he rips off his rag of a shirt and we see him run and ride and fight shirtless for some time. At the end of the film, we see two of the three Mesquiteers—Stony and Lullaby— with women. Stony has Betty on his arm and Lullaby, wearing a white suit and pith helmet, is with Henrietta. But Tucson is by himself, reading *Detective* magazine. The sexed male must not appear in a situation that will remind us of the physical fact of sexuality. We look at Tucson's bare torso only as an example of masculine beauty and strength, the strength that the white male needs to quell the libidinous forces of the Other.

A similar coding of the Other as libidinous occurs in the 1934 Bob Steele western *A Demon for Trouble* (a remake of the 1932 Ken Maynard film *Arizona Terror*). Here Bob encounters a woman sunbathing. She quickly puts on her robe, but her action draws attention to the possible erotic effect of her posing in a swimsuit. The erotic theme finds reinforcement later in the film when Bob moves in with the Mexican bandit, Galindo (Don Alvarado), and his lover, Carmen (Carmen LaRoux). Carmen takes a fancy to Bob and flirts with him and makes it clear that she wants to take him to bed. Carmen is a sex-driven woman, and Bob has to insist that he loves another woman and that he is Galindo's friend. Carmen, however, does not take no for an answer, at least not without pressing herself on the desiring and desirable young Bob. *Mexican* is synonymous with sexuality in this film, just as it will be, later, in the two series of Cisco Kid films starring Duncan Renaldo and Gilbert Roland (Monogram, 1945–47). *A Demon for Trouble* ends with Galindo and Carmen riding away together, while Bob and his sweetheart remain north of the border. The randy couple travels south; the chaste couple stays in America.

The B westerns of the 1930s deal with sexuality in an explicit manner that disappears in the flashier films of the 1940s, when the target audience became more clearly identified with children. For example, in *Between Men* (1935), John Wellington (William Farnum) is a Virginia blacksmith and a single father. His wife is dead and his son has a terrible burn on his chest. Sir George Thorn (Lloyd Ingraham) has a daughter who leaves home with a man named Gentry (Frank Ball); some say, insinuating impropriety, that she has to get married. Wellington fights three men who cast aspersions on her. During the fight, one man pulls a gun and shoots John, Jr. Thinking his son is dead, Wellington picks up the gun and shoots one of the fighters and runs after the others. He is not heard from in Virginia again. He turns up in Arizona as a rancher by the name of Rand. Living nearby is Gentry, now under the name Winters, and the daughter, Gayle (Beth Marion), who was born to Sir George's daughter. This daughter/mother is now dead. Meanwhile John, Jr. (Johnny Mack Brown), survives the gunshot and grows up as ward of Sir George, and when he is an adult he decides to travel west to search for Sir George's granddaughter.

Out in Arizona, Trent (Earl Dwire), who works for Rand, has eyes for Gayle, but her father (Gentry/Winters) sends him packing. The film is noteworthy for its clear presentation of men's brutish desires. Trent wants to ravish Gayle. At one point, two of Rand's other men chase Gayle with the clear intention of raping her. A montage of scenes shows Johnny as he courts Gayle. The final fight between Rand and Johnny, necessary for the revelation of paternity, results in Johnny bare-chested. The father sees the scar on Johnny's chest and recognizes him as his son but does not reveal his true identity. The significance of the film's title likely lies in Gayle's situation between men: between Gentry and Sir George, between Trent and Rand, between men who want to rape her and men who want to protect her.

Sexuality in these films is usually associated with non-white American characters or foreigners—Mexicans and French Canadians. But the white American cowboy, especially as he evolves into the singing cowboy (Gene Autry, Roy Rogers, Eddie Dean, Monte Hale, Dusty King, and others), avoids sex with the same self-consciousness and assiduity with which he avoids alcohol. The absence of overt sexuality in the majority of B westerns with white heroes is thrown into relief by the brief series of black westerns made in the late 1930s with Herbert Jefferies. *Two-Gun Man from Harlem* (1940) is an amazing black western that differs from the white films in its overt sexuality. The plot turns on an adulterous love affair. The bad guy seduces the willing wife, Mrs. Ruth Steel (Mae Turner). Her husband, the rancher John Steel (Tom Southern), is the hero's boss. Caught *in flagrante delicto*, the bad guy shoots the woman's husband. When the hero, Bob Blake (Herbert Jefferies), comes running, the wife surreptitiously exchanges his gun for the murder weapon and then testifies that he, Blake, is the murderer. He flees in a montage of shots that see him hitching rides north, first to Chicago and then to Harlem, where we see him in a nightspot listening to jazz.

Back at the ranch, the bad guy has the wife kidnapped. He plans to have her killed so she cannot rat on him. Blake returns disguised as a notorious bad guy called the Deacon. This hero-in-disguise is the two-gun man from Harlem, wearing two gats under his long black coat. (Blake apparently killed the real Deacon in a fight over the Deacon's girl, back in Harlem. Sex pervades the film.) Blake/Deacon joins the bad guys' gang and eventually sorts things out. It is worth noting that Blake's/Deacon's treatment of the good girl, Sally Thompson (Margaret Whitten), the girl whom Blake will end up with, is harsh and even violent. He shouts at her and also manhandles her. Sex and violence go together in these films. I note also that the fights in the film are photographed with many close-ups that focus on fist striking jaw. We might argue that the sexuality and violence derive from a black culture that manifests such themes in its music. I think of blues songs such as "Stag-o-Lee" or "Frankie and Johnny."

Phil Hardy asserts that another of these black westerns, *Harlem Rides the Range* (1939), despite being a "routine film," illustrates the "inflexibility of the genre." He goes on: "though written by blacks, the film aped white westerns totally and was far removed from black interests" (92). Another Jefferies western, *Harlem on the Prairie* (1937), Hardy says, "is played entirely straight" (70). The black westerns appear to reinforce stereotypes of the black person, as Leab notes in his comments on *Harlem Rides the Range* (174). But *Two-Gun Man from Harlem* strikes me as distinctly different from the more familiar white westerns. Imagine a young black male watching a film such as *Two-Gun Man from Harlem* in the late 1930s. Seeing a black person riding, shooting, and fighting with confidence and control must have been revelatory. Julia Leyda, in "Black-Audience Westerns and the Politics of Cultural Identification in the 1930s," argues for the crucial importance of these films for a black audience, especially an audience of young African Americans. The emergence of the black person from black stereotype—what the *BFI Companion* terms "the eye-rolling, necrophobic Negro" (Buscombe, 69)—is perhaps coded in the character played by Mantan Moreland. Moreland features in many non-westerns of the period (notably as Charlie Chan's driver in several films with the Chinese detective), and he invariably plays the buffoon. In *Two-Gun Man from Harlem*, however, Moreland plays the cook and the hero's pal. In the final shot of the film, he takes off his apron and emerges into independence.

I suspect the changes in these westerns occurred progressively. Hardy's reading of the films is insensitive to the cultural context, and his use of the word *aped* is insensitive and inappropriate. We might consider too the context in which these films were made—with a director (Richard C. Kahn, who also wrote the scripts) and crew consisting of white people and a production company operated by white people (Hollywood Pictures Corporation, Merit Pictures).

A later film in this series, *The Bronze Buckaroo* (1939), is more conventional than *Two-Gun Man from Harlem*. It disturbs in its sadistic violence and its presentation of the black person as gullible and simple. One character is fooled into thinking a donkey talks, and in a saloon scene a bad guy makes someone smoke three cigars simultaneously and another fellow drink three drinks simultaneously without dropping an ash or a drop of liquor. Later the bad guys use a branding iron to make a character talk. The violence and sexuality of these films suggests questions. Why was this series as short-lived as it was? How do these films work historically? For whom were they made? The conventional answer to the last question is that these were films made for black audiences and played at what Daniel J. Leab terms "Jim Crow theaters" (180; see also Merlock and Nachbar, 58). But Hardy observes that *Harlem on the Prairie* "was surprisingly successful in non-ethnic theatres, grossing some $50,000 in its first year of distribution" (70). If this is true, we might see the growing audacity of these films as one reason they were short-lived. What is becoming apparent by 1940 and the release of *Two-Gun Man from Harlem* is that these films parody the white westerns. But *parody* is perhaps too soft a word. We might see the violence and sexuality as monstrous, and, if so, these films constitute a sort of teratology. The twist is that the monstrousness revealed by these films is the white cowboy whose monstrousness lies hidden behind all that whiteness. The black westerns show what lies just below the surface of the white westerns.

One other black western appeared before the B western disappeared in the early 1950s, *Look-Out Sister* (1947), a film that is mostly an excuse for a series of loosely-held-together musical numbers. The star of this film is Louis Jordan, a saxophone player and singer who had many R&B hits in the 1940s and '50s. In the film, Louis' doctors order him to rest from touring, and we find him in a rest home where Billy (Glenn Allen), a young boy on crutches, asks him to tell stories about cowboys. Talk of cowboys results in Jordan's falling asleep and dreaming of a holiday dude ranch for sick children, but in the dream the ranch hosts no children except for the one on crutches, who is instrumental in foiling the bad guy. This kid teaches Louis, the nominal hero, to shoot, and this is how they discover the shenanigans. The plot, such as it is, involves a crook trying to gain control of the holiday ranch because it has oil on it. Two-Gun Jordan is really rather inept as a cowboy and this is part of the fun. The film burlesques the white singing-cowboy B westerns by pointing up those films' reliance on music and on their function as fantasies for boys. The hero requires the aid of a boy because the hero is, in effect, a boy himself—at least he imagines himself playing boys' cowboy games.

Harlem on the Prairie, the first of the black westerns, appeared in 1937, and its producer was Jed Buell. In 1938, Buell produced another western, one that remains infamous in film history. The film is *The Terror of Tiny Town*, a western with an all-midget cast. This film makes clear the monstrousness of the conventional B western and the smallness of the manly hero. The film contains several jokes that turn on someone's being the "biggest man in the territory," and the irony about inversion—the small person being big and the big person being small—is apparent. Tiny Town is a euphemism for the fake towns, the partial towns, that are in reality Hollywood backlots and sound stage sets or perhaps a few buildings on someone's ranch outside of Los Angeles, and the true terror of this tiny town is the masculinity that appears benign but disguises violence and libidinous energy of a rather basic sort. This film is all about artificiality and performance. The opening scene—on a stage with two actors and a master of ceremonies in front of a curtain discussing the film—sets the tone of self-conscious artifice.

The Terror of Tiny Town is a western send-up. It has just about everything we might expect in a western: feuding ranchers set against each other by an unscrupulous bad guy who wants both ranches and the niece of one of the ranchers, a runaway stagecoach stopped by the hero on white horse (in this case, a Shetland pony), saloon gals singing, a corrupt sheriff, an attempted mob lynching, a good guy escaping bad guys by hiding behind a rock as they ride by, cattle rustling and altered brands, a bare-chested blacksmith, a woman-beating bad guy, and a foreign cook (is he Italian, Swedish, or German?). The barbershop scene is a key to the film. In it, the notion of the traditional all-male, all-white barbershop quartet is upended, as here the performing unit consist of five people, of both genders and two races: three white barbers, a white woman, and a black person. The vision of this group in *The Terror of Tiny Town* suggests absurdity, satire, and dislocation, partly because of the other characters in the barbershop. In this scene a fellow reading a newspaper looks distinctly like a child, but when he sings it is with a deep, mature male voice. Also in this scene is shot of a penguin. Here is a throwaway shot that works a bit like the Jew in *The Rogue of the Range*. Why a penguin? The penguin reminds us of the animal behind the man. But of course a penguin is a flightless bird, its inability to fly perhaps signalling the hero's inability to fulfill every manly function. Is flightlessness a form of emasculation?

The world this film conjures is artificial and monstrous. In this world, a bartender drains—twice—a glass of beer as big as his head. The hero and his girlfriend sing a song about Jack and Jill, and this same song is performed by various characters in the saloon. The song is a reminder of both the nursery quality of this film and the cowboys in it, and a reminder too that sexuality is inherent in a west where men are men and women are willing and waiting. The monsters here are not the midgets but the characters they represent, especially the hegemonic male white hero of the B westerns. The emphasis here is on a masculinity that drips testosterone and yet remains stunted and immature. The cowboys are boys playing men. These men are half-men.

In this film, everyone is a stranger in town. When we see the characters walk under hitching rails and almost under swinging saloon doors,
when we see them struggling to manage their recalcitrant Shetland ponies,
when we see them scrambling to board a stagecoach, and when we see
them literally step *up* to the bar, we are aware of how awkward they are
in the spaces they occupy. If the cowboy hero in most B westerns is our
Ideal-I, our Imaginary Other, and if the villain is a reminder of the Otherness we do not desire, a stand-in for the truly Other in terms of race and
ethnicity, then all the characters in *The Terror of Tiny Town* represent
that undesirable Otherness for "big" people who view the film. The film
contains the black singer in the barbershop scene and the foreign cook
to remind us of race and ethnicity, of foreignness generally. But the message is that everyone is foreign. The masculinity that parades as hegemonic in the films of Bob Steele, Johnny Mack Brown, and the others
here looks aberrant, strange, awkward, and even misguided. After this film
and the series of Herb Jefferies westerns, the B western would not flirt
with the sexuality we see in *Between Men* or *A Demon for Trouble*, and
its violence would limit itself to confrontations between hero and bad guy
or to violence on the part of the bad guy that accentuates his villainy.

Just as the first of the black westerns and *The Terror of Tiny Town*
appeared, Monogram Pictures released *Gun Packer* (1938). In this film,
Jack Randall plays a character known variously as Jack Denton, Jack
Drake, and Trigger Smith. Jack and his trusty steed, Rusty, have a black
sidekick, Pinkie (Raymond Turner), who rides a dancing mule. The mule
sits every now and then, making for some familiar comedic moments
that poke fun at racial minorities. Although Jack and Pinkie are friends,
Pinkie seems to do all the work. At one point he rides into town leading
Rusty, and the local sheriff (Glenn Strange) locks him in jail, assuming
he has stolen the horse. How could a black person have a horse like
Rusty? At the film's end, we see Jack with the girl, Ruth Adams (Louise
Stanley), and no sign of Pinkie. Once the hero finds a girl to his liking, he
has no use (apparently) for Pinkie. Pinkie can once again become invis-
ible, out of sight. A character such as Pinkie serves to decorate space
and amuse for a while, but he is not integral to the society the films see
as valuable. His absence at the end of *Gun Packer* should remind us just
how callous and insensitive people such as Jack are. The offhand use of
the black person here is precisely what a film such as *The Terror of Tiny
Town* critiques. Space in the B western is filled with Otherness, but in fact
it has room only for normal people: white, upright, and strong.

Virgin Land
Landscape, Nature, and Masculinity

All this used to be a wilderness and now it's a garden! You must be proud.
—Mrs. Stoddart in *The Man Who Shot Liberty Valance*

[H]eroic deeds and character grow out of the western landscape and wild and unsettled nature and lead to fulfillment and happiness on the part of those protagonists who are strong and true enough to meet the challenge of lawless openness by purging the evil forces that also flourish in this environment.
—John G. Cawelti (239)

My sister recently reminded me that when we were young we used the railings on our front porch as horses and rode pell-mell through our imaginary western landscape. I remember placing a pillow over the banister upstairs in our house, securing it with a belt, and, using the cord from my nightgown for reins, galloping through my imaginary landscape. Of course, we needed no such assistance to ride around the backyards and adjacent streets as though they were the wide-open spaces, high mesas, and rocky barrens we saw in the western movies we loved. In our minds we saw the landscapes of the western films with Gene and Roy and Hoppy and the rest. Mostly, this landscape was the desert and rock country of California and Nevada that appeared in B western after B western. To this day I think of the landscape in many B westerns as "Hoppy rocks," because so many of the Hopalong Cassidy films were shot in the same rocky area in southern California. This area is most likely Lone Pine, where films such as *Somewhere in Sonora* (1933), *Blue Steel* (1934), *Hop-a-Long Cassidy* (a.k.a. *Hopalong Cassidy Enters* 1935), and several Gene Autry films were shot. I could list many locations where B westerns were filmed: Bronson Canyon, Iverson Movie Ranch, Monogram (later Melody) Ranch, Oliver Drake Ranch, Red Rock Canyon, Vasquez Rocks, Walker Ranch (all in California), and other locations in Nevada, Arizona, and elsewhere. Anyone interested can find information on these and other locations at Jerry L. Schneider's website, Movie Making Locations. Links to this site, as well as to other movie location sites, are available at the Old Corral (http://www.b-western.com). The many locations meld into one mythical place: the west. Perhaps the sense of place I am trying to explain is best indicated by the series of Rough Riders films (with Buck Jones, Tim McCoy, and Raymond Hatton) and Johnny Mack Brown films produced by Monogram Studio in the early 1940s. The opening credits appear over a panoramic shot of Monument Valley, on the Utah–Arizona border, that the studio took from John Ford's *Stagecoach* (1939). The stagecoach from that film is visible in these credit sequences. Yet none of these films, and I think I can also say no B western, was ever filmed in Monument Valley. The point is that the picture of Monument Valley signifies "the west," and this west never existed in material reality.

What mattered was the sense of a place distinct from both urban and pastoral landscapes. Western landscape at its most intense is sublime landscape, to match the sublime power of the hero. Often the films deal with cattle ranchers or sheep ranchers, and sometimes homesteaders who plant crops, but rarely do we see a landscape suited to such workaday pursuits. We do see the hill country of southern California—country that is arable, no doubt—but in the films what sticks in the memory are the often-used locations such as Bronson Canyon and Lone Pine. These locations are distinctive because of their aridity and barrenness. Films shot in Lone Pine, for example, give us a terrain of high rocks of noteworthy shapes, rounded and often phallic. This is a landscape later associated with films of Anthony Mann such as *Winchester 73* (1950) and especially *Man of the West* (1958), in which the hero confronts his adversary among the rocks. We see a similar reckoning among the rocks in Bud Boetticher's *The Tall T* (1957). In these films, landscape serves to accentuate the psychic struggle of the hero, who must face his demons and come to terms with the failures and traumas of his past. In the B western, this is landscape stripped to its essentials to mirror the morality the films champion. The hero is as strong and steadfast as the land is hard and implacable. He rides through a space removed from time and even from reality. His is a liminal zone, a place for passage, but passage that never ends. We are in the realm of fantasy, in the sense Slavoj Žižek describes in *Looking Awry* (1991, 1995). Normally, as Žižek points out, fantasy is a form in which the subject's desire is "fully satisfied" (6). For Žižek, such a view of fantasy needs to be extended to include the observation that fantasy "stages" or constructs desire itself. He articulates the idea succinctly and in italics: "*through fantasy, we learn how to desire*" (6). Learning how to desire means learning to navigate a terrain that has no end, no final satisfaction. In the B western, we see many scenes of riding—riding back and forth from town to ranch, riding from ranch to hideout, riding from hideout to town, and so on. Often we have tracking shots, especially of the hero riding. These are the only tracking shots these films use. As Žižek argues, "the usual tracking shot is obsessional, forcing us to fix on a detail" (94). Žižek is speaking about tracking shots in Hitchcock that are most often slow. In the western, however, the tracking shots are most often swift, as the camera tracks galloping horses. In the case of the tracking of the hero and his horse, the camera is often placed below the level of the horse's back, so we gaze up to the hero as he rides heroically to the rescue. We view horse and rider as Ideals devoutly to be emulated but never actualized. Shots of the hero riding illustrate the fluid connection between man and mount, the mastery of the skilled rider, the heroic stature of the hero. Further, the riding to and fro captures the impossibility of final fulfillment in these films. The fantasy is only as fantastic as its necessity. We need to repeat the performance, the performance both of the cowboy and of ourselves as psychic participants in the repeated action. That landscape is, in a very real sense, the space for fantasy. This is why young boys felt (and feel) compelled to repeat the performance of their heroes once they return from the cinema to their backyards and bedrooms.

Landscape as Fantasy

The western landscape, in other words, is a landscape of the mind rather than any specific landscape. The setting of these films is, more or less, like the setting of the traditional fairy tale: "ahistoric and acartographic" (qtd. in Tucker, 6). The same locations were used for both westerns and Tarzan films, as well as a variety of serials with modern and exotic settings, and what these locations lacked in naturalistic detail, the Hollywood designers and set makers provided. Republic Studios had its manmade caves to serve for mines and hideouts, its forest sets and campsite sets, while MGM provided Johnny Weissmuller with circus acrobatic equipment to make his vine swinging easier. All the studios had their simulated wagons and stagecoaches with suitable process shots to give the impression of movement through an appropriate, if not always continuous, landscape. We can find films shot in a variety of landscapes, from arid desert to lush forest to rolling range to high mountains, and in geographical regions from the American southwest to the Dakotas, from the Mexican border area to the South American pampas, and from South African jungle to Arabian sand dunes. But this variety fits into the landscape symbolized by Monument Valley. What resonates most strongly in terms of landscape are the rocks. The rocks—the Hoppy rocks—are virtually fetishes. Like the guns the heroes use, like the snappy clothes the heroes wear, the rocks symbolize or signify the hero's strength of purpose, his masculinity. The landscape in these films reminds us of the hero's phallic power. This is especially the case when the films are shot among the Hoppy rocks. These rocks express the sublime, and we can trace this impulse to convey sublimity back to Romantic landscape painting and poetry of the nineteenth century. The grand canvasses of John Martin, some large works and sketches by John Constable, the fantastic designs of William Blake, and the daring swirls of light in paintings by J.M.W. Turner inaugurate the sublime in landscape, and these artists' visions transferred easily to North America, where we find similarly impressive landscapes in paintings by Thomas Moran and Albert Bierstadt. Lee Clark Mitchell sees Bierstadt as the first artist to recognize the potential in depictions of the Far West. He created, Mitchell argues, "a realm of optic lawlessness" (57; see also McGillis).

Watching B westerns might well confirm Mitchell's observation. These films show no interest in verisimilitude when it comes to placing their action in landscape. One shot may show a rider in a forest and the next a different view of the same rider among the dramatic rocks of Lone Pine. Consider the opening of the Roy Rogers film *North of the Great Divide* (1950). This film, which deals with salmon fishing in the northwest, near the Canadian border, opens with a series of shots of a lake, an Indian village by the lake, swimming salmon, salmon leaping up a waterfall (these shots of the fish are clearly stock footage), and finally Roy Rogers on Trigger alongside a Native American who is also on horseback. First we see the riders from a distance as they pose on the lakeshore, and then we cut to a full frontal shot. In this medium close-up, the two riders are on a sound stage with suitable backdrop. Roy and his Native companion speak of the importance of the fish to the Native's way of life, and the camera cuts to a shot of the lake from behind the figures and the horses. They are still on the sound stage, but now we see a waterfall with fish leaping up it, the same stock footage we saw just a minute before in the opening montage. When we cut back to the lake, no waterfall is in sight. This disregard for the continuity of people in space is common in the B western.

Stock footage of a racing stagecoach or a cattle drive or night raiders or burning ranches appears in film after film, whether its location meshes with that of the main action or not. In film after film we see the same shots of rodeo events. This "optic lawlessness" is not so much a challenge to our sense of perspective or a clever *trompe l'oeil* as it is a fantasy of absorption. The viewer—usually a young male—is drawn so close to the actions of the hero that landscape is simply an extension of the hero, and since the hero is capable of anything—he might shoot one way and have his bullet travel the opposite way or even around a corner—the space he occupies is capable of anything, too. The landscapes of these westerns are as fantastic as the cowboy hero who moves through these scenes of grandeur with an authority that suggests ownership.

The landscape in these films constitutes, in other words, a fantasy chronotope—time and space exist in free-flowing combinations that disregard temporal and spatial realities. Time and space relate only loosely to history. Films set prior to 1850 or after 1865 take place in similar locations, and the characters who inhabit the cinema space, whether that space is temporally located before or after the Civil War, wear similar clothing and use similar firearms—even in those films that purport to move the action into the 1930s or later. And even those films that draw attention to datable world events (see Loy, "Soldiers in Stetsons")—films such as *Cowboy Commandos* (1943), *Valley of Hunted Men* (1942), or *King of the Cowboys* (1943)—set the action in familiar B western locations. Eventually the viewer becomes as familiar with the settings of these films as he or she does with the faces of the actors who appear in them, over and over again. In film after film we see the same cabin in the woods, the same pass, the same rocky terrain, the same saloon, the same mine shaft, the same lake, the same trees, the same roads. We see the same bits of scenery, literally, in film after film, because often the filmmakers used the stock footage that served them several times in the past. The series of John Wayne films produced by Warner Brothers in the early 1930s (e.g., *Haunted Gold*, 1932, and *Ride Him, Cowboy*, 1932) are remakes of silent Ken Maynard films and use many shots from the silent films when Wayne (actually Maynard) is riding. Looking closely, we can discern that the cowboy in one set of shots wears a different shirt from the one in shots taken specifically for this film. And of course the cowboy in the stock footage rides a landscape different from the one John Wayne rides; we see the landscape change from shot to shot as we move from silent footage to the sound footage. Another of many possible examples is the Lash LaRue series of films in the late 1940s. One scene with a runaway stagecoach appears repeatedly in films such as *Cheyenne Takes Over* (1947), *Border Feud* (1947), and *Stage to Mesa City* (1947), despite the fact that the figure of a falling driver does not fit the circumstances in all these films.

I daresay that the fantasy here is uncanny. The landscape in the B westerns is as familiar as a Saturday afternoon at the Bijou, and yet it remains the place where anything can and does happen. It remains a strange and forbidding land. Without doubt, the best example is Gene Autry's debut film, *The Phantom Empire* (1935), in which the western landscape is a cover, literally, for an underground kingdom that is home to a futuristic society. This extreme fantasy is, however, rare in the western. More to the point are the Durango Kid films of the late 1940s and early '50s. In *Law of the Canyon* (1947), *Whirlwind Raiders* (1948), and *Bonanza Town* (1951), the character played by Charles Starrett (playing Steve Langtry, Steve Lanning, and Steve Ramsey, respectively) arrives in town without luggage or any sign of an extra horse. Despite this austerity, when trouble occurs the Starrett character rides out of town to a convenient clump of trees or large boulder or to an even more convenient cave, into which he disappears to emerge dressed in black, wearing a black mask, and riding the white stallion, Raider—a horse quite unlike the one he rode in on. This is magic indeed. The very land births the Durango Kid and his horse.

The Durango Kid is the male hero as fetish. Like the Shadow, he knows what evil lurks in the hearts of men, and he knows how to eradicate this evil. When the Durango Kid rides, he purifies the land. As an Imaginary for the viewer, this cowboy balances the Real and the Symbolic. He takes the viewer to the pure source of being, that original place where no difference exists between self and Other, between land and inhabitant, or between desire and its satisfaction. He also represents, as forthrightly as possible, the law of the father. He is the figure who descends, like a *deus ex machina*, to set things right, to ensure that civilized behaviour returns to a lawless land. He represents the taming of the land. He embodies both the wilderness and the town. The Durango Kid is fetish because he provides the young viewer with a fantasy of capability. As long as we continue to believe that the Durango Kid exists, we believe in the possibility of purity and green earth. The Durango Kid ensures victory over fears of castration and impotence. Strange as it may seem, the green-earth fantasy overlays the actuality of the arid desert and barren rocks that we see in so many B westerns. The space contained in the film frame suggests openness and extension to the far horizon, but we might remember that the suggestion of expansiveness is an illusion. What we see is landscape captured within a frame, and this framed space has something in common with what Aaron Betsky identifies as "queer space." Queer space "finds its origin in the closet, the place of hiding and constructing one's own identity" (21). The cave or hiding place behind a boulder is the Durango Kid's closet, and from it he emerges dressed in a costume that both hides his identity and gives him an identity. For Betsky, queer space "proposes a world of fantasy that is directly related to the body and has no definite space" (21). We have noted that these westerns focus attention on the body with cowboy clothes and spectacular mounts and guns and gun belts. The land in which the cowboy hero rides draws attention to the body, too—the body in space, the body in movement, the body climbing and running and riding in an environment that mirrors the phallic power of the hero.

"If queer space starts in the closet," Betsky argues, "it forms itself in the mirror" (17). And Metz regards the cinema as a sort of mirror for the spectator, reflecting the spectator's fantasies. That the young boy who watched the B westerns saw himself reflected in the heroes he gazed upon was apparent in the cowboy games he played, prompted by the action he saw on film. But Betsky notes that the "free and open space" in the mirror is also "shifting and ephemeral"—it is, in short, "unreal." Again, as Betsky notes, such queer space is potentially "liberating" (5). His description is worth quoting: "It is a useless, amoral, and sensual space that lives only in and for experience. It is a space of spectacle, consumption, dance, and obscenity. . . . It is a space in between the body and technology, a space of pure artifice" (5).

The queer space Betsky writes about is distinctly urban, as opposed to the frontier spaces of the western. And yet the western films continually contrast a straitlaced east with its urban centres and business codes and effete rules of etiquette with the wide and open spaces of the west with its camaraderie and song, its room to roam, and its codes of honour and freedom. Betsky's words *amoral* and *obscenity* are a stumbling block in any attempt to make the western landscape queer. However, we might remember that the cowboy, despite the codes and despite his role as peacemaker and bringer of law to the lawless, acts with impunity when he shoots and carries out distinctly unlawful acts in order to get the job done. The cowboy is a vigilante, someone who does not accept that the laws are for him. He rides the man down any way he can. In this sense, he is not subject to the laws of the land. He takes the law into his own hands, as the saying goes. His personal morality is curiously amoral. As for *obscene*, the space the cowboy inhabits is quite literally forbidding (one 1941 film has the title *Forbidden Trails*) and foreboding. The *west* is a place offensive to eastern sensibilities. And it is a space where men, rather than women, are most at home.

Landscape as Paradise

The west as queer space, a space associated with dust and dirt and the earth in all its fundamental bodily activity, is not the whole story. The viewer of the B western is left in no doubt that the land the cowboy roams is a land beautiful enough to be paradise. The film titles indicate this: *Blue Montana Skies* (1939), *Land of the Open Range* (1942), *The Man from Music Mountain* (1938 Gene Autry; 1943 Roy Rogers), *Paradise Canyon* (1935), *Pals of the Golden West* (1951), *Homesteaders of Paradise Valley* (1947), *Near the Rainbow's End* (1930), *Rainbow Valley* (1935), *The Rainbow Trail* (1932), *Rainbow over Texas* (1946). The land of the west is that pot of gold at the end of the rainbow where music sounds under blue skies. This is open land where fences spell trouble, but trouble set to rights by Knights of the Range (the title of a 1940 film). We might remember what Horace Greeley was supposed to have said: "Go west, young man." The west was a land of opportunity. It beckoned to all those with grit and a spirit of entrepreneurship. We think of the cowboy as a man free of ties to institutions and routines associated with jobs, yet he proves himself capable of turning his hand to any number of things—from ranching to wildcatting, from turning out a newspaper to upholding the law, from running a stagecoach line to working for the railroad, from overseeing an orphanage to working for the forestry service.

The west as a place in which anything is possible is at the centre of the famous Turner thesis. In 1893, Frederick Jackson Turner celebrated the closing of the American frontier in his essay "The Significance of the Frontier in American History." Although historians have vigorously contested Turner's argument, it was and continues to be hugely influential. I think its influence is discernible in the B westerns. I quote from the final paragraph of Turner's essay:

From the conditions of frontier life came intellectual traits of profound importance. The works of travelers along each frontier from colonial days onward describe certain common traits, and these traits have, while softening down, still persisted as survival in the place of their origin, even when a higher social organization succeeded. The result is that to the frontier the American intellect owes its striking characteristics. That coarseness and strength combined with acuteness and inquisitiveness; that practical, inventive turn of mind, quick to find expedients; that masterful grasp of material things, lacking in the artistic but powerful to effect great ends; that restless, nervous energy; that dominant individualism, working for good and for evil, and withal that buoyancy and exuberance which comes with freedom—these are traits of the frontier, or traits called out elsewhere because of the existence of the frontier. Since the days when the fleet of Columbus sailed into the waters of the New World, America has been another name for opportunity, and the people of the United States have taken their tone from the incessant expansion which has not only been open but has even been forced upon them. He would be a rash prophet who should assert that the expansive character of American life has now entirely ceased. Movement has been its dominant fact, and, unless this training has no effect upon a people, the American energy will continually demand a wider field for its exercise. But never again will such gifts of free land offer themselves. For a moment, at the frontier, the bonds of custom are broken and unrestraint is triumphant. There is not tabula rasa. The stubborn American environment is there with its imperious summons to accept its conditions; the inherited ways of doing things are also there; and yet, in spite of environment, and in spite of custom, each frontier did indeed furnish a new field of opportunity, a gate of escape from the bondage of the past; and freshness, and confidence, and scorn of older society, impatience of its restraints and its ideas, and indifference to its lessons, have accompanied the frontier.

That "dominant individualism, working for good and for evil," nicely describes the characters that inhabit the B western. What rings in Turner's words are the rational powers brought to bear upon a land to create a space fit for habitation by an enterprising people. It is an imperial call to expansion and goes some way to explain why the B westerns move their action from Montana and Oklahoma and Texas to South America and Arabia and Africa. The cowboys are people on the move, imperial guards expanding the American empire, taking "freshness, and confidence, and scorn of older society" to the far-flung frontiers they seek. Turner's vision has something of the utopian in it, and much of the masculine.

We can find this same turn to utopian vision in Roger Horrocks's treatment of nature in the western. Horrocks focuses on the big-budget westerns such as *Shane* and *She Wore a Yellow Ribbon*, but what he says resonates with what we see in the B western. Rather than serving as mere background to the action, nature "is the central 'character'" in western films and fiction, according to Horrocks (70). In keeping with the queer theme, he adds that one might say the landscape in westerns is "a homoerotic landscape" (71). He is thinking of the "hard" and "sculptural" (his words) rocks. Horrocks goes on to suggest "that the western also symbolically restores to men something they have lost—not simply being able to live in nature and its beauty, but *their own nature*, their own beauty" (73; italics in original). From this perspective, the landscape of westerns is "utopian," "a recovery of lost harmony with nature" (73). As is so often the case, however, the vision is not one-dimensional. Landscape is both a reflection of the male beauty invested in the cowboy and a reflection of his alien and dislocated life. The cowboy suffers just as the land suffers in so many ways: lack of water (desert), abuse and overuse (sheep and cattle wars), fencing (the closed range), damming of valleys (wiping out farms and ranches), mining and drilling and exploding (finding ore and oil and building roads and railroads).

If we see any change in the B western from the 1930s to the late '40s and early '50s, then we might note that often in the 1930s the hero settles down at the end of the adventure. Often we see him framed against a tree or a house or a horizon with his arm around the girl. The vision is of a utopian new world before the man and woman and around them. Hand in hand they will make their way into the future. This theme is not so blatant in the Hopalong Cassidy films of the 1930s, but again we have the young hero fascinated by a woman but choosing another kind of family—the family of men—to face the future with. But by the 1940s and the arrival of the singing cowboy, we have the lone rider who departs from civilization at the end to roam the vast reaches of the west. Now the utopian vision is not of a man and a woman ready to work together and not in vain but rather of the cowboy who rides free of all constraint in a pristine land of profound beauty.

When I write of the utopian vision, I draw on the "myth of the garden" that Henry Nash Smith examined in *Virgin Land* (1949). Many B westerns focused on the hero defending groups of small farmers or homesteaders. The result of this focus on the land as garden is a tension between the garden myth and the romantic myth of the wanderer. Smith posits the "stout yeoman" and the "wild horseman of the plains" (207) as the two figures representing, respectively, the garden and the open plains (the desert in Smith's study). Opening the west through exploration and settling the west through homesteading are chronological rather than coterminous. The tension is between the settled life and the itinerant life—the one mode of living working the land and the other taking what nature has to offer. We see something of the same tension today. The cry "Drill, baby, drill" (heard at the Republican National Convention in Minneapolis, September 2008) and the drive to transform the land and seabed through excavation clashes with the desire to protect the wilderness for continuing outdoor activity—hiking, climbing, birdwatching, hunting, and so on. In other words, the B western tries to take account of the closing of the frontier while at the same time it tries to perpetuate the mythic frontier that was home to the gallant frontiersman.

Landscape as Ecosystem

By the late 1940s we see a growing sense of the land as precious, as a resource that can be ruined. This theme is present in greater or lesser intensity in a number of films, and, from the perspective of the early twenty-first century, the sensitivity to ecology may appear naive. But it is an indication of things to come. In *Border Saddlemates* (1952), for example, Rex Allen plays a veterinarian sent to fill in for a colleague who lives near the Canadian border. The plot has villains catching foxes in Canada and transporting them to a fox farm on the US side of the border. The fox business is a cover for more nefarious goings-on, however. The bad guys are placing counterfeit money in false-bottomed fox cages. Mel Richards (Forrest Taylor) runs the fox farm on the US side of the border, and he has a niece and nephew, Jane (Mary Ellen Kay) and Danny (Jimmy Moss). Danny has a pet fox called Smokey. Smokey becomes ill, forcing Dr. Allen (the character takes the name of the actor) to quarantine all animals and thus thwart the villains in their bid to move the counterfeit money. The bad guy is Baxter (Roy Barcroft). Rex and his sidekick, Slim Pickens (again, the character takes the name of the actor), eventually sort things out. Rex is a kindly country doctor who is a father figure to young Danny. In the end, Rex departs, leaving everyone happy. He rides down the street and then raises KoKo in that familiar heroic cowboy salute.

The film's plot has to do with counterfeiting, a fairly common theme in these westerns. However, the hero is a veterinarian and therefore someone close to animals. Rex's job is to keep animals healthy. The film provides us with plenty of information about the raising of foxes and tells us why some people raise foxes. The foxes are used to make fur coats, providing, as one character puts it, "frosty to a woman's wardrobe." Fox fur, we learn, is becoming to a woman. To calm our possible outrage at any cruelty done to foxes, Mel says that some foxes are "tame but liable to bite." When Smokey becomes sick, Rex comforts Danny by telling him that the "same friendly eyes that watch over you and me watch over Smokey." Man and animal inhabit God's world and come under God's protection. The strange combination of fox farming and foxes as pets is never strained in this film. Just as the young girl in *Trail of Robin Hood* eats turkey on Thanksgiving and yet has a pet turkey, so Danny has a pet fox without thinking of the fate of the other foxes. The connection between animals and children is important because of the implications of dealing with the human species' connection to nature.

Just how naive this film is, however, is evident in the role played by Slim Pickens. Slim is the town dog catcher, and the film opens and closes with amusing vignettes involving Slim's wagon with its cage for the dogs he catches. Providing a little comedy are the two instances in which Slim finds himself caged and dogs outside looking in on the imprisoned catcher. Of course Slim bemoans his situation and cries to be let out. He wants sympathy from Rex and the others. The keeping of dogs and foxes in cages does not, however, elicit any sympathy from Slim or anyone else in the film. Animals are important as long as they provide something useful for humans. The difference between animals and humans seems to be that animals suit cages and humans do not.

Consciousness concerning the importance of nature is especially apparent in Roy Rogers's films of the late 1940s and early '50s. *Apache Rose* (1947) has Roy as a wildcatter whose friend, Carlos Vega (Russ Vincent), owns a ranch with his sister Rosa (Donna Martell). Carlos has run up a gambling debt of $147,000 on the Casino Del Mar, an offshore floating casino. The owners of the casino want rights to the oil deposits on the Vega ranch, and Roy wonders aloud why Carlos hasn't tried to develop the oil himself, since the oil deposits there are the best Roy has seen. Carlos tells him that Rosa has the "silly, sentimental idea that oil derricks will spoil the ranch." Because she opposes the development of the oil deposits, the bad guys shoot Rosa. The rest of the film concerns Billy (Dale Evans), disguised as Rosa so that Roy can flush out the bad guys, and we hear little more about oil or its development or its environmental impact. As important as the oil theme is the gambling theme. Gambling is risky business for anyone, and the crooked casino owners take advantage of the innocent Mexican, Carlos. Roy must come to his rescue, and Roy, we hear early in the film, "pays off like a slot machine." In other words, if you are going to bet, bet on a man like Roy, not on business-suited gents out to make a fast buck.

Roy's sidekick in this film is a fellow named Alkali (Olin Howland), and it is Alkali who tells Billy that Roy pays off like a slot machine. His metallic name is perhaps suggestive of oil and its uses or of the detrimental properties of an oil-based economy to agriculture. Little is made of this theme of rural versus urban uses of the land, although the film rounds to its close with a lengthy chase scene in which the good guys on horseback chase the bad guys in sedans and catch them. The last battle takes place on an ocean beach near the caves in which the oil deposits lie. The beach, with its pounding waves, nicely signals the inexorable passing of time and change, along with elemental things.

More forthright in its presentation of nature as a dominant theme is another Rogers film from the same year, *Springtime in the Sierras*. This one begins with Roy and his group herding horses down a dusty road. Cut to a set with a fawn. Roy sees that the fawn has lost its mother, so he decides to take it to Cap Foster's place for sick animals, a place Roy and his friends used to call Cap's Sanitarium when they were kids. The place is outdoors; it has a cabinet on a tree with a Red Cross on it to indicate hospital. When Roy arrives with the fawn, Cap (Harry Cheshire) is tending to a doe that has been shot. Roy and Cap figure that this doe is the fawn's mother; hunters shot her and she "dragged herself" to Cap's. We surmise that the doe knew Cap Foster would take care of her. Roy notes that it is not hunting season. Now we learn that hunting out of season is "big business." Cap angrily tells Roy that the professional hunters are "racketeers" who are "wiping out natural wildlife." The scene cuts to a courtroom in which a judge is serving sentence on out-of-season hunters. The judge says these hunters are "robbing every American boy of his natural heritage to hunt as a sport in season." He goes on to call these illegal hunters the "lowest, most contemptible breed of criminals."

We cut back to Roy as he arrives with his horses at the Lazy W ranch, owned by Jean Loring (Stephanie Bachelor). Her foreman is Matt Wilke (Roy Barcroft). Jane expresses interest in the pinto that Roy has, but he tells her it is not for sale. In fact, he has brought it as a gift for Taffy Baker (Jane Frazee).

Now we cut to Cap's ranch, where we meet Taffy, who lives with Cap. Her brother Bert (Harold Landon), we learn, is going bad. In a scene in which we see hunters shooting deer, one of these hunters wears a camouflage jacket and head scarf. It turns out that this fellow is Bert. Cap notes that the professional hunters use silencers and telescopes and wear camouflage—in other words, they are not truly sportsmen. Cap discovers the bad guys, but Jean Loring shoots him in cold blood. At film's end, Taffy pursues Jean just the way Roy pursues Matt Wilke on horseback, and both she and he leap from their horses to throw the other riders and then fight them on the ground. During the fight, Roy demonstrates how to punch the baddie and Taffy proves a good learner. At the end, Roy leaves, although he makes it clear he will miss Taffy.

The message of *Springtime in the Sierras* is clear: animals are the friends of humans. Along with the doe and fawn, the film shows Cap Foster with a pet squirrel that has the run of his house, and a pet crow that shakes a claw with anyone who offers a hand in friendship. This is 1947, however, and although animals may be friends of humans, they also serve human needs. They allow for sport hunting, and what the film criticizes is hunting out of season, the undisciplined killing of animals for profit, rather than hunting per se. A more contemporary view of animals as part of an ecosystem is presented in another Roy Rogers film.

This one is *Susanna Pass* (1949). The opening shot shows a deer and a fawn on a studio set that is supposed to be a forest. The camera tracks across a sign that reads: "State Game Preserve: No Firearms Allowed." Cut to a wagon with two escaped convicts. One, a character named Del Roberts (Douglas Fowley), jumps down with a knife and catches the fawn and kills it. Then the two convicts build a fire to cook their prey. Cut to a fire lookout, where the spotter notices a great patch of smoke. Roy and the firefighters ride to investigate. Meanwhile, the convicts fight over whether to stay together. Roberts knifes the other fellow, Bob Oliver (Robert Bice) and flees in the wagon. Oliver is only wounded, however, and gets away on foot. Their quarrel was over oil. Bob's father runs a fish hatchery near a local lake, and under the lake is oil. Bob was framed for murder by his uncle Martin, who is plotting to gain control of the lake and the oil. Bob now wants to clear his name. Roberts just wants money and, since he is a seismic engineer, he wants to work for whomever will develop the oil deposit.

The next cut takes us to the local jail, where Rita (Estella Rodriguez) is singing "Two-Gun Rita from Down in Gower Gulch." (The reference to Gower Gulch, the intersection of Sunset Boulevard and Gower Street in Hollywood, is an in-joke to aficionados of the B western. In the silent film era, cowboys gathered at this intersection in the hope of finding work.) The cook at the jail is Rita's father, Carlos (Martin Garralaga), and these two Mexican characters provide light comic relief. At one point Roberts remarks that Carlos "wouldn't know an accident if he saw one." If these characters offer anything more than light relief, then it is their connection to food and the staples of life. The Mexican people here, like the fish and the animals and the women, need protection. As in *Springtime in the Sierras*, we have a squirrel that has the run of the house and a raven (here called Jim) that shakes hands. In the final conflict between Roy and Roberts, Jim is instrumental in helping Roy discover Roberts.

The plot turns on Martin Masters's (Robert Emmett Keane) desire to obtain his brother Russell's (Lucien Littlefield) property so he can benefit from the oil under Russell's lake. Dale Evans as Doc Parker (who has been in the Marines) works for Russell. We have several shots of the fish hatchery. Later in the film, Doc explains to Walter P. Johnson (Roberts in disguise) how the hatchery functions, and we see the incubation of fish eggs, fish hatching, minnows, and so on. The film emphasizes the scientific know-how needed to breed fish and restock lakes. The final scene in the film has Roy explaining the importance of fish hatcheries: "Sportsmen and the youth of America can get away from the city and go fishing like our forefathers." As in *Springtime in the Sierras*, the vision of the country is of a vast game preserve for the benefit of American sports hunters. The bad guys are bad because they explode dynamite in the water to take seismic tests. In the process, they kill fish, and they determine to kill all the fish later so they can run the hatchery out of business. In other words, they have no sympathy for nature, its creatures, sportsmen, or the youth of America.

Another film that deals with fish is *North of the Great Divide* (1951). This film opens with written information about the great salmon runs in the northwest and how the "greed of a few" endangers the salmon and the lives of people living in the region. Stock footage shows salmon swimming upriver to spawn, leaping falls, and swimming in shallows with their backs exposed above the water line. Native Americans, dressed like Plains Indians, dance by fires on a lakeshore. They are giving thanks for the return of the salmon. In medium close-up we see Roy Rogers and his friend, Tacona (Keith Richards—not the one most familiar to a later generation), as they sit astride their horses. In a distant shot we see them by the lake, but another shot, from behind, shows a waterfall with leaping fish in front of them. Here's an example of editing that takes no account of continuity and realism. What immediately follows, in a rather abrupt turn of events, is a horse race, during which Tacona falls from his horse and is attacked by a wolf. Roy comes to his friend's aid, only to have the wolf turn on him. Trigger comes to the rescue and kills the wolf. Roy hears whim-pering, and behind a bush he finds a wolf pup whose tail is caught in a trap. Without commenting on the cruelties of spring traps, Roy decides to raise the pup. The goings-on we have witnessed turn out to be part of the annual Salmon Run Celebration, which is set on the international border and includes three nations—the United States, the Oseka Nation (I cannot find information on this nation of Native Americans, leading me to believe they are a fantasy among other fantasies in this film), and Canada. (The Canadian fort we see in this film is the same one that appears in Rex Allen's *Border Saddlemates*.) Before the celebration ends, Tacona and Roy become blood brothers, with the ritual slicing of the hand and mix-ing of blood. Roy has been working for the game reserve, but he is now leaving to study for the Indian Affairs department.

Time passes. Roy's boss at Indian Affairs (Al Bridge, uncredited) assigns him back to the Oseka Nation, because trouble is brewing between the new fish cannery and the Natives. The situation is complicated by the fact that the owner of the cannery, Banning (Roy Barcroft), and his henchman Stagg (Jack Lambert) plan to destroy the Canadian cannery across the lake and blame the destruction on the Oseka. Roy uncovers the chicanery and the film comes to a close with a vicious whip fight between Roy and Stagg (Stagg has used a bullwhip throughout the film).

The film contains plenty of stock footage of fish swimming and fish-ing boats and machines to move and process fish. Banning asserts at one point that he won't let "a few stray Indians interfere with our business." He argues that the Indians did not use the river and lake properly for fish-ing; they just caught enough fish to eat. Even Roy's boss in Indian Affairs states, "We can't have Indians fighting businessmen." The Indians, he says, have to learn to live peaceably with modern industry. Roy, however, warns that the salmon can become extinct if overfished the way the cannery business wants. Ultimately we have to side with Roy and see the cannery business as greedy and insensitive to natural resources. The film's title song speaks of the "Wilderness calling north of the Great Divide," where a "man has lots of elbow room," and the vision in this film is of a roman-tic wilderness needing protection, not exploitation. Roy argues that there should be "uniform international laws" to protect salmon and regulate fishing. He also says "our countries always co-operate." Here is an early version of Canadian–American trade relations in the making.

I'll close this discussion of the B western's sensitivity to matters of eco-logical health with a look at a Gene Autry picture, *Riders of the Whistling Pines* (1949). The concern here is the devastation of forests. As the credits roll, we see behind them a beautiful forest and lake. The camera cuts to a lodge—Cedar Ridge Sportmens Camp—and a banner saying "Welcome Gene." Two elderly people, Abner (Leon Weaver) and Loie (Loie Bridge), quarrel because she wants to own a place and not work for someone else. Up ride Carter (Jason Robards, Sr., uncredited), who is a forestry person, and a man called Bill Wright (Damian O'Flynn). Carter goes into the lodge to use the phone, and outside Wright sneakily cuts the phone line. So begins the adventure.

Gene Autry has resigned from the Forestry Service to run a sportsman's lodge in the piney woods. On the way to his lodge he tries out his new rifle on a cougar, which he calls a "deer killer." He misses a couple of times, but then he and his friend, Joe Lucas (Jimmy Lloyd), find a Forest Ranger shot. Wright is the murderer; he uses Gene's shooting as a blind to murder Carter. But Gene thinks he did the deed, and an inquest agrees, although the judge deems Carter's death "accidental." Crestfallen, Gene sells his lodge to the old folks who had run it while he was away. He gives the money, anonymously, to Helen Carter (Patricia Barry), the daughter of the man he supposedly shot.

We learn that Wright shot the ranger because the ranger had discovered tussock moth killing trees on government property. The local lumber dealer, Mitchell (Douglas Dumbrille), can use these trees because he has a large order that he cannot fill using the trees he has a legal right to log. Once the trees infected with the tussock moth are dead or assured of dying, Mitchell can offer to take them away and use them to fill his order. But Gene finds the insects, too, and reports the problem to the Forestry Service. They offer him the job of spraying the trees from the air with DDT. He refuses, but he changes his mind when he finds out that his friends had altered the sight on his rifle and that he could not, therefore, have killed the ranger. We have some discussion about the safety of using DDT; the bad guys claim it will kill livestock. To ensure this happens, the bad guys fly at night and spray a lethal dose of DDT. Gene's friend Joe finds out they are doing this, and Wright shoots him. Joe survives the gunshot and tells Gene about the bad guys. Gene rides to the lumberyard to find out what is going on, but he finds nothing. He is, however, captured after assaulting Mitchell. Mitchell's men lock Gene in a shed, where he finds the DDT and the equipment used to spray it. He escapes and does brief battle with Pete (an unshaven Clayton Moore). Riding to save the day, but riding into a trap, Gene gallops on Champion. Joe takes a plane, but is taken hostage by Wright. With Wright in the plane, Joe crashes into the cabin where Mitchell is waiting to ambush Gene.

The interest in this film is in the use of DDT to control a threat to the forest. Gene assures local ranchers that DDT is safe; it will kill the tussock moth but do no harm to wildlife or to domestic stock. We see shots of great tankers being filled with DDT, and a fleet of airplanes, one of which Gene flies, spraying the forest. Great swathes of DDT fall from the sky, blanketing the forest. Not until 1973 was DDT banned in the United States, and so we can only smile ruefully at the means the government took to save the forest in this film. But we also note that the government did save the forest and prevent its being logged by an unscrupulous and greedy lumber baron. The B western offers its young viewers a view of the male as protector not only of animals, women, and children but also of natural resources. It sides, for the most part, with the beauty of nature against the blight of industry.

Man and Rocks

What strikes me most forcefully in the B western with regard to landscape is the Hoppy rocks. Many times we see villain and hero come to a reckoning among the rocks. These rocks are where finality occurs; they represent fulfillment, a location in which desire comes, for the time being, to an end. In other words, the rocks represent a Lacanian Real, a place of amorphous and chaotic impossibility, a place of elemental and primeval importance. The rocks are where manhood comes to its apotheosis and to its end. One man dies, the other rides back to town triumphant. No one can remain among the rocks. The cowboy returns to the realm of the symbolic, to town with its lawyers and banks and newspapers. But usually he rides away again, out of town, back to the trail that leads to those rocks. The cowboy is a fantasy precisely because he remains a denizen of the rocks. He and the rocks are one.

What I am arguing here is best illustrated in two big-budget westerns: George Stevens's *Shane* and Clint Eastwood's *High Plains Drifter* (1972). In both of these films, the hero comes riding down from the high country, from the far horizon, to a valley or a town where trouble needs fixing. Once the hero has accomplished his task, he returns to the mountains from which he had emerged. He returns to the Real, where he will await the call to another mission. The Eastwood movie makes this point by having the hero emerge from a heat haze and return into this same haze at the end. He dissolves into the heat of the distant horizon. Both Shane and the Eastwood character are associated with death, one departing with a bullet in his stomach and the other having been killed in a previous incarnation. Eastwood's *Pale Rider* (1985) is similar thematically to the other two films. The B westerns activate this idea by having the hero ride away on another trail where he waits the call to another adventure. The hero belongs among the rocks, not in town, not on a ranch, not in some domestic situation.

We might, then, add a dimension to the implications of landscape in these films. Whereas Jane Tompkins sees the land as a replacement for the female in the western and Horrocks sees it as a sign of the genre's homoeroticism, we might just as well see the relationship between the hero and the land as autoerotic. These films are about the man's desire to be the Ideal-I, to be that which he desires—implacable and sure and permanent. The cowboy hero is a fantasy through and through, and naturally he inhabits a fantasy landscape. These films are about what goes on in the mind of a man, and what goes on in the mind of a man is just as inscrutable as that sublime landscape he roams. Jim Kitses notes that in the western, "the land and its awesome vistas" "incorporate the picturesque and the sublime" (19). True, but the hero is associated most intensely with sublimity. Žižek's definition of the sublime object seems to me to fit the notion of the hero I am working out here. Quoting Lacan on the ethics of psychoanalysis, Žižek writes:

> The sublime object is precisely "an object elevated to the dignity of the Thing," an ordinary, everyday object that undergoes a kind of transubstantiation and starts to function, in the symbolic economy of the subject, as an embodiment of the impossible Thing, i.e. as materialized Nothingness. (83)

The sublimity of the land and the sublimity of the hero are manifestations of fantasy in the sense of the impossible. Any attempt to actualize the fantasy of the cowboy can end only in disappointment and defeat.

Corporate Cowboys and the Shaping of a Nation

Children are the darlings of corporate America. They're targets for marketers of everything from hamburgers to minivans. And it's not good for them.
—Susan Linn, 1

[The cowboy] may be part of a mythic construct of America's past, and his image in popular culture may be rife with sociological and psychological implications, but he exists in the first place because of a superior act of marketing.
—William W. Savage, Jr.

Bring 'em back, dead or alive.

G eorge W. Bush lives much of the time in Texas; he wears a cowboy hat; he speaks a cowboy lingo; he is just about my age. George W. Bush grew up pretty much at the same time I grew up, and no doubt he was as immersed in the culture of his time as I was. And that culture was a cowboy culture. I'm speaking of the 1940s and '50s when cowboys were everywhere. And I mean everywhere. As we have seen, they were most obviously in the movies and by the end of the 1950s they were definitely on television; as many as fifty prime-time western programs appeared from the late 1950s to the early '60s. Cowboys also turned up on cereal boxes, on belts, on stationery, on Thermos bottles and lunch boxes, on bicycles and guitars, on pins and earmuffs, and on a variety of clothing, toys, and games. Roy Rogers's son, Dusty Rogers, tells us that he "grew

163

up in Roy everything. I had bedspreads and sheets and pillow shams and curtains and carpet—everything Roy. Most kids put R and L on their boots to tell right from left and I had a double R on each boot. I didn't know which one was which for years. I had Roy Rogers pajamas to neckties to hats to boots to scarves—everything" (qtd. in George-Warren and Freedman, 148). And of course the cowboy heroes turned up in books and comics for children of all ages. They were my generation's Captain Underpants, appearing in a series called Better Little Books, marketed to the very young. The cowboy was ubiquitous in the 1940s and '50s, and the values he inculcated in an entire generation have not diminished in recent years. If anything, these values have intensified. Anglo-American culture continues to validate cowboy virtues of aggression, enterprise, and expansion. The cowboy is not one-dimensional. However, a one-dimensional version is available and this is the version we have seen acted out on the world stage by George W. Bush.

By a one-dimensional version, I do not mean something simple. I mean a hegemonic version of masculinity, a version of masculinity that serves as a standard devoutly to be reached for by the North American male. The hegemonic male is an ideal rather than an actuality, but he is an ideal that has direct effect on the ways of being male. "You can run, but you can't hide," George W. Bush is fond of saying, and he says these words in his posture of the aggressive male, the male who supposedly manifests the strong traits of the hegemonic male. George W. Bush aspires to be the cowboy. His language and the language of his administration consists, to a significant extent, of cowboy lingo, as Wendy Christensen (2005) points out. The cowboy mentality has worked its way into our sense of what it is to be masculine; it did so in the 1950s and it does so now. The cowboy inhabits many of us like an inflection or should I say "infection"? The cowboy is a symptom of male desire. We see the tall rangy man of few words and efficient action not only in an ideology of aggression but also in posture, body language, facial expression, manner of speech, and so on. If the cowboy has become for some men (and some women) habitus, a socially acquired mindset, the reason for this is simple: he was ubiquitous for most of the mid-twentieth century.

Before going on, I note a paradox. The cowboy is a populist figure; he appeals to the rural working person close to the land, to the urban enforcer, to the urban person who feels nostalgia for a simpler time and a simpler place, and to the young. He seems to represent an egalitarian ethic as he fights to set things right for the little guy, the small rancher and homesteader. His adversaries invariably are the big ranchers, big bankers, big eastern syndicates who represent a corporate America and who make life impossible for the small entrepreneur who just wants to fashion a life modest in material and strategic gains (see the Kevin Costner film *Open Range*, 2003). The paradox emerges when we grasp the implications of the cowboy ethic—might is right, freedom means the freedom to expand one's holdings, and the rule of law benefits those who can pay for the law to work in their favour. The cowboy is a capitalist. (This insight was captured directly by many of the western films made in Italy, the so-called spaghetti westerns. See for example, Sergio Corbucci's *The Compañeros* [1970] or Sergio Leone's *A Fistful of Dynamite* [1971], a.k.a. *Duck, You Sucker*. A more naive example is the 1939 Roy Rogers film *Wall St. Cowboy*.) The cowboy as conceived by the Hollywood western is George W. Bush, whose tax reductions benefit mostly the wealthiest Americans and whose vision of social security places responsibility for social protection in the hands of the individual, not the government.

We find the emphasis on lucre tucked into some of the cowboy creeds. We might find the interest in good business tucked away in Gene Autry's seventh dictum: "A cowboy is industrious and always works hard." This interest is, however, explicit in the sixth dictum of Hopalong Cassidy's creed: "If you waste time or money today, you will regret it tomorrow. Practice thrift in all ways" (TV Acres, Oaths & Pledges). In the films, most cowboys have money the way the animals in Kenneth Grahame's *The Wind in the Willows* have money: they do not seem to work for it. However, in *Heroes of the Saddle* (1940), the Three Mesquiteers (played in this film by Robert Livingston as Stony, Duncan Renaldo as Rico, and Raymond Hatton as Rusty) do work for their money. Early in the film, the daughter of their pal Montana (Kermit Maynard) finds herself an orphan and left in the care of an orphanage. The Mesquiteers visit the girl, Peggy (Patsy Lee Parsons), and bring her a great pile of gifts, games, toys, and a doll that she holds close to her for the rest of the film. In other words, they have gone shopping in a big way. Trouble follows, when they discover that Peggy has broken her foot and needs traction equipment if her foot is to get better. The orphanage is unable to afford the equipment, so the Mesquiteers promise to make the required $400. What follows is a montage of the three cowboys working at various ranch jobs, interspersed with shots of rodeos and rodeo advertisements. In other words, these cowboys work hard to earn the money they need to help their friend Peggy.

Complications arise when they learn that the director of the orphanage is corrupt and the whole business is a scam to make money from government grants. The Mesquiteers not only make the money for the traction equipment, but they uncover the nefarious doings of the bad guys. By the end of the film, the three cowboys have become the directors of the orphanage. In the final scene, Stony and Rico are about to depart on their horses; they want nothing to do with office work and have given their positions as directors to the nurse, Ruth Miller (Loretta Weaver). Just then, Rusty shows up in a fancy car, from which he emerges wearing top hat and tails. He appears ready to take his place as businessman and administrator. But he is only fooling to entertain the children. Beneath his expensive clothes he wears his familiar buckskin. He disrobes to reveal his riding outfit, much to the delight of the children, and joins Stony and Rusty. The cowboy wants his freedom, but he is quite capable of earning money and administering institutions. In the fantasy these films deliver, the cowboy can have and be the best of both worlds.

Let's go back to the pile of toys the Mesquiteers bring to Peggy. The connection with capitalism, material goods, and the market is explicit in the many consumer items related to cowboys, and the target for many of these items is and has been children, especially boys. I mention toys and games and pins and earmuffs in the first paragraph of this chapter to signal the connection between the cowboy and the child, especially but not exclusively the male child. Corporate America has for a long time been selling masculinity to the young. Susan Linn notes that "kids today are growing up in a marketing maelstrom" (1), and this is true everywhere, not just in America. She argues that the intensity of marketing to children has increased immensely since the 1980s and so too has the glorification of market practices as the solution to all social and economic problems. This glorification manifested itself in the 1980s and '90s in the privatization of many areas of social and economic practice that had been in an earlier time closely tended by governments.

To give an example that strikes me as absurd, I cite the privatization of provincial parks in the province where I live (Alberta, Canada). The idea that private enterprise can tend our wilderness areas better than governments can, even that they should wish to protect the environment instead of make money from it, strikes me as ridiculous. My government sees no contradiction between a zeal to make money and a desire to protect the environment, because it sees the marketplace as the answer to all of life's little and big problems. Even the Green Party (in Canada at least) champions the marketplace, arguing that environmentally sensitive practices can also be economically sound practices. But this idealization of the market is not new; it has been with us for a long time. My concern here is with the connection between modern market practices as they relate to the young, and those practices as they existed when I was a boy. Viewers who sit through the credits of the 1997 film *L.A. Confidential* (D. Curtis Hanson) are rewarded with some original footage from the 1954 Rose Bowl Parade in Pasadena, California, in which a smiling, white-haired, black-clad figure with a brace of pistols rides a white horse. The rider is Hopalong Cassidy, cowboy hero to thousands of boys in the 1940s and '50s. Hoppy is also evident in an earlier film, by Sidney Lumet, that deals with political manipulation and the drive for power (*Power*, 1986); in one scene we see a photograph of Hoppy decorating a corporate wall. Here Hoppy signals the paradox I mentioned earlier: he is a kindly elder statesman of the cowboy ethic who represents at once the desire for freedom and justice and the business savvy of the big entrepreneur.

The TV Acres website notes that William Boyd (Hopalong Cassidy) "realized his importance as a role model to children and so, set forth principles by which they should behave." I cannot resist quoting these "ten commandments of good citizen ship" [*sic*]:

1. The highest badge of honor a person can wear is honesty. Be mindful at all times.

2. Your parents are the best friends you have. Listen to them and obey their instructions.

3. If you want to be respected, you must respect others. Show good manners in every way.

4. Only through hard work and study can you succeed. Don't be lazy.

5. Your good deeds always come to light. So don't boast or be a show off.

6. If you waste time or money today, you will regret it tomorrow. Practice thrift in all ways.

7. Many animals are good and loyal companions. Be friendly and kind to them.

8. A strong, healthy body is a precious gift. Be neat and clean.

9. Our country's laws are made for your protection. Observe them carefully.

10. Children in many foreign lands are less fortunate than you. Be glad and proud you are an American.

This "Creed for American Boys and Girls" amounts to a code of citizenship. The emphasis here, as in all the codes, is on the American way. Note that numbers 7 and 10—which instruct boys and girls to be kind to animals that are "good and loyal companions" and to be proud of their nationality—do not suggest that boys and girls might help animals that are not companions or those children in foreign lands who are less fortunate. Despite nods to good deeds and kindness, this code and others like it are unfailingly self-serving. Their most insistent instruction is obedience to parents and the country's laws.

Those of us who grew up with Hoppy and idolized him wanted to show our affection and loyalty to him, and corporate America was not slow to show us how we could do so. Not only could we dress like Hoppy but we could buy toys that replicated Hoppy's pistols. We could buy a whole slew of Hoppy items from cereal to sweaters. Here's an incomplete list: bicycles, crayon and stencil sets, tablecloths, wrapping paper, dolls of various sizes including a full-size cut-out doll, wood-burning sets, pyjamas, a Pony Express Toss Game and a variety of board games, drums, binoculars, a frontier set, spurs, hats of various types and sizes, pillows and cushions, pictures, pocket knives, cameras, cookie jars, scarves, plates, cups and mugs, pins, comics, and of course guns and holsters. Hoppy's name and face appeared on just about anything you can imagine. But it wasn't only Hoppy who endorsed these multifarious objects. So too did Roy Rogers, Gene Autry, and other cowboy stars. I recall having a Roy Rogers toy guitar. I longed for pistols that resembled Roy's and a stetson that had the distinctive blocking that Roy's had. But what captured my imagination more than anything was the Red Ryder BB rifle.

The Daisy Manufacturing Company, maker of a variety of firearms, marketed a BB rifle directly to children. I saw the ad for the Red Ryder rifle in many of the comics I read. Red Ryder was a cowboy who began his life in the comic strip created by Fred Harman, but he quickly migrated to the screen, where such cowboy heroes as "Wild Bill" Elliott, Alan "Rocky" Lane, and Jim Bannon played him. Daisy clearly marketed their Red Rider BB rifle as a replica of the Winchesters the cowboys carried in the films we watched. The 1983 film *A Christmas Story* is about a boy growing up in 1950s America who desperately wants a Red Ryder BB gun. He manages to acquire one; I was not as fortunate—or unfortunate, depending on how you view these things. After the kid from the house behind ours used his BB rifle to shoot a hole through our bathroom window and through the bathroom windows of the houses on either side of ours, my mother was adamant that I would never have an opportunity to do something similar, at least not while she had anything to say about the matter.

Before I make my point concerning the marketplace, I need to emphasize the connection between the cowboy heroes and children. Just as today we continue to see film heroes and their spinoffs appeal to children—I think of Spider-Man, the X-Men, Lara Croft, Batman, and other superheroes from the comics and computer games—so too did the cowboy heroes of my youth appeal to children. And books were part of this. Buck Jones, Gene Autry, Roy Rogers, and the rest had their own line of novels and Big Little Books for younger readers. These were published by Whitman Publishing Company of Racine, Wisconsin, beginning in 1932. In 1938, Whitman changed the name of these books to Better Little Books. Whitman also published Roy Rogers and Gene Autry books for older readers. Another publisher, Samuel Lowe Company of Kenosha, Wisconsin (Lowe had been president of Whitman Company until he opened his own company in 1940), in 1949 issued a series of ten small books for young readers that deal with cowboy themes. The Hollywood cowboys also had fan clubs and codes that appeared to identify upright and socially responsible behaviour. Gene Autry informs us that his famous cowboy code consisted of a "set of rules . . . to govern the role of the B Western hero." And we know that when Autry says these rules govern the B Western hero, he means that they should also govern the boys and girls who follow the B western hero. He acknowledges that "we took such matters seriously then [in the 1940s and '50s] and the code tapped a spirit that was alive in the land" (184). That spirit is no less alive today than it was in Autry's heyday. Autry's code, and those codes and creeds of the other cowboy heroes, constitute a set of ethics that no one could find sinister. In fact, *The Village Voice*, as recently as 28 September 2004, published an article by Erik Baard ("George W. Bush Ain't No Cowboy") in which Baard tests Bush against Autry's cowboy code and finds him wanting in every area. Baard's point is that Bush aspires to behave in the manner set out in the code but fails in his aspiration; and this failure, Baard assures us, is unfortunate, since the code is worthwhile.

When we reflect on the business empire that Autry established after he left filmmaking, we might make the connection between his cowboy code and his success in the corporate world. Autry wants us to make the connection. This code looks good on paper; it presents a sound portrait of the man of strength and honour who can be trusted with everything from protecting the social fabric to tending the coffers of stockholders. In his autobiography, *Back in the Saddle Again*, Autry includes a chapter titled "The Corporate Cowboy," and this about sums up what I am saying (166–81). In the chapter that follows, "Riding into the Sunset," he sets out his cowboys' code and insists that what may appear to be a set of old-fashioned values continues to be relevant: "I never felt there was anything wrong with striving to be better than you are" (185). The figure Autry cuts in the stories he inhabits is rugged and persistent. He is a capable organizer of men, often leading posses or advising groups of ranchers. In the Better Little Book *Gene Autry and the Mystery of Paint Rock Canyon* (1943), when Gene loses the trail of a bad guy, the narrator points out that "another man, discouraged at losing the trail so completely, might have given up the search" but that "Gene Autry was only strengthened in his determination to bring the killer to justice" (250). Striving, calculating, and never giving up are traits of a good corporate cowboy.

The connection between cowboys and children may be a form of nostalgia, but this nostalgia serves corporate masters. We see this most persistently and most disturbingly in the championing of guns. From the perspective of the early twenty-first century when we have experienced many school shootings—the most infamous being the Columbine High School shootings of 1999 (fictionalized in the 2003 Gus Van Sant film, *Elephant)*—the Red Ryder BB gun now seems rather harmless. But Daisy's marketing of this rifle to children stands as the advent of the marketing of more dangerous guns to children. We have come from the Daisy Red Ryder BB rifle to the automatic weapons marketed by Feather Industries as a source of comradeship between father and son. The photograph from Feather Industries 1991 catalogue that I discussed in Chapter 4 shows father and son in the healthy outdoors happily handling a machine gun. The western heritage also turns up in the marketing of six-guns like those we saw in the movies. A company called Freedom Arms (echoing the Second Amendment) proudly markets its Mid-Frame revolver (.357 Magnum), which must remind us of the pistols used by the cowboy heroes. Another company, America Remembers, specializes in pistols and rifles manufactured as tributes to famous Americans, some of whom are Roy Rogers, Gene Autry, Hopalong Cassidy, Clayton Moore, and Monte Hale (see http://www.americaremembers.com). Not only are children the target of mass marketing, but they are also exploited in the service of mass marketing. We see this in the Fleming Firearms advertisement, and also in the fashion magazine *Kid's Wear*. In this glossy and expensive publication, we have page after page of children photographed in a great range of clothing, including underwear. Looking at the photographs in this magazine, I find it difficult to miss what James Kincaid calls "erotic innocence."

But I return to Hoppy and Gene and the boys. These film performers were used to sell a host of manufactured products in a way that was not entirely different from the way the brand name sells products today. Today children learn early to desire products emblazoned with the Gap logo or the Nike or the Calvin Klein or the Game Boy or the Speedo or the Mattel. As Naomi Klein has chronicled at length, the practice of branding products with corporate names has spread like a virus. No longer do we purchase products, Klein notices; we purchase brand names. She notes that celebrities such as "Michael Jordan, Puff Daddy, Martha Stewart, Austin Powers, Brandy . . . mirror the corporate structure of corporations like Nike and the Gap, and they are just as captivated by the prospect of developing and leveraging their own branding potential as the product-based manufacturers." Klein speaks of a "fluid partnership between celebrity people and celebrity brands" (30). Susan Linn speaks of "imprinting" brand names on children at an early age. The words "imprint" and "brand" remind us of cowboy culture; we are the cattle and consumer products are the brand. Just as contemporary brand names sell a lifestyle rather than a product, the cowboys of my youth sold a lifestyle or at least a set of values that perpetuated a way of life. We used to call this the American way of life, although today we might call it "globalization." Despite the ostensible individualism of the cowboy, what he promoted was a homogenized existence in which everyone plays the market game.

The branding of children with images of their heroes in order to sell products of one kind or another inevitably connects the hero to the marketplace and market values. What the Hoppy or Roy name on a huge variety of products testifies to is the rightness of market practices. If Roy or Gene is willing to have his name on pyjamas or board games or bicycles, then Roy or Gene must approve of these products and the products must be worth buying. Roy and Gene taught us to be good consumers. What we could not see was the paradox. Roy and Gene represented the west, the cowboy who wandered free of market practices and who championed the small farmer who lived close to the land and needed little in the way of material goods. The cowboy rode miles living off the land, rarely changing his shirt, and needing few material possessions aside from saddle and guns. In other words, the cowboy consumer and the cowboy hero were both critical of and complicit with the marketplace. The cowboy championed business, self-reliance, entrepreneurship, professionalism, craft, leadership, and all those attributes that make up the American Way. The cowboy was the embodiment of Second Amendment rights and what these rights imply about democracy. He was also the embodiment of control and governing through fear. To cross the cowboy was to face the intimidating barrel of a gun. We too, as young children drawn into the world of our heroes, could have it both ways; we could long for freedom and distance from crass bourgeois values and indulge these same crass consumer values; we could follow the leadership of a strong and intrepid hero, someone capable of bringing 'em back dead or alive. Our heroes from films and their spinoff books pretended to offer strong moral guidance and innocent pleasure, but they offered something else—they connected the notion of freedom with the notion of capitalist competition and social Darwinism.

The masculinity represented in the movies and books is a capitalist notion of masculinity. Shirley Burggraf, in *The Feminine Economy and Economic Man* (1997), describes *Homo economicus* as manifesting the following characteristics: "individualism, selfishness, competitiveness, and above all rationality" (19). With the possible exception of "selfishness," these characteristics fit the cowboy to a tee, and even selfishness works when we think of the cowboy remaining aloof from domesticity and social activity, and preferring the lonely life of the trail. Time after time, the cowboy rejects the offer of a job or a home or even of a reward at the end of an adventure. For example, at the end of the Snowden Miller novel *Roy Rogers and the Rimrod Renegades* (1952), Roy refuses to accept the reward for capturing the gang of bad guys because, as he says, "I was only doin' my duty" (280). Instead, the reward is divided among local ranchers who had suffered at the hands of the outlaws. As for Roy, he reckons he'll "be hittin' the trail" (281). The fantasy perpetrated on youngsters who read this book or see the films with their cowboy heroes is that the real man is the Ideal-I—he who rides free and yet who has business sense and a seemingly endless supply of money whenever he is called upon to buy clothing, equipment, or food. This is the Ideal-I every boy should seek to be. While he disdains material wealth for himself, he has such wealth as if by magic, by virtue of his very manliness. To be a real man is to be rich.

We do well to remember that films and books are part of the marketplace, and the cowboys I followed in my childhood, in both films and books, worked over and over again to make things possible for men to do business. The cowboys we idolized went to work to make places safe for business, albeit small business. They uncovered corrupt bankers, corrupt railroad magnates and cattle barons, corrupt lawyers and judges, and corrupt oilmen. The worst thing a villain could do, in the westerns I grew up with, was to indulge in usury. Time and again, the villain plans to acquire land or goods through lending money, acting to ensure the borrower cannot repay the loan, and foreclosing on the deal. One example is the novel *Roy Rogers and the Gopher Creek Gunman*, by Don Middleton (1945). The title page of this book says the volume is an "authorized edition," which must mean that Roy Rogers himself has lent his imprimatur to the story. As the story begins, a nameless narrator gives us a thorough description of Roy Rogers, cowboy hero. He is "young" and "bronzed" (11). Roy is uneasy for a reason he cannot explain, and the narrator gives us the following description:

> It was the first time Roy had ever felt this uneasiness. He had traveled countless miles in the dark of night, with only Trigger and the stars for companions. Because he had spent half his life in the saddle, complete solitude and trackless country were nothing new to him.
>
> Roy had been a cowboy for as long as he could remember. He loved the wild, free life of the plains. He had tamed broncs, hazed cattle, ridden point on trail drives, bulldogged the toughest steers and won a dozen rodeo championships.
>
> He knew the mountains and plains in all kinds of weather. He was familiar with every detail of the country through which he traveled. He could identify the call of every creature of the West and he knew the name of every tree and shrub. He was completely at home in the moonlit silence of the night. (12)

Here is the cowboy of romance, a figure noble and wise. He is close to nature, and he is skilled in reading its every facet. He is completely at home on the range, with only his horse and nature itself for companions. He is the personification of self-reliance.

The narrator informs us that Roy is "heading for country where oil had recently been discovered" (11–12). Having heard from an old prospector about this discovery of oil, "Roy had decided to take a look at this new world of derricks and machines and grim-faced men" (12). His motive is curiosity; he has no desire to involve himself in the oil business. He is an itinerant knight, an unattached samurai, out to see new things, ready for adventure.

Roy and Trigger come across a murdered man and later find this man's brother and his partner (characters named Dick Collins and Gimlet Lonergan), who are drilling for oil. Roy learns that a usurer named Geesel holds the mortgage on the land and equipment that Dick and Gimlet have had to take out in order to carry out their drilling. He learns too that another man, named Clayton, holds a second option on the land in case Dick and Gimlet fail to strike oil by a certain date. The description of Geesel indicates his miserly nature. He wears "a suit of black, but age had turned it to a greenish hue. His face was lean and hawklike, with eyes set far back beneath shaggy brows" (72). Later we learn that he is both "shrewd" and "cowardly," hiring "others to do his rough work" (78). These "others" are often half-breeds and Indians such as Indian Pete. The Indians have a "notion," Dick tells Roy, that they "owned this land," but Roy (using italics) emphatically assures him that "the Indians never *did* have title to land around here" (53). The irony in this statement is apparent only to readers of this novel, not to Roy. Neither the Indians nor the hawk-faced man, Geesel, has title to this land. What the novel does not make clear is that Geesel desires ownership, whereas the Native Americans' idea of ownership challenges notions of private property taken for granted by Roy and the white community. The reader is supposed to think that neither Geesel nor the Indians ought to have such title precisely because they are other than white, upright, and true. The narrator never tells us directly Geesel's racial or ethnic origin, but the description we have of him fits the Jewish stereotype. In other words, the bad guys often smack of the foreign; xenophobia as well as racial prejudice rear their unpleasant heads in these works. The market, the money, and the land that supplies the market with money belong to good God-fearing, hard-working Americans who can trace their ancestry to solid European stock. Gimlet Lonergan and Dick Collins represent such European stock. So does Roy Rogers.

The novel ends with Dick and Gimlet becoming rich, drenched in oil, as Gimlet tells Roy. As for Roy, he returns to the X-Bar-X Ranch because "he had had his fill of the oil game and he had decided that the life of a cowboy was the life for him" (247). As the book ends, Roy receives a package from Gimlet. In the package are Gimlet's oil-soaked old clothes. Gimlet's note refers to these clothes as a "souvenir." Roy receives a bundle of smelly dirty clothes while the two men whose land he saved so they could become rich will live high on the hog from now on. Roy Rogers may just be a cowhand, but those he befriends become rich. The message could not be clearer. Readers of this book and the many like it most likely read the books while wearing their Roy Rogers or Hopalong Cassidy or Gene Autry pyjamas, perhaps lying on Roy Rogers sheets, after having breakfasted on cereal recommended by Roy or Hoppy. Wealth awaits at trail's end.

In other words, the cowboys I grew up with were brand names as much as they were personalities or celebrities. Or perhaps it is more accurate to say that they were brand names because they were celebrities. Today we may have different celebrities who appeal to young people, but the meaning of celebrity remains much the same as it was. Take, for example, the celebrity writer J.K. Rowling. She began as a writer and she is now a celebrity whose books infiltrate the market in a massive way. My point is that we have been teaching our children for a long time the virtues of consumerism. True, we do not see Dick and Gimlet in the Roy Rogers novel take their new-found wealth and buy homes and clothes and gadgets and so on, but we know they have the ability to do so. Perhaps the message was more subtle back then. Now we know Harry covets and gets a special Quiditch broomstick. Nancy Drew drives hot cars. And even board books ask that we buy Cheerios cereal in order to take part in the interactive fun.

My point is simple: books for children are (or can be and often are) complicit with market forces that try to convince us that we are one market under God and that we may enjoy the good life if only we purchase enough things, books being one of those things, along with theatre tickets so we can watch our heroes perform onscreen. We buy things in a futile attempt to fulfill our fantasy of returning to the Real from which we departed at about eighteen months of age. Books and films are as much about how we can achieve the good consumer life as they are about anything else. Their trangressive potential finds itself compromised by the market that controls what films are produced and what books are published and how these are marketed. And if these books and films present a world that valorizes male achievement, male cunning and strength, male action and aggression, and male control of institutions, this is no accident. The cowboy is, after all, the ultimate patriarch.

Postscript

The Frontiersman (1938)

You're a man's man, and satisfied being that.
—June Lake addressing Hopalong Cassidy in *The Frontiersman*

I conclude with a discussion of the Hopalong Cassidy film *The Frontiersman*. The title pretty much tells it all. The American frontier supposedly closed in 1892, and in 1893 Frederick Jackson Turner celebrated its influence on the American character in his famous essay. But the man who represented the frontier continues to occupy our cultural attitudes to masculinity today. The strong, silent, lanky fellow, perhaps capable of singing a song, and assuredly capable of shooting straight and riding fast remains a large part of our sense of masculinity. This guy is a paradox: both civilized and wild, both boy and man, both situated in the past and pointing the way to the future, both sensitive and brutal. This man exists only in our imaginations. But we insist on seeing him as a big brother, as a guide to ways of being male, as a mentor for youth. What I am suggesting is meticulously articulated in the Hopalong Cassidy film that I now view.

As the credits roll, we note that they appear placed on small chalkboards, signalling that this film is to be about education and schooling. What we think is didactic material for youngsters is what this film sets out to be; it announces its educational theme. We enter the world of the Bar-20 watching Windy Halliday (George "Gabby" Hayes) building an outdoor shower. Then Lucky Jenkins (Russell Hayden) enters the scene chasing a young boy, Archie (Dickie Jones). Lucky is angry because the

177

"little weasel" Archie has put cactus needles in his bunk. It turns out that Archie is a little devil, causing trouble at the ranch and at school and wherever he goes.

"I don't want to go to school, and I don't want to take a bath," he whines. "I ain't gonna take no shower."

The story turns on the education of this spoiled brat, and Hoppy is the person who undertakes to carry out this education.

Hoppy tells Archie's aunt, and later he tells Buck Peters, that Archie is not a bad kid, he's just been spoiled. Concerned that Archie is doing poorly in school and even resisting going to school, Hoppy takes Archie aside early in the movie and says: "Man to man, what about this school?" Archie replies by saying he admires Hoppy's spurs, and Hoppy tells him that a man has to earn his spurs. The film will literalize this old adage when Hoppy gives Archie a pair of spurs near the film's close, telling him that he's earned them. During their first man-to-man conversation, however, Archie makes clear his belief that cowboys have all the fun.

"Look at all the fun you have, riding, shooting, and fighting," he says to Hoppy. Archie represents the young male viewer of this film and other B westerns. For Archie and young viewers, the cowboys do have all the fun playing with their horses and guns and engaging in fisticuffs and shootouts. Hoppy tries to temper the boy's enthusiasm for cowboy ways, saying that the future is for men with brains and that education is important. Archie is not convinced, because when Buck rides up to say that Dan Rawley (Charles A. Hughes) and his rustlers are making off with the cattle, and Hoppy and the rest of the ranch hands ride off for some shooting, Archie moans, "I always miss all the fun."

Meanwhile, at the school the kids, led by the "little imp" Archie, have gone on strike. They misbehave terribly, tying up their teacher and doing a war dance, complete with war whoops and a burning brand, around her cringing figure. When Hoppy and Windy arrive they find the students singing sweetly, conducted by Archie. Loud knocking then reveals that the kids have locked the teacher in a closet. When Hoppy sets her free, she resigns in high dudgeon. A replacement teacher arrives. The town's mayor, Jud Thorpe (Charles A. Hughes—and this casting indicates that Jud is also Rawley, the villain of the piece), had asked for a male teacher, but instead the position is filled by a beautiful young woman. Her name is June Lake (Evelyn Venable). The mayor and other townspeople want to send her back where she came from, but Hoppy comes to her defence and takes June to stay at the Bar-20, where she causes a stir among the ranch hands, who haven't seen a pretty young woman in a long time.

June quickly wins the affection of Archie by interesting him in a book about Sir Galahad. Galahad, Archie and the viewer learn, is a knight in shining armour who always fought for that which was right. June compares Galahad with Hoppy, saying that they both have "shining armour and a brave heart," but young Archie thinks Hoppy is better than Galahad. When asked if he has heard of this shining knight, Hoppy says he has read about Galahad and Lancelot.

"Anyone can understand Tennyson, even me," he says. Modesty dictates that he distance himself from the legendary knight, but we know that Hoppy is the complete man—a reader, rider, and crusader for justice.

June soon brings changes to the ranch and to the cowboys. Even Windy thinks he will use his "Floridy water" to spruce up so he'll look and smell good when he proposes to June. Lucky disobeys Hoppy's orders to get the fencing done, and takes June for a buggy ride. Even Hoppy finds himself in an apron cleaning the blackboard at the school. The presence of a young woman from the east makes the changes coming to the west easy to discern. When the ranch hands should be out tending to stock and other ranch chores, they go instead to the schoolhouse to repair shingles and paint walls so that the place will look spiff for the new schoolmarm. June brings order and cleanliness to the west, but she also brings disruption to the manly acts of corral building, fence mending, and branding. She threatens to sow dissension among friends and co-workers.

At one point in the film, Hoppy earnestly informs Buck that the future will not be the same as the past the two of them have known. The scene is shot in close-ups, something relatively rare in these movies. The close-ups convey the intimacy and intensity between the two men. Buck insists that a "fellow had to be a man" in his day, and Hoppy replies that Archie will have to be a "different kind of man" in order to cope with the changing times. Hoppy tells Buck that the Bar-20 brand and the land will exist long after the two of them have gone; mills and factories and packing houses will spring up where now they have the far horizon. The picture Hoppy describes is of a new industrial reality in which the land disappears under the smoke of the mills and factories. And the law of the gun will no longer be viable or even acceptable. But we never get a clear sense of this "different kind of man." Later in the film, Buck gives a speech that echoes Hoppy's words, indicating not that he truly grasps the implications of change but that the words are ultimately empty. Buck repeats what he has heard Hoppy say simply because he wants to sound knowledgeable and in control.

The ending of the movie assures the viewer that riding a man down the way the cowboy heroes do in film after film is the true measure of manhood. Hoppy chases Thorpe/Rawley into the rocks, where the final reckoning takes place. This film contains other features we have considered. At the end of the school year, students and teacher have a graduation ceremony that centres on the raising of the flag, the Pledge of Allegiance, and the singing of patriotic songs. In the various shots of the school throughout the film, we see mostly male students, with a couple of token females and two black students. In the scenes where the students sing, the camera rests on these two black boys. During the montage of scenes that occurs when the cowboys round up the children to take them back to school once June Lake has arrived, we have a throwaway shot that is as offensive as the scene with the Jewish character in *Rogue of the Range* (1936). What we see is a visual equivalent of W.C. Fields's line about the "Ubangi in the fuel supply" (*You Can't Cheat an Honest Man*, 1939). We see two cowboys wrestling a black boy from amidst a huge woodpile. In other words, this film champions the patriotic vision of a white masculinity that uses minority people for amusement and entertainment. But they do not take part in any foreground action.

What *The Frontiersman* ultimately communicates is the rightness of good old boyishness, and white boyishness at that. The man to admire is white, unfettered by a female, quick on the draw, close to his horse and other men. The final scene has Hoppy, Windy, and Lucky saying goodbye to June, who is going back to Boston. Hoppy has convinced her to return in the fall to teach again because the students need her, but the ending communicates a distinct sense of closure. The three cowboys, all of whom have contemplated proposing to June (with the possible exception of Hoppy), wave their goodbyes and turn their backs to the departing wagon and head away from the camera. Interestingly, they head back toward the ranch house. This film gives us an ambivalent ending in that our heroes do not climb aboard their stallions and head for the hills. Rather, they head for the house. The important thing, however, is that they remain friends, the only friends they need. As they head for the house, we might reflect that they constitute their own family—truly the family of man. And so a man's a man for all that.

List of Films Mentioned

The Alamo (Batjac, 1960). Dir. John Wayne. John Wayne, Richard Widmark.

Annie Get Your Gun (MGM, 1950). Dir. George Sidney. Betty Hutton, Howard Keel.

Apache Rose (Republic, 1947). Dir. William Witney. Roy Rogers, Dale Evans.

Arizona Bound (Monogram, 1941). Dir. Spencer G. Bennett. Buck Jones, Tim McCoy.

The Arizona Terror (Tiffany, 1931). Dir. Phil Rosen. Ken Maynard, Edmund Cobb.

The Ballad of Little Jo (Joco, 1993). Dir. Maggie Greenwald. Suzy Amis, Bo Hopkins.

Barbarosa (ITC Films, 1982). Dir. Fred Schepsi. Willie Nelson, Gary Busey.

Bar Z Badmen (Republic-Supreme, 1937). Dir. Sam Newfield. Johnny Mack Brown, Tom London.

Bells of San Angelo (Republic, 1947). Dir. William Witney. Roy Rogers, Dale Evans.

Below the Border (Monogram, 1942). Dir. Howard Bretherton. Buck Jones, Tim McCoy.

Between Men (Republic-Supreme, 1935). Dir. Robert N. Bradbury. Johnny Mack Brown, William Farnum.

Billy the Kid Returns (Republic, 1938). Dir. Joseph Kane. Roy Rogers, Smiley Burnette.

Billy the Kid's Fighting Pals, a.k.a. *Trigger Men* (PRC, 1941). Dir. Sherman Scott (Sam Newfield). Bob Steele, Al St. John.

Blackboard Jungle (MGM, 1955). Dir. Richard Brooks. Glenn Ford, Sidney Poitier.

Blue Montana Skies (Republic, 1939). Dir. B. Reeves Eason. Gene Autry, Smiley Burnette.

Blue Steel (Lone Star, 1934). Dir. Robert N. Bradbury. John Wayne, George Hayes.

Boiling Point (Allied, 1932). Dir. George Melford. Hoot Gibson, George Hayes.

Bonanza Town (Columbia, 1951). Dir. Fred F. Sears. Charles Starrett, Smiley
   Burnette.
Border Devils (Artclass, 1932). Dir. William Nigh. Harry Carey, George Hayes.
Border Feud (PRC, 1947). Dir. Ray Taylor. Lash LaRue, Al St. John.
Border Saddlemates (Republic, 1952). Dir. William Witney. Rex Allen, Slim
   Pickens.
Breed of the West (National Players, 1930). Dir. Alvin J. Neitz (Alan James). Wally
   Wales, Lafe McKee.
Bronze Buckaroo (Hollywood Productions, 1939). Dir. Richard C. Kahn. Herbert
   Jeffries, Artie Young.
Bucket of Blood (American International, 1959). Dir. Roger Corman. Dick Miller,
   Antony Carbone.
Bullwhip (Allied Artists, 1958). Dir. Harmon Jones. Guy Madison, Rhonda
   Fleming.
Bury Me Not in the Lone Prairie (Universal, 1941). Dir. Ray Taylor. Johnny Mack
   Brown, Fuzzy Knight.
Buzzy Rides the Range (Ellkay Productions, 1940). Dir. Richard C. Kahn. Dave
   O'Brien, Claire Rochelle.
Carson City Kid (Republic, 1940). Dir. Joseph Kane. Roy Rogers, "Gabby" Hayes.
Casablanca (Warner Brothers, 1941). Dir. Michael Curtiz. Ingrid Bergman,
   Humphrey Bogart.
Cheyenne Takes Over (PRC, 1947). Dir. Ray Taylor. Lash LaRue, Al St. John.
A Christmas Story (Christmas Tree Films, 1983). Dir. Bob Clark. Darren McGavin,
   Melinda Dillon.
Code of the Cactus (Victory, 1939). Dir. Sam Newfield. Tim McCoy, Ben Corbett.
Code of the Fearless (C.C. Burr Productions, 1939). Dir. Raymond K. Johnson. Fred
   Scott, John Merton.
Code of the Rangers (Monogram, 1938). Dir. Sam Newfield. Tim McCoy, Rex
   Lease.
Code of the Saddle (Monogram, 1947) Dir. Thomas Carr. Johnny Mack Brown, Ray-
   mond Hatton.
Code of the Silver Sage (Republic, 1950). Dir. Fred Brannon. Allan "Rocky" Lane,
   Eddy Waller.
Code of the West (RKO Radio Pictures, 1947). Dir. William Berke. James Warren,
   Steve Brodie.
Colt Comrades (Harry Sherman Productions, 1943). Dir. Lesley Selander. William
   Boyd, Andy Clyde.
Come On, Tarzan (World Wide, 1932). Dir. Alan James. Ken Maynard, Roy Stew-
   art.
Compañeros (Tritone Filmindustria, 1970). Dir. Sergio Corbucci. Franco Nero,
   Tomas Milian.
Conquest of Cheyenne (Republic, 1946). Dir. R.G. Springsteen. "Wild Bill" Elliott,
   Peggy Stewart.

Corpus Christi Bandits (Republic, 1945). Dir. Wallace Grissell. Allan "Rocky" Lane, Helen Talbot.

Cowboy Commandos (Monogram, 1943). Dir. S. Roy Luby. Ray Corrigan, Dennis Moore.

The Crooked Trail (Supreme Pictures, 1936). Dir. S. Roy Luby. Johnny Mack Brown, Lucile Browne.

Dead or Alive (PRC, 1944). Dir. Elmer Clifton. Tex Ritter, Dave O'Brien.

Death Valley Rangers (Monogram, 1943). Dir. Robert Tansey. Ken Maynard, Hoot Gibson.

A Demon for Trouble (Supreme, 1934). Dir. Robert Hill. Bob Steele, Lafe McKee.

Die Hard (Fox, 1988). Dir. John McTiernan. Bruce Willis, Bonnie Bedelia.

Down in the Valley (Element Films, 2005). Dir. David Jacobson. Edward Norton, Evan Rachel Wood.

Drum Taps (KBS Productions, 1933). Dir. J.P. McGowan. Ken Maynard, Dorothy Dix.

Elephant (HBO, 2003). Dir. Gus Van Sant. John Robinson, Alex Frost.

False Colors (Harry Sherman Productions, 1943). Dir. George Archainbaud. William Boyd, Andy Clyde.

The Fast and the Furious (Universal, 2001). Dir. Rob Cohen. Vin Diesel, Paul Walker.

The Fighting Champ (Monogram, 1932). Dir. J.P. McCarthy. Bob Steele, George Hayes.

The Fighting Parson (Allied, 1933). Dir. Harry Fraser. Hoot Gibson, Marceline Day.

A Fistful of Dynamite, a.k.a. *Duck, You Sucker* (Rafran/San Marco/Miura, 1971). Dir. Sergio Leone. Rod Steiger, James Coburn.

Forbidden Trails (Monogram, 1941). Dir. Robert N. Bradbury. Buck Jones, Tim McCoy.

Fort Apache, the Bronx (Producers Circle, 1981). Dir. Daniel Petrie. Paul Newman, Edward Asner.

Friendly Persuasion (Allied Artists, 1956). Dir. William Wyler. Gary Cooper, Dorothy McGuire.

The Frontiersman (Paramount, 1938). Dir. Lesley Selander. William Boyd, Russell Hayden.

Fuzzy Settles Down (PRC, 1944). Dir. Sam Newfield. Buster Crabbe, Al St. John.

The Gay Buckaroo (Allied, 1932). Dir. Phil Rosen. Hoot Gibson, Charles King.

Ghost Patrol (Puritan, 1936). Dir. Sam Newfield. Tim McCoy, Claudia Dell.

Ghost Town Gold (Republic, 1936). Dir. Joseph Kane. Robert Livingston, Ray Corrigan.

The Golden Stallion (Republic, 1949). Dir. William Witney. Roy Rogers, Dale Evans.

Gun Code (PRC, 1940). Dir. Peter Stewart (Sam Newfield). Tim McCoy, Dave O'Brien.

Gun Glory (MGM, 1957). Dir. Roy Rowland. Stewart Granger, Rhonda Fleming.

Gun Packer (Monogram, 1938). Dir. Wallace Fox. Jack Randall, Louise Stanley.

Guns and Guitars (Republic, 1936). Dir. Joseph Kane. Gene Autry, Smiley Burnette.

Gunsmoke Ranch (Republic, 1937). Dir. Joseph Kane. Robert Livingston, Ray Corrigan.

Hair-Trigger Casey (Berke-Perrin Productions, 1936). Dir. Harry Fraser. Jack Perrin, Betty Mack.

Harlem on the Prairie (Associated Features, 1937). Dir. Sam Newfield, Jed Buell. Herbert Jeffries, Lucius Brooks.

Harlem Rides the Range (Hollywood Pictures, 1939). Dir. Richard C. Kahn. Herbert Jeffries, Lucius Brooks.

Haunted Gold (Warner Brothers, 1932). Dir. Mack V. Wright. John Wayne, Sheila Terry.

Haunted Ranch (Range Busters, 1943). Dir. Robert Emmett Tansey. John "Dusty" King, David Sharpe.

Hearts of the West, a.k.a. *Hollywood Cowboy* (MGM, 1975). Dir. Howard Zieff. Jeff Bridges, Andy Griffith.

Hellfire (Republic, 1949). Dir. R.G. Springsteen. "Wild Bill" Elliott, Marie Windsor.

Heroes of the Saddle (Republic, 1940). Dir. William Witney. Robert Livingston, Duncan Renaldo.

Hidden Valley (Monogram, 1932). Dir. Robert N. Bradbury. Bob Steele, Gertrude Messinger.

High Plains Drifter (Malpaso, 1972). Dir. Clint Eastwood, Clint Eastwood, Verna Bloom.

High School Confidential (MGM, 1958). Dir. Jack Arnold. Russ Tamblyn, Jan Sterling.

Hit the Saddle (Republic, 1937). Dir. Mack V. Wright. Robert Livingston, Ray Corrigan.

Home in Oklahoma (Republic, 1946). Dir. William Witney. Roy Rogers, Dale Evans.

Home in San Antone (Columbia, 1949). Dir. Ray Nazarro. Roy Acuff, Jacqueline Thomas.

Home in Wyomin' (Republic, 1942). Dir. William Morgan. Gene Autry, Smiley Burnette.

Home on the Prairie (Republic, 1939). Dir. Jack Townley. Gene Autry, Smiley Burnette.

Home on the Range (Republic, 1946). Dir. R.G. Springsteen. Monte Hale, Adrian Booth.

Homesteaders of Paradise Valley (Republic, 1947). Dir. R.G. Springsteen. Allan "Rocky" Lane, Bobby Blake.

Hop-a-long Cassidy, a.k.a. *Hopalong Cassidy Enters* (Paramount, 1935). Dir. Howard Bretherton. William Boyd, Jimmy Ellison.

Hoppy's Holiday (Hopalong Cassidy Productions, 1947). Dir. George Archainbaud. William Boyd, Andy Clyde.

Ironman (Paramount, 2008). Dir. Jon Favreau. Robert Downey, Jr., Gwyneth Paltrow.

The Jack Bull (HBO, 1999). Dir. John Badham. John Cusack, John Goodman.

Jesse James at Bay (Republic, 1941). Dir. Joseph Kane. Roy Rogers, "Gabby" Hayes.

Kansas Terrors (Republic, 1939). Dir. George Sherman. Robert Livingston, Duncan Renaldo.

The Kentuckian (Hecht-Lancaster, 1955). Dir. Burt Lancaster. Burt Lancaster, Walter Matthau.

King of the Cowboys (Republic, 1943). Dir. Joseph Kane. Roy Rogers, Smiley Burnette.

Knights of the Range (Paramount, 1940). Dir. Lesley Selander. Russell Hayden, Victor Jory.

L.A. Confidential (Warner Brothers, 1997). Dir. Curtis Hanson. Russell Crowe, Kevin Spacey.

Land of the Open Range (RKO, 1942). Dir. Edward Killy. Tim Holt, Ray Whitley.

Law of the Canyon (Columbia, 1947). Dir. Ray Nazarro. Charles Starrett, Smiley Burnette.

Law of the Lash (PRC, 1947). Dir. Ray Taylor. Lash LaRue, Al St. John.

Law of the Pampas (Paramount, 1939). Dir. Nate Watt. William Boyd, Russell Hayden.

Lonely Are the Brave (U/JOEL, 1962). Dir. David Miller. Kirk Douglas, Gena Rowlands.

Look-Out Sister (Ascot Pictures, 1947). Dir. Bud Pollard. Louis Jordan, Monte Hawley.

The Man from Music Mountain (Republic, 1938). Dir. Joseph Kane. Gene Autry, Smiley Burnette.

The Man from Music Mountain (Republic, 1943). Dir. Joseph Kane. Roy Rogers, Ruth Terry.

Man of the West (Ashton Productions, 1958). Dir. Anthony Mann. Gary Cooper, Lee J. Cobb.

The Man Who Shot Liberty Valance (Ford Productions/Paramount, 1962). Dir. John Ford. John Wayne, Jimmy Stewart.

The Matrix (Village Roadshow, 1999). Dir. Andy and Larry Wachowski. Keanu Reeves, Laurence Fishburne.

Midnight Cowboy (Florin Productions, 1969). Dir. John Schlesinger. Dustin Hoffman, Jon Voight.

My Pal Trigger (Republic, 1946). Dir. Frank McDonald. Roy Rogers, "Gabby" Hayes.

The Mystery of the Hooded Horsemen (Grand National, 1937). Dir. Ray Taylor. Tex Ritter, Charles King.

Near the Rainbow's End (Tiffany, 1930). Dir. J. P. McGowan. Bob Steele, Lafe McKee.

'Neath Arizona Skies (Lone Star, 1934). Dir. Harry Fraser. John Wayne, Sheila Terry.

North of the Great Divide (Republic, 1950). Dir. William Witney. Roy Rogers, Gordon Jones.

Open Range (Touchstone, 2003). Dir. Kevin Costner. Kevin Costner, Robert Duvall.

Out California Way (Republic, 1946). Dir. Leslie Selander. Monte Hale, Lorna Gray.

Outcasts of the Trail (Republic, 1949). Dir. Philip Ford. Monte Hale, Paul Hurst.

Outlaws of the Desert (Paramount, 1941). Dir. Howard Bretherton. William Boyd, Brad King.

Pale Rider (Malpaso, 1985). Dir. Clint Eastwood. Clint Eastwood, Michael Moriarty.

Pals of the Golden West (Republic, 1951). Dir. William Witney. Roy Rogers, Dale Evans.

Parade of the West (Ken Maynard Productions, 1930). Dir. Harry Joe Brown. Ken Maynard, Gladys McConnell.

Paradise Canyon (Monogram, 1935). Dir. Carl Pierson. John Wayne, Marion Burns.

The Phantom Empire (Mascot, 1935). Dir. Otto Brower, B. Reeves Eason. Gene Autry, Smiley Burnette.

Pony Post (Universal, 1940). Dir. Ray Taylor. Johnny Mack Brown, Fuzzy Knight.

Powdersmoke Range (RKO, 1935). Dir. Wallace Fox. Harry Carey, Hoot Gibson.

Power (Fox, 1986). Dir. Sidney Lumet. Richard Gere, Gene Hackman.

Public Cowboy #1 (Republic, 1937). Dir. Joseph Kane. Gene Autry, Smiley Burnette.

The Purple Vigilantes (Republic, 1938). Dir. George Sherman. Robert Livingston, Ray Corrigan.

Rainbow over Texas (Republic, 1946). Dir. Frank McDonald. Roy Rogers, Dale Evans.

The Rainbow Trail (Fox Film Corporation, 1932). Dir. David Howard. George O'Brien, Cecilia Parker.

Rainbow Valley (Lone Star Productions, 1935). Dir. Robert N. Bradbury. John Wayne, Lucile Browne.

Range Defenders (Republic, 1937). Dir. Mack V. Wright. Robert Livingston, Ray Corrigan.

Rebel without a Cause (Warner Brothers, 1955). Dir. Nicholas Ray. James Dean, Natalie Wood.

The Red Rope (Republic-Supreme, 1937). Dir. S. Roy Luby. Bob Steele, Charles King.

Renegades of Sonora (Republic, 1948). Dir. R.G. Springsteen. Allan "Rocky" Lane, Eddy Waller.

Renegade Trail (Paramount, 1939). Dir. Lesley Selander. William Boyd, George Hayes.

Repo Man (Edge City, 1984). Dir. Alex Cox. Emilio Estevez, Harry Dean Stanton.

The Return of Frank James (Fox, 1940). Dir. Fritz Lang. Henry Fonda, Gene Tierney.

Ride Him, Cowboy, a.k.a. *The Hawk* (Warner Brothers, 1932). Dir. Fred Allen. John Wayne, Ruth Hall.

Riders of Pasco Basin (Universal, 1940). Dir. Ray Taylor. Johnny Mack Brown, Fuzzy Knight.

Riders of the Black Hills (Republic, 1938). Dir. George Sherman. Robert Livingston, Ray Corrigan.

Riders of the Whistling Pines (Columbia, 1949). Dir. John English. Gene Autry, Patricia White.

Riders of the Whistling Skull (Republic, 1937). Dir. Mack V. Wright. Robert Livingston, Ray Corrigan.

Riding Avenger (Diversion, 1936). Dir. Harry Fraser. Hoot Gibson, Ruth Mix.

Roarin' Lead (Republic, 1936). Dir. Mack V. Wright. Robert Livingston, Ray Corrigan.

Rogue of the Range (Supreme, 1936). Dir. S. Roy Luby. Johnny Mack Brown, Lois January.

Romance of the Rockies (Monogram, 1937). Dir. R.N. Bradbury. Tom Keene, Earl Dwire.

Romance of the West (PRC, 1946). Dir. Robert Emmett (Tansey). Eddie Dean, Joan Barton.

Romance on the Range (Republic, 1942). Dir. Joseph Kane. Roy Rogers, "Gabby" Hayes.

Romance Rides the Range (Spectrum Pictures, 1936). Dir. Harry Fraser. Fred Scott, Marion Shilling.

Rough Riding Rhythm (Conn Pictures, 1937). Dir. J.P. McGowan. Kermit Maynard, Dave O'Brien.

Round-up Time in Texas (Republic, 1937). Dir. Joseph Kane. Gene Autry, Smiley Burnette.

Rustler's Rhapsody (Paramount, 1985). Dir. Hugh Wilson. Tom Berenger, Patrick Wayne.

Santa Fe Stampede (Republic, 1938). Dir. George Sherman. John Wayne, Ray Corrigan.

Santa Fe Uprising (Republic, 1946). Dir. R.G. Springsteen. Allan "Rocky" Lane, Bobby Blake.

Scouts to the Rescue (Universal, 1939). Dir. Alan James and Ray Taylor. Jackie Cooper, David Durand.

The Searchers (Warner Brothers, 1956). Dir. John Ford. John Wayne, Jeffrey Hunter.

Shane (Paramount, 1953). Dir. George Stevens. Alan Ladd, Jean Arthur.

She Wore a Yellow Ribbon (RKO, 1949). Dir. John Ford. John Wayne, John Agar.

Shoot 'Em Up (New Line Cinema, 2007). Dir. Michael Davis. Clive Owen, Paul Giamatti.

Shooting High (Fox, 1940). Dir. Alfred E. Green. Gene Autry, Jane Withers.

Singing Guns (Palomar Pictures, 1950). Dir. R.G. Springsteen. Vaughn Monroe, Walter Brennan.

Smoking Guns (Ken Maynard Productions/distrib. Universal, 1934). Dir. Alan James. Ken Maynard, Gloria Shea.

Somewhere in Sonora (Warner Brothers, 1933). Dir. Mack V. Wright. John Wayne, Paul Fix.

Son of Paleface (Paramount, 1952). Dir. Frank Tashlin. Bob Hope, Roy Rogers.

South of Caliente (Republic, 1951). Dir. William Witney. Roy Rogers, Dale Evans.

Springtime in the Rockies (Republic, 1937). Dir. Joseph Kane. Gene Autry, Smiley Burnette.

Springtime in the Sierras (Republic, 1947). Dir. William Witney. Roy Rogers, Jane Frazee.

Stagecoach (Walter Wanger Productions, 1939). Dir. John Ford. John Wayne, Claire Trevor.

Stage to Mesa City (PRC, 1947). Dir. Ray Taylor. Lash LaRue, Al St. John.

Starlight over Texas (Monogram, 1938). Dir. Al Herman. Tex Ritter, Carmen LaRoux.

Stars over Arizona (Monogram, 1937). Dir. Robert N. Bradbury. Jack Randall, Kathleen Eliot.

Star Trek: The Next Generation (TV series, 1987–1994).

Stella Dallas (Samuel Goldwyn Company, 1925). Dir. Henry King. Ronald Coleman, Alice Joyce.

Stone of Silver Creek (Universal, 1935). Dir. Nick Grinde. Buck Jones, Noel Francis.

Sunset (TriStar, 1988). Dir. Blake Edwards. Bruce Willis, James Garner.

Sunset Trail (Paramount, 1939). Dir. Lesley Selander. William Boyd, George Hayes.

Susanna Pass (Republic, 1949). Dir. William Witney. Roy Rogers, Dale Evans.

Tall in the Saddle (RKO, 1944). Dir. Edwin L. Marin. John Wayne, Ella Raines.

The Tall T (Columbia, 1957). Dir. Bud Boetticher. Randolph Scott, Richard Boone.

Terminator 2: Judgment Day (Amblin Entertainment, 1991). Dir. James Cameron. Arnold Schwarzenegger, Linda Hamilton.

The Terror of Tiny Town (Columbia, 1938). Dir. Sam Newfield. Billy Curtis, Little Billy.

Tex Rides with the Boy Scouts (Grand National, 1937). Dir. Ray Taylor. Tex Ritter, Charles King.

¡Three Amigos! (HBO, 1986). Dir. John Landis. Steve Martin, Chevy Chase.

Three Godfathers (MGM, 1948). Dir. John Ford. John Wayne, Harry Carey, Jr.

The Three Mesquiteers (Republic, 1936). Dir. Ray Taylor. Robert Livingston, Ray Corrigan.

Three on the Trail (Harry Sherman Productions, 1936). Dir. Howard Bretherton. William Boyd, James Ellison.

Three Texas Steers, a.k.a. *Danger Rides the Range* (Republic, 1939). Dir. George Sherman. John Wayne, Ray Corrigan.

Thundering Trails (Republic, 1942). Dir. John English. Bob Steele, Tom Tyler.

Touch of Evil (Universal International, 1958). Dir. Orson Welles. Orson Welles, Vivien Leigh, Charlton Heston.

Toy Story (Disney/Pixar, 1995). Dir. John Lasseter. Tom Hanks, Tim Allen.

Toy Story 2 (Disney/Pixar, 1999). Dir. John Lasseter, Ash Brannon. Tom Hanks, Tim Allen.

Trail Dust (Paramount, 1936). Dir. Nate Watt. William Boyd, George Hayes.

Trailing Double Trouble (Monogram, 1940). Dir. S. Roy Luby. Ray Corrigan, John King.

Trail of Robin Hood (Republic, 1950). Dir. William Witney. Roy Rogers, Gordon Jones.

Trigger, Jr. (Republic, 1950). Dir. William Witney. Roy Rogers, Dale Evans.

Triggerman (Monogram, 1948). Dir. Howard Bretherton. Johnny Mack Brown, Raymond Hatton.

The Trigger Trio (Republic, 1937). Dir. William Witney. Ray Corrigan, Max Terhune.

The Truman Show (Paramount, 1998). Dir. Peter Weir. Jim Carrey, Laura Linney.

Two-Gun Man from Harlem (Merit Pictures, 1938). Dir. Richard C. Kahn. Herbert Jeffries, Clarence Brooks.

Two-Gun Sheriff (Republic, 1941). Dir. George Sherman. Don Barry, Lynn Merrick.

Under Arizona Skies (Monogram, 1946). Dir. Lambert Hillyer. Johnny Mack Brown, Raymond Hatton.

Under California Stars (Republic, 1948). Dir. William Witney. Roy Rogers, Jane Frazee.

Under Fiesta Stars (Republic, 1941). Dir. Frank McDonald. Gene Autry, Smiley Burnette.

Under Montana Skies (Tiffany, 1930). Dir. Richard Thorpe. Kenneth Harlan, Dorothy Gulliver.

Under Nevada Skies (Republic, 1946). Dir. Frank McDonald. Roy Rogers, Dale Evans.

Under Western Stars (Republic, 1938). Dir. Joseph Kane. Roy Rogers, Smiley Burnette.

Unforgiven (Malpaso, 1992). Dir. Clint Eastwood. Clint Eastwood, Gene Hackman.

The Unknown Ranger (Columbia, 1936). Dir. Spencer G. Bennett. Bob Allen, Harry Woods.

Valley of Fire (Gene Autry Productions, 1951). Dir. John English. Gene Autry, Pat Buttram.

Valley of Hunted Men (Republic, 1942). Dir. John English. Bob Steele, Tom Tyler.

Wall Street Cowboy (Republic, 1939). Dir. Joseph Kane. Roy Rogers, George Hayes.

Warlock (Twentieth Century-Fox, 1959). Dir. Edward Dmytryk. Henry Fonda, Anthony Quinn, Richard Widmark.

Whirlwind Raiders (Columbia, 1948). Dir. Vernon Keays. Charles Starrett, Smiley Burnette.

The Wild Bunch (Warner Brothers, 1969). Dir. Sam Peckinpah. William Holden, Ernest Borgnine.

Wild Horse (Allied, 1931). Dir. Richard Thorpe, Sidney Algier. Hoot Gibson, Stepin Fetchit.

Wild Horse Canyon (Monogram, 1938). Dir. Robert F. Hill. Jack Randall, Charles King.

The Wild One (Columbia, 1953). Dir. László Benedek. Marlon Brando, Lee Marvin.

Winchester 73 (Universal, 1950). Dir. Anthony Mann. Jimmy Stewart, Dan Duryea.

Winds of the Wasteland (Republic, 1936). Dir. Mack V. Wright. John Wayne, Phyllis Fraser.

You Can't Cheat an Honest Man (Universal, 1939). Dir. George Marshall. W.C. Fields, Edgar Bergen.

References

America Remembers, "Roy Rogers & Dale Evans Tribute Revolver." Accessed 20 April 2003, http://www.americaremembers.com/F118150.asp.

Anderson, Chuck. The Old Corral. Accessed 28 January 2005, http://www.surfnetinc.com/chuck/trio.htm.

Autry, Gene, with Mickey Herskowitz. Back in the Saddle Again. Garden City, NY: Doubleday, 1978.

Baard, Erik. "George W. Bush Ain't No Cowboy." Village Voice, 28 September 2004. Accessed 2 October 2004, http://www.villagevoie.com/print/issues/0439/baard.php.

Baden-Powell, Robert. Scouting for Boys: A Handbook for Instruction in Good Citizenship. Edited by Elleke Boehmer. Oxford: Oxford University Press, 2004 (1908).

Barbour, Alan G. The Thrill of It All. New York: Collier Books, 1971.

Battaglia, Debbora. "On Practical Nostalgia: Self-prospecting among Urban Trobrianders." In Rhetorics of Self-Making, ed. Debbora Battaglia, 77–97. Berkeley: University of California Press, 1995.

Bazin, André. What Is Cinema? Vol. 2. Essays selected and translated by Hugh Gray. Berkeley: University of California Press, 1967.

Beard, Tyler, and Jim Arndt. 100 Years of Western Wear. Layton, UT: Gibbs Smith, 1993.

Beaugrand, Bob. Gene Autry and the Mystery of Paint Rock Canyon. A Better Little Book. Racine, WI: Whitman, 1943 (1947).

Betsky, Aaron. Queer Space: Architecture and Same-Sex Desire. New York: William Morrow, 1997.

Bordo, Susan. The Male Body: A New Look at Men in Public and in Private. New York: Farrar, Straus and Giroux, 1999.

191

Boym, Svetlana. *The Future of Nostalgia.* New York: Basic Books, 2001.

Bull, Debby. *Hillbilly Hollywood: The Origins of Country and Western Style.* New York: Rizzoli International, 2000.

Burggraf, Shirley P. *The Feminine Economy and Economic Man: Reviving the Role of the Family in the Postindustrial Age.* Reading, MA: Perseus Books, 1997 (1999).

Buscombe, Edward, ed. *The BFI Companion to the Western.* New York: Atheneum, 1988.

———, and Roberta E. Pearson, eds. *Back in the Saddle Again: New Essays on the Western.* London: British Film Institute, 1998.

Cahill, Greg. "Guns & Kids." *MetroActive News and Issues.* Accessed 21 April 2003, http://www.metroactive.com/papers/sonoma/07.29.99/guns-9930.html.

Calder, Jenni. *There Must Be a Lone Ranger: The Myth and Reality of the American Wild West.* London: Abacus, 1976 (1974).

Carrier, Roch. "The Sorcerer." *The Hockey Sweater and Other Stories.* Trans. Sheila Fischman. Toronto: Anansi, 1979, 149–53.

Carter, Ann, and David McPhail. *Tall in the Saddle.* Victoria, BC/Custer, WA: Orca, 1999.

Cary, Diana Serra. *The Hollywood Posse: The Story of a Gallant Band of Horsemen Who Made Movie History.* Boston: Houghton Mifflin, 1975.

Cawelti, John G. *Adventure, Mystery, and Romance.* Chicago: University of Chicago Press, 1976.

Chapman, Art. "Fashion Statement with a Western Accent." *Star-Telegram,* 16 February 2003. Online at http://www.dfw.com/mld/startelegram/news/columnists/art_chapman/5194398.htm?template=contentModules/printstory.jsp.

Christensen, Wendy M. "Cowboy of the World? Gendering Discourse and Iraq War Debate." Paper presented at the annual meeting of the American Sociological Association, Marriott Hotel, Loews Philadelphia Hotel, Philadelphia, PA, 12 August 2005. Online at www.allacademic.com//meta/p22889_index.html.

Clum, John M. *"He's All Man": Learning Masculinity, Gayness, and Loving from American Movies.* New York: Palgrave, 2002.

Connell, Bob. *Masculinities.* St. Leonards: Allen & Unwin, 1995.

Copeland, Bobby. *B-Western Boot Hill: A Final Tribute to the Cowboys and Cowgirls Who Rode the Saturday Matinee Movie Range.* Madison, NC: Empire, 1999.

Coyne, Michael. *The Crowded Prairie: American National Identity in the Hollywood Western.* London/New York: I.B. Tauris, 1997.

Crow, J. Brim, and Jack H. Smith. *The Cowboy and the Kid.* Irving, TX: Wind River, 1988.

D'Angelo, Rudy A. The Spaghetti Western. Accessed 26 February 2003, http://members.tripod.com/rudydangelo/about.htm.

Davis, Fred. *Yearning for Yesterday: A Sociology of Nostalgia.* New York: Free Press, 1979.

Diaz, Tom. *Making a Killing: The Business of Guns in America*. New York: New Press, 1999.

Dibb, Mike. "A Time and Place: Bud Boetticher and the Western." In *The Movie Book of the Western*, ed. Ian Cameron and Douglas Pye, 161–66. London: Studio Vista, 1996.

Durgnat, Raymond, and Scott Simmon, "Six Creeds That Won the Western." In *The Western Reader*, ed. Jim Kitses and Gregg Rickman, 69–83. New York: Limelight, 1998.

Dyer, Richard. *The Culture of Queers*. London/New York: Routledge, 2002.

Empson, William. *Some Versions of Pastoral*. Harmondsworth, England: Peregrine Books, 1966.(1935).

Engeman, Thomas S. "In Defense of Cowboy Culture." Claremont Institute, CA. Accessed 21 January 2005, http://www.claremont.org'writings/crb/summer2003/engeman.html.

Fiedler, Leslie. *Love and Death in the American Novel*. New York: Dell, 1966 (1960).

———. *No! In Thunder*. New York: Stein and Day, 1972 (1960).

Freud, Sigmund. "Analysis of a Phobia in a Five-Year-Old Boy: 'Little Hans' (1909)." In *Case Histories I*, ed. James Strachey, 167–305. Harmondsworth, England: Penguin, 1983.

———. *On Sexuality*. Ed. Angela Richards. Harmondsworth, England: Penguin, 1981 (1953).

Frye, Northrop. *The Secular Scripture*. Cambridge, MA: Harvard University Press, 1976.

Gaines, Jane Marie, and Charlotte Cornelia Herzog. "The Fantasy of Authenticity in Western Costume." In *Back in the Saddle Again: New Essays on the Western*, ed. Edward Buscombe and Roberta E. Pearson, 172–81. London: British Film Institute, 1998.

Galbraith, Mary. "Hear My Cry: A Manifesto for an Emancipatory Childhood Studies Approach to Children's Literature." *The Lion and the Unicorn* 25 (2001): 187–208.

Garber, Marjorie. *Vested Interests: Cross-Dressing and Cultural Anxiety*. New York: Routledge, 1997 (1992).

Garner, Alan. *Red Shift*. London: Collins, 1973.

———. *The Owl Service*. London: Collins, 1967.

George-Warren, Holly, and Michelle Freedman. *How the West Was Worn*. New York: Harry N. Abrams, 2001.

"Ghost Town Gold." *Weekly Variety*, 1 August 1936. Accessed 23 February 2003, http://www.angelfire.com/ms/3mesqueteers/film2rep.html.

Gibson, William James. *Warrior Dreams: Violence and Manhood in Post-Vietnam America*. New York: Hill & Wang, 1994.

Grahame, Kenneth. *The Wind in the Willows*. New York: Scribner's, 1983 (1908).

Granger, Brian. "Barbershop Quartets." *St. James Encyclopedia of Pop Culture.* Accessed 7 January 2009, http://findarticles.com/p/articles/mi_g1epc/is_/ai_2419100090.

Hage, Ghassan. *White Nation: Fantasies of White Supremacy in a Multicultural Society.* New York: Routledge, 2000.

Halberstam, Judith. *In a Queer Time and Place: Transgender Bodies, Subcultural Lives.* New York: New York University Press, 2005.

Halperin, David M. *Saint Foucault: Towards a Gay Hagiography.* New York: Oxford University Press, 1995.

Hardy, Phil. *The Western: The Complete Film Sourcebook.* New York: William Morrow, 1983.

Hintz, J.F. *Horses in the Movies.* South Brunswick/New York: A.S. Barnes, 1979.

Hitt, Jack. "Mighty White of You: Racial Preferences Color America's Oldest Skulls and Bones." *Harper's,* 25 July 2005, 39–55.

Horrocks, Roger. *Male Myths and Icons: Masculinity in Popular Culture.* London: Macmillan, 1995.

Horwitz, James. *They Went Thataway.* New York: Ballantine Books, 1976.

Huizinga, Johan. *Homo Ludens.* Boston: Beacon Press, 1971.

Jackson, Mary V. *Engines of Instruction, Mischief, and Magic: Children's Literature in England from Its Beginnings to 1839.* Lincoln: University of Nebraska Press, 1989.

Jackson, Ronald. *Classic TV Westerns.* New York: Citadel, 1994.

Jameson, Fredric. *The Ideologies of Theory: Essays 1971–1986.* Vol. 1. Minneapolis: University of Minnesota Press, 1988.

Kincaid, James. *Erotic Innocence: The Culture of Child Molesting.* Durham, NC: Duke University Press, 1998.

Kitses, Jim. *Horizons West: Directing the Western from John Ford to Clint Eastwood.* London: British Film Institute, 2004.

Klein, Naomi. *No Logo: Taking Aim at the Brand Bullies.* Toronto: Vintage, 2000.

Kramer, Jane. *The Last Cowboy.* New York: Washington Square Press, 1977.

Lacan, Jacques. "The Topic of the Imaginary," *The Seminars of Jacques Lacan: Book 1, Freud's Papers on Technique 1953–1954.* Ed. Jacques-Alain Miller, 73–88. New York, London: W.W. Norton, 1988.

Leab, Daniel J. *From Sambo to Superspade: The Black Experience in Motion Pictures.* Boston: Houghton Mifflin, 1976.

Lewis, C. Jack. *White Horse, Black Hat: A Quarter Century on Hollywood's Poverty Row.* Lanham, MD: Scarecrow Press, 2002.

Leyda, Julia. "Black-Audience Westerns and the Politics of Cultural Identification in the 1930s." *Cinema Journal* 42 (2002): 46–70.

Linn, Susan. *Consuming Kids: The Hostile Takeover of Childhood.* New York: New Press, 2004.

Lott, John R., Jr. *More Guns, Less Crime: Understanding Crime and Gun Control Laws.* 2nd ed. Chicago: University of Chicago Press, 2000.

Loy, Philip R. "Soldiers in Stetsons: B-Westerns Go to War." *Journal of Popular Film and Television*, Winter 2003. Accessed 5 April 2004, http://www.findarticles.com/cf_dis/m0412/4_30/97629462/print.jhtml.

Lunn, Janet. *The Root Cellar*. Toronto: Lester and Orpen Dennys, 1981.

Lyman, Rick. *Watching Movies: The Biggest Names in Cinema Talk about the Films That Matter Most*. New York: Henry Holt, 2002.

MacDonald, George. *Phantastes and Lilith*. Grand Rapids, MI: Wm. B. Eerdmans, 1964.

MacDonald, Robert H. *Sons of Empire: The Frontier and the Boy Scout Movement, 1890–1918*. Toronto: University of Toronto Press, 1993.

MacDonald, William Colt. *Powdersmoke Range*. New York: G.K. Hall, 1997 (1934).

Mallan, Kerry, and Roderick McGillis. "Between a Frock and a Hard Place: Camp Aesthetics and Children's Culture." *Canadian Review of American Studies/Revue canadienne d'études americaines* 35, no. 1 (2005): 1–19.

Manchel, Frank. *Cameras West*. Englewood Cliffs, NJ: Prentice-Hall, 1971.

Marcuse, Herbert. *One-Dimensional Man*. Boston: Beacon, 1964.

Marx, Karl. *Das Kapital: A Critique of Political Economy*. Ed. Serge L. Levitsky. Chicago: Henry Regnery, 1970.

McGillis, Roderick. "Westering of the Spirit: Wordsworth Out West." *Journal of Popular Culture* 18 (1984): 85–95.

Merkin, Daphne. "Lemony Snicket Says, 'Don't Read My Books!'" *New York Times Magazine*, 29 April 2001.

Merlock, Ray, and Jack Nachbar. "Gene Autry: Songs, Sidekicks, and Machines." In *The Hollywood West: Lives of Film Legends Who Shaped It*, ed. Richard W. Etulain and Glenda Riley, 44–62. Golden, CO: Fulcrum, 2001.

Metz, Christian. *The Imaginary Signifier: Psychoanalysis and the Cinema*. Bloomington: Indiana University Press, 1977.

Middleton, Don. *Roy Rogers and the Gopher Creek Gunman*. Racine, WI: Whitman, 1945.

Miedzian, Myriam. *Boys Will Be Boys: Breaking the Link between Masculinity and Violence*. New York: Doubleday, 1991.

Miles, Rosalind. *Rites of Man: Love, Sex and Death in the Making of the Man*. London: Grafton, 1991.

Miller, Snowden. *Roy Rogers and the Rimrod Renegades*. Racine, WI: Whitman, 1954 (1952).

Mitchell, Lee Clark. *Westerns: Making the Man in Fiction and Film*. Chicago: University of Chicago Press, 1996.

Nikolajeva, Maria. *Children's Literature Comes of Age*. New York: Garland, 1995.

Nodelman, Perry. *The Hidden Adult: Defining Children's Literature*. Baltimore: Johns Hopkins University Press, 2008.

Nye, Doug. "My Heroes Have Always Been Cowboys." *The State*, 22 June 2003. Accessed 26 January 2005, http://www.thestate.commld/thestate/living/6135123.htm?template=contentModules/printstory.jsp.

Nye, Douglas E. *Those Six-Gun Heroes: 25 Great Movie Cowboys*. Spartanburg, SC: ETV Endowment of South Carolina, 1982.

O'Meara, Dina. "There's Something about a Well-Seasoned Cowboy That Makes Women Wild about the West," *Calgary Herald*, 26 June 1998, D1.

Parrish, James Robert. *Great Western Stars*. New York: Ace Books, 1976.

Pearce, Philippa. *Tom's Midnight Garden*. Oxford: Oxford University Press, 1958.

Phillips, Robert W. *Singing Cowboy Stars: The Guys, the Gals, the Sidekicks*. Salt Lake City, UT: Gibbs-Smith, 1994.

Pollack, William. *Real Boys: Rescuing Our Sons from the Myths of Boyhood*. New York: Henry Holt, 1998.

Pumphrey, Martin. "Why Do Cowboys Wear Hats in the Bath? Style Politics for the Older Man." In *The Movie Book of the Western*, ed. Ian Cameron and Douglas Pye, 50–62. London: Studio Vista, 1996.

Rainey, Buck. *Saddle Aces of the Cinema*. New York: A.S. Barnes, 1980.

Reimer, Mavis, ed. *Home Words: Discourses of Children's Literature in Canada*. Waterloo, ON: Wilfrid Laurier University Press, 2008.

Robertson, Pamela. *Guilty Pleasures: Feminist Camp from Mae West to Madonna*. Durham, NC: Duke University Press, 1996.

Rogers, Roy, and Dale Evans, with Jane and Michael Stern. *Happy Trails: Our Life Story*. New York: Fireside, 1994.

Rose, Jacqueline. *The Case of Peter Pan, or the Impossibility of Children's Fiction*. London: Macmillan, 1984.

Rosenberg, Bruce A. *Code of the West*. Bloomington: Indiana University Press, 1982.

Rosenthal, Michael. *The Character Factory: Baden-Powell and the Origins of the Boy Scout Movement*. New York: Pantheon, 1984.

Rotundo, Anthony E. *American Manhood: Transformations in Masculinity from the Revolution to the Modern Era*. New York: Basic Books, 1993.

Russo, Vito. *The Celluloid Closet: Homosexuality in the Movies*. New York: Harper & Row, 1981.

Said, Edward. *Orientalism*. New York: Vintage, 1979 (1978).

Sarup, Madan. *Jacques Lacan*. Toronto: University of Toronto Press, 1992.

Savage, William W., Jr. *The Cowboy Hero: His Image in American History and Culture*. Norman: Oklahoma University Press, 1979.

Savran, David. *Taking It Like a Man: White Masculinity, Masochism, and Contemporary American Culture*. Princeton, NJ: Princeton University Press, 1998.

Sedgwick, Eve Kosofsky. *Between Men: English Literature and Male Homosocial Desire*. New York: Columbia University Press, 1985.

———. *Tendencies*. Durham, NC: Duke University Press, 1993.

Seiler, Robert M., and Tamara P. Seiler. "The Social Construction of the Canadian Cowboy: Calgary Exhibition and Stampede Posters, 1952–1972." *Journal of Canadian Studies* 33 (Fall 1998): 51–82.

Shavit, Zohar. *Poetics of Children's Literature*. Athens: University of Georgia Press, 1986.

Slotkin, Richard. *Gunfighter Nation: The Myth of the Frontier in Twentieth-Century America*. New York: Harper Perennial, 1992.

Smith, Henry Nash. *Virgin Land: The American West as Symbol and Myth*. New York: Vintage Books, 1950.

Sontag, Susan. *Against Interpretation and Other Essays*. New York: Delta, 1966 (1961).

Stanfield, Peter. "Dixie Cowboys and Blue Yodels: The Strange History of the Singing Cowboy." In *Back in the Saddle Again: New Essays on the Western*, ed. Edward Buscombe and Roberta E. Pearson, 96–118. London: British Film Institute, 1998.

Stephens, John. *Language and Ideology in Children's Fiction*. London and New York: Longman, 1992.

Strathern, Marilyn. *Partial Connections*. Savage, MD: Rowan and Littlefield, 1991.

Studlar, Gaylyn. "Wider Horizons: Douglas Fairbanks and Nostalgic Primitivism." In *Back in the Saddle Again: New Essays on the Western*, ed. Edward Buscombe and Roberta E. Pearson, 63–76. London: British Film Institute, 1998.

Sullivan, Tom R. *Cowboys and Caudillos: Frontier Ideology of the Americas*. Bowling Green, OH: Bowling Green State University Popular Press, 1990.

Tennyson, Alfred Lord. *A Collection of Poems by Alfred Tennyson*. Ed. Christopher Ricks. Garden City, NY: Doubleday, 1972.

"The Three Mesquiteers." *Motion Picture Herald*, 12 September 1936. Accessed 27 February 2003, http://www.angelfire.com/ms/3mesquiteers/film1rep.html.

"Thundering Trails." *Weekly Variety*. 4 December 1942. Accessed 27 February 2003, http://www.angelfirre.com/ms/3mesquiteers/film49.html.

Tirman, John. "The Future of the American Frontier." *The American Scholar* 78 (Winter 2009): 30–40.

Tompkins, Jane. *West of Everything*. Oxford: Oxford University Press, 1992.

Tucker, Holly. *Pregnant Fictions: Childbirth in the Fairy Tale in Early Modern France*. Detroit, MI: Wayne State University Press, 2003.

Turner, Frederick Jackson. "The Significance of the Frontier in American History." 1893. Accessed 7 June 2005, http://history.sandiego.edu/GEN/text/civ/turner.html.

TV Acres. Oaths and Pledges. Accessed 3 November 2003, http://www.tvacres.com/oaths_pledges.htm.

———. "Trail Boss" *Rawhide*. Accessed 6 January 6 2009, http://www.tvacres.com/westrns_coverpage.htm.

"The Valley of the Hunted Men." *Weekly Variety*, 23 October 1942. Accessed 27 February 2003, http://www.angelfire.com/ms/3mesquiteers/film48.html.

Warshow, Robert. *The Immediate Experience: Movies, Comics, Theatre and Other Aspects of Popular Culture.* New York: Atheneum, 1975.

White, Ray. "The Good Guys Wore White Hats: The B Western in American Culture." In *Wanted Dead or Alive: The American West in Popular Culture*, ed. Richard Aquila, 135–59. Urbana: University of Illinois Press, 1996.

White, Raymond E. "Ken Maynard: Daredevil on Horseback." In *Shooting Stars: Heroes and Heroines of Western Film*, ed. Archie P. McDonald. Bloomington: Indiana University Press, 1987.

Whitehead, Stephen M. *Men and Masculinities.* Cambridge: Polity Press, 2002.

Williams, Raymond. *Keywords: A Vocabulary of Culture and Society.* London: Fontana Press, 1976.

Wright, Will. *Sixguns and Society: A Structural Study of the Western.* Berkeley: University of California Press, 1975.

Yoggy, Gary. "When Television Wore Six-Guns: Cowboy Heroes on TV." In *Shooting Stars: Heroes and Heroines of Western Film*, ed. Archie P. McDonald, 218–57. Bloomington: Indiana University Press, 1987.

Žižek, Slavoj. *Looking Awry: An Introduction to Jacques Lacan through Popular Culture.* Cambridge, MA: MIT Press, 1995 (1991).

Index

Books in the Film and Media Studies Series
Published by Wilfrid Laurier University Press

The Young, the Restless, and the Dead: Interviews with Canadian Filmmakers / George Melnyk, editor / 2008 / xiv + 134 pp. / photos / ISBN 978-1-55458-036-1

Programming Reality: Perspectives on English-Canadian Television / Zoë Druick and Aspa Kotsopoulos, editors / 2008 / x + 344 pp. / photos / ISBN 978-1-55458-010-1

Harmony and Dissent: Film and Avant-garde Art Movements in the Early Twentieth Century / R. Bruce Elder / 2008 / xxxiv + 482 pp. / ISBN 978-1-55458-028-6

He Was Some Kind of a Man: Masculinites in the B Western / Roderick McGillis / 2009 / xii + 210 pp. / photos / ISBN 978-1-55458-059-0

9 647